Mom's Big Book of Baking

Mom's **Big** Book of
BAKING

200 SIMPLE, FOOLPROOF FAMILY FAVORITES FOR BIRTHDAY PARTIES, BAKE SALES, AND MORE

LAUREN CHATTMAN

The Harvard Common Press

Boston, Massachusetts

For the children in my family:
Rose, Eve, Sophia, Grace, Sam, Cara, John, and Ian

The Harvard Common Press
535 Albany Street
Boston, Massachusetts 02118

Printed in China

The ISBN for this hardcover edition of *Mom's Big Book of Baking* is 978-1-55832-395-7.
It was originally published with the ISBN 1-55832-192-6.

Library of Congress Cataloging-in-Publication Data
   Mom's big book of baking : 200 simple, foolproof recipes for delicious family treats
to get you through every birthday party, class picnic, potluck, bake sale, holiday, and
no-school day / Lauren Chattman.
      p. cm.
   Includes index.
   ISBN 1-55832-192-6 (hc : alk. paper) — ISBN 1-55832-194-2 (pbk : alk. paper)
1. Baking.   2. Quick and easy cookery.   I. Title.
   TX763.C49   2001
   641.8'15—dc21
                                                                                2001024369

Special bulk-order discounts are available on this and other Harvard Common Press
books. Companies and organizations may purchase books for premiums or resale, or
may arrange a custom edition, by contacting the Marketing Director at the address
above.

Cover design by Night & Day Design
Interior design by Marysarah Quinn
Photography by Becky Luigart-Stayner
Food styling by Jan Moon
Prop styling by Fonda Shaia
Illustrations by Laura Tedeschi

10 9 8 7 6 5 4 3 2 1

acknowledgments

Thanks to Angela Miller, who came up with the idea for this book and then helped me through every stage of its development; to Dan Rosenberg, who first wanted me to write a baking book for Harvard Common Press; to Bruce Shaw, for making sure that it happened; to Maggie Carr, for smart and careful copyediting; to Valerie Cimino, who keeps me in close touch with everything that happens at HCP; to Adrienne Anifant, who often does her job in spite of me. Skye Stewart has worked hard to put the word out about this book. Thanks to Virginia Downes and Jodi Marchowsky for their work on the cover and for producing such a pretty book, and to Becky Luigart-Stayner for the beautiful photos. Pam Hoenig is an editor of unsurpassed intelligence, humor, and integrity. I was surprised and delighted to find myself working with her again.

It would not have been possible to bake so much in such a short time without Yvette Willock, babysitter and good friend. If I know anything about family baking, it is because of my daughters Rose and Eve, whose likes and dislikes certainly contributed to the shaping of this book. And thanks once again to my husband, Jack Bishop, the best baking partner ever, whose contributions to this book are too numerous to mention.

contents

baking basics for moms

Before you had kids, you had a particular relationship with your oven. Maybe you were uninterested in cooking. Like one of my sisters during her single years, you might even have used this large, empty box to store the sweaters that wouldn't fit in your closet. Or you may have been a passionate baker who clipped recipes from *Gourmet's* "You Asked for It" column and attempted to duplicate desserts from the country's best restaurants for your frequent dinner party guests.

Either way, once you had kids you probably started using your oven differently. Out went the sweaters and in went the slice-and-bake cookies. The individual chocolate soufflés are history; chocolate cupcakes have taken their place. Like everything else in your life, your cooking now revolves around your kids. Not only must you satisfy their basic nutritional needs; you must also keep in mind their likes and dislikes. You must produce items that you probably haven't made since you yourself were in seventh grade—cupcakes with sprinkles for a classroom birthday party, marshmallow treats for a snow day—items essential to kids' happiness, if not their health. Needless to say, you now have about as much time to bake as you have to take that shower in the morning

while the little ones attempt to break down the bathroom door.

Why bake at all, you might ask, if you barely have time for basic grooming? First, let me say this: If making cupcakes for the whole class means staying up past midnight, by all means buy them at the supermarket on the way to school. You will not enjoy something that has robbed you of sleep. But if you do have a little free time before bed, why not spend it making something good to eat? Sure, homemade cupcakes will always be superior to store bought, but the benefits of baking go beyond better tasting cupcakes.

The activity itself—selecting the recipe, mixing the batter, spreading the frosting, decorating the cupcakes with sprinkles—can be creative, relaxing, and fun. Baking is a therapeutic way to spend what little free time you have by yourself, when your kids are napping, in school, or in bed. Involving your kids—in deciding what to bake, gathering the ingredients, choosing the decorations—will give them a sense of accomplishment, help them develop good taste, and teach them a few things about cooking (and maybe math and science) at an early age.

It sounds corny, but it's true: the blueberry muffins, blondies, or popovers you regularly make for and with your child become the stuff of memories. If your mom made apple pie every year for Thanksgiving or the world's best marble pound cake, you know what I mean. Baking is certainly not a requirement for the job of motherhood, and it's true that some of the world's best moms couldn't tell you the difference between molasses and maple syrup. But baking is one of the sweetest and most memorable ways to nourish and spend time with your kids. Who knows? Invest in that first jar of molasses and they might still be talking about mom's famous gingerbread twenty years from now.

Before you can make any warm and fuzzy memories, you need the right recipes, ones that will allow you to bake without stress and fear. Mom's Big Book of Baking gathers together over two hundred kid-friendly baking recipes, all of them tested in a real mom's kitchen (mine) and tasted by real kids (mine, too). This book is my own recipe file, which I began to compile over five years ago, when my first daughter was born. Back then I was embarking on a career as a pastry chef. Little did I know that as my family grew I would become more interested in making chocolate pudding than chocolate soufflés. But that's what happened, and this book is the result.

From Pastry Chef to Baking Mom

This book comes out of my own particular experience as a pastry chef and baking mom. When my older daughter was a newborn, I left my job as a teacher to attend a professional pastry and baking course at night. At 5 P.M. my husband took over at home. I left our apartment for cooking school and learned to bake the kind of fancy cakes you might see at a Parisian *pâtisserie*. We moved to the East End of Long Island, and I took a job as the pastry chef at a casual but chic Hamptons restaurant where I made desserts for New York sophisticates on vacation.

While I was making grown-up desserts at school and work, I was making simple pancakes, muffins, and cookies for my family. The two types of baking could not have been more different. The restaurant desserts required special equipment, expensive ingredients, and sauces and garnishes to dress them up. The stuff I made at home was simple and unadorned. But both the restaurant desserts and the homemade cookies satisfied my sweet tooth and gave me satisfaction in a job well done.

I left my restaurant job to write about simple cooking. It was a natural progression. Now that I had kids I was less interested in challenging cooking projects and more interested in figuring out ways to make good food quickly and without hassle. With my first two books, I developed a repertoire of streamlined recipes that allowed me to put together delicious and interesting family dinners in minutes. When I baked for fun, I thought in the same terms. What would be the simplest way to make memorable brownies?

Because of my training and my passion for pastry, I set high standards for my recipes. If I'm going to bake chocolate chip cookies, I want them to be utterly delicious. Because I am a busy mom, I'm realistic about the time I'll have to bake. So I've come up with recipes that produce the highest quality baked goods with the least amount of fuss. If I've discovered a trick or shortcut, I reveal it in the recipe. After making countless batches, I've come to believe that melting the butter makes better chocolate chip cookies. It's also quicker—you don't have to wait for the butter to soften.

I love beautiful bakery desserts, but while baking for this book I've come to appreciate the charm of obviously homemade cookies, cakes, and pies. Children are unimpressed by the fancy stuff pictured in magazines anyway. If you decorate cookies with your kids, you will quickly find out that they are less interested in piping perfect polka dots with royal icing than they are in piling on as many multicolored sprinkles as they can. Appreciate your handiwork the way your kids appreciate theirs. When you're at home, it's not about the perfect looks of the finished product. It's about the fun of making something yourself and eating what you've made when you're done admiring it.

Building a Repertoire of Mom's Recipes

As a baking mom, I wanted to collect comforting and familiar recipes, but I didn't want to write a book that was boring. So in each chapter I have tried to strike a balance between the tried and true and the new. There are old favorites and new ideas that I think are good enough to become old favorites in time.

If your kids are like mine, they prefer plain and simple baked goods to more elaborate desserts. I can't tell you how many times I've watched one of my girls scrape away the jelly, frosting, and chopped nuts in order to get a few bites of plain birthday cake. With this image in my head, I've come up with recipes that won't scare kids off. For the most timid eaters, there are Homemade Vanilla Wafers (page 108), Baking Powder Biscuits (page 71), Fluffy White Sandwich Bread (page 247), and much more.

That said, you don't have to make the same chocolate brownies over and over again. Your whole family will get a wonderful sugar rush from brownies made with rich Homemade Caramel Sauce swirled through the batter (page 233). If your kids like grapes, they'll love Sweet Focaccia with Grapes (page 256) even if they've never had anything like it before. If they are peanut butter fanatics, give them Chocolate–Peanut Butter Cups (page 92) instead of peanut butter cookies.

In each chapter, I begin with the basics and move through to the less obvious choices.

Chapter 1 focuses on the breakfast standbys, pancakes and waffles. Here you'll find a variety of pancakes, from buttermilk to cornmeal-cheddar. Each recipe is simple enough to make on a weekday morning. If your kids think that waffles come from a toaster, amaze them by pulling out the waffle iron and conjuring a batch of Pumpkin Waffles (page 39) on Halloween or Bittersweet Chocolate Waffles (page 40) topped with ice cream for a special dessert. Because I am a cereal fanatic, I've included my favorite granola recipes too.

Chapter 2 contains my best recipes for muffins, quick breads, and scones. I'll give you two reasons to try these recipes: Home-made muffins, quick breads, and scones are much better than even the "gourmet" versions you can buy at upscale coffee bars, and they are among the easiest baked goods you can make. Mix up a batch of my rich but light Sour Cream Corn Muffins (page 57; you don't even need an electric mixer) and compare them to the heavy, greasy muffins sold at your local bakery. I'm sure you will agree.

Not surprisingly, the cookie chapter is the biggest in the book. Of course, there's a recipe for chocolate chip cookies, but there are also recipes for crunchy almond biscotti, oatmeal lace cookies, and meringues. These cookie recipes are simple but not run-of-the-mill. If you could have seen the way the mothers at my daughter's last birthday party were gobbling up my Cranberry-Walnut Hermits (page 102), you would know that this recipe alone is worth the price of the book. Try some of the holiday recipes at the end of the chapter if you reserve cookie baking for special occasions. Stained-Glass Butter Cookies (page 126) are a fun project and a nice contribution to a schoolroom party in December.

Brownies and bars are a necessity for moms. They are quicker than cookies, since the batter is just poured into the pan. They are portable; you can carry them right in the pan to a potluck dinner or wrap them individually in plastic and drop them into lunch bags before school. They are adaptable. Instant Homemade Microwave Brownies (page 142) are perfect for those times when you and your family have to have a pan of warm brownies in less than 15 minutes. Blueberry-Cornmeal Crumb Squares (page 163) take a little more time and planning; they are a suitable dessert for company.

What would a mom's baking book be without apple pie and all the other pie, cobbler, and tart recipes that moms are famous for? **Chapter 5** covers the basics of making and rolling dough, and gives you recipes for pumpkin, apple, and blueberry pie, peach cobbler, berry crisp, lemon tart, and more. I finish with a few pie and tart recipes with pat-in-the-pan crumb crusts for those times when only pie will do but you don't have time for pastry.

There is a cake for every occasion in **Chapter 6**. Is New York Cheesecake (page 237) your dad's favorite? Go ahead and make it for Father's Day. Intrigued by the idea of upside-down cakes but never had the courage to try one? It's not as hard as it looks—bake a Plum Upside-Down Cake (page 212) and see for yourself. Always wanted to make a Devil's Food Layer Cake (page 216) with Chocolate Butter Icing (page 227) that looks like the photo on the Betty Crocker box but tastes homemade? It's here. A surplus of cupcake recipes, from Strawberry Cupcakes with Vanilla Whipped Cream (page 219) to Granola Cupcakes with Orange Cream Cheese Frosting (page 221), will keep you covered for a year's worth of kids' parties.

The last chapter of the book features recipes for simple breads and pizzas. To cut down on rising times, I call for rapid-rise yeast in all of them. You can begin making any of the breads after lunch and have them for dinner. Bread is the perfect thing to make if you love to bake but don't want to feed your family sweets every day (personally, I don't have a problem with this). Bread is an important part of a healthy diet but still fills your house with an incredibly sweet aroma. I probably use the recipe for Thin and Crispy Pizza Dough (page 260) more than any other in this book. Once a week I'll make a batch in my food processor, freeze half, and have enough for two nights' worth of dinners. I've written up some of my favorite topping combinations, but once you've got the dough recipe down, feel free to improvise using your favorite topping ingredients.

Good Excuses for Baking

I've written the recipes in this book keeping in mind the typical occasions and events that might call for baking: birthday parties, picnics, potlucks, bake sales, holidays, and those dreaded days when there's no school. But when I'm baking for my family I certainly don't limit myself to these occasions. If there is no holiday or birthday in sight when I'm in the mood for something sweet, I'll think of an excuse to satisfy my craving. I've jotted down some of these reasons, under the heading "A Good Excuse to Make..." at the end of many recipes in this book.

Whenever I need an excuse to make Oatmeal Scones (page 76), for example, I just look at the year's supply of rolled oats that I recently purchased at the local warehouse club. What on earth am I going to do with all those oats if I don't bake with them whenever I get the chance? If I need a reason to make a Chocolate Chip–Pecan Tart (page 177), I remind myself that this simple dessert (it's like a big chocolate chip cookie baked in a tart shell) packs very well, so I plan a picnic and bring it along. Take these suggestions literally, or use them to help you think of ways to incorporate baking into your family life.

Kids Can Help

Some kids love to bake, some love to watch you bake, and some just love to eat. I encourage my older daughter to help me whenever she wants, but I don't push her if she'd rather color while I bake a batch of cookies. Many of the recipes in this book are simple enough that interested older kids (ten and up) will be able to make them while you look on. Younger kids will need closer supervision. You know your kids, and common sense will dictate what is safe for them to do, what they might enjoy, and what they can and can't do. When there is a recipe that I think is particularly suitable for kid cooks, I've noted this under the heading "Kids Can Help."

Mom's Pantry

In the following pages I provide some information on the ingredients I use most often, to help you shop and stock your pantry. A well-stocked pantry will make the difference between fantasizing about homemade brownies and actually making them. If you keep the following ingredients on hand, you will always be able to find something to bake when the class mother calls at 8 P.M. to remind you about the PTA bake sale or picnic scheduled for tomorrow.

Butter: All the recipes in this book call for unsalted butter. It has a purer flavor than the salted variety and is better for desserts. If salt is necessary in a dessert, you can always add it yourself.

Buttermilk: Buttermilk gives all kinds of baked goods a nice, tangy flavor. If you've never baked anything with it, try making some buttermilk biscuits or waffles and see what I mean.

Chocolate: If you have enough self-control so that you won't snack on handfuls of semisweet chocolate chips, you'll save money if you buy extra-large bags at a warehouse club to keep around for impulse baking. I won't spend a lot of money on imported bittersweet chocolate for baking, since I've found that inexpensive Baker's brand makes wonderfully rich, fudgy brownies. On the other hand, cheap cocoa powder doesn't deliver the same way that more expensive brands of Dutch-process cocoa do. When a recipe calls for unsweetened cocoa powder, I use either Pernigotti or Van Leer (see Mail-Order and Online Resources, page 273).

Cornmeal: Yellow cornmeal adds great color and crunch to pan-cakes, waffles, cookies, bars, muffins, and cakes. White cornmeal is too bland for baking. When it's available, I buy stoneground cornmeal, but Quaker and other national brands stocked in the cereal aisle are just fine.

Eggs: All recipes in this book have been tested with large eggs. There is no difference in flavor or quality between brown and white eggs; use whichever color you like.

Flour: I use either King Arthur or Hecker's unbleached all-purpose flour. For most cakes, I use Soft-As-Silk cake flour (not self-rising), which has a lower protein content and produces very light baked goods.

Food Coloring: A must for cookie and cake decorating. The four-color packages that you can buy at the supermarket are plenty for most projects. Invest in a decorator set of six or eight colors (see Mail-Order and Online Resources, page 273) if you are a real artist. No matter how much they beg, try to keep smaller children away from food coloring jars! One drop on the wrong hands can color a whole kitchen in the ten seconds that you have your back turned.

Graham Cracker Crumbs: Graham cracker crumbs are great for making quick pie and cheesecake crusts. Buy them pre-ground in the baking aisle of your supermarket or grind them yourself in the food processor. Chocolate wafer cookie crumbs also make good crusts. I've recently seen pre-ground Oreo crumbs in the baking aisle, but if I can't find these, I grind Nabisco Famous Chocolate Wafers.

Maple Syrup: If you make pancakes or waffles with any frequency, buy pure maple syrup in one-quart jugs at your local warehouse store.

Meringue Powder: This is the secret ingredient in shiny Royal Icing (page 123) and fluffy Birthday Cake Frosting (pages 225 and 226). Look for it in the baking aisle at your supermarket, or order it from King Arthur (see Mail-Order and Online Resources, page 273).

Nonstick Cooking Spray: This is an item I cannot bake without. Using cooking spray is quicker than greasing a pan with butter and much more reliable. I prefer the "original" flavor (which is flavorless) to "butter" flavor, which tastes artificial to me.

Nuts: Nuts are expensive and go rancid quickly if not frozen. Pack them in zipper-lock plastic bags and freeze them to preserve freshness.

Peanut Butter: Most supermarket peanut butters have added corn syrup, which makes them too sweet. I use Smuckers "Natural" peanut butter, which doesn't contain corn syrup or any other additives. Don't buy freshly ground peanut butter at supermarkets or natural foods stores; it is too coarse and grainy for most desserts.

Rolled Oats: They're not just for breakfast. Buy quick-cooking (not instant) oats to use in cookies, muffins, and cupcakes as well as pancakes, waffles, and granola.

Spices: Small jars of ground cinnamon, nutmeg, ginger, allspice, and mace should keep you covered baking-wise.

Sprinkles: Any kid will tell you that the sprinkles are the best part of the cupcake or cookie. Tiny jars sold in supermarkets are relatively expensive and don't last long. If you bake a lot of cupcakes and cookies, buy sprinkles in quantity by mail (see Mail-Order and Online Resources, page 273). Store them in airtight containers or zipper-lock plastic bags and they will keep a good, long time in your pantry.

Sugar: There is no dessert without sugar. I keep granulated sugar, light and dark brown sugar, and confectioners' sugar in airtight containers or zipper-lock plastic bags in my pantry. I also have a selection of colored sanding sugars to sprinkle on cookies and cupcakes. Look for them in the supermarket baking aisle or mail order (see Mail-Order and Online Resources, page 273).

Vanilla Extract: I once purchased a bottle of imitation vanilla extract in the interest of economy, and the difference in the flavor of my baked goods was striking. Everything I made with imitation extract tasted weird and artificial. So I try to cut corners in other ways and always use the real stuff when it comes to vanilla.

Mom's Equipment

If you bake at all, you probably already have most of the equipment used in my recipes. Here's a rundown of the items I use most frequently, with some shopping notes just in case you have to buy one of these items.

Baking Sheets: I like insulated baking sheets, which prevent cookies from scorching on the bottom before they are cooked through. They cost a little extra and are available at cookware stores. It's good to have baking sheets with and without rims. It's easier to lift warm cookies from the rimless sheets; rimmed sheets

are good for catching drips from bubbling pies.

Biscuit Cutters: You can always use a juice glass to cut your biscuit dough into rounds, but a metal cutter slices through dough more easily. Buy a set of three or four in descending size and you'll have the option of making extra-large or tiny biscuits.

Cake Dome: You can't wrap a frosted cake in plastic. To keep it fresh, store it in an airtight plastic cake dome.

Cake Pans: You'll need two 9-inch round cake pans for layer cakes; an 8-inch square baking pan for brownies and bars; a 9 x 5-inch loaf pan for pound cakes and breads; a 12-cup Bundt pan for simple but pretty cakes like Sour Cream Coffee Bundt Cake (page 206) and Apple-Raisin Bundt Cake (page 209); a 9-inch springform pan for cheesecakes; and a 9-inch angel food tube pan if you want to make angel food cake.

Cookie Cutters: Metal cookie cutters have sharper edges and cut through cookie dough more efficiently than do plastic ones. Collect sets of holiday-themed cookie cutters and you'll use them year after year.

Craft Sticks: When you're decorating cookies with a crowd of kids, craft sticks make great icing spreaders. Use them for Cookie Pops (page 128), too. I buy mine at the local five-and-dime. You can get them at any craft or toy store.

Double Boiler: The gentle heat of a double boiler melts chocolate so that it is smooth and not grainy. If you don't own a double boiler, you can improvise by placing a metal bowl over a saucepan filled with an inch or two of simmering water.

Electric Mixer: I use a heavy-duty KitchenAid standing mixer. It's expensive but it will last long enough for you to use with your great-grandchildren. For cookie dough and cakes, I use the paddle attachment. To whip egg whites or cream, I use the whisk. Standing mixers and handheld mixers fitted only with beater attachments will do the same jobs, just not as quickly.

Food Processor: For me, baking without this appliance would be like doing laundry without the washing machine. I use a food processor for everything from chopping nuts to puréeing raspberries. I have a Cuisinart model with an 11-cup capacity, and I recommend one at least this size for big jobs like kneading bread dough.

Measuring Cups and Spoons: Successful baking requires precise measuring. Use clear "liquid" measuring cups for liquid ingredients, plastic or metal "dry" measuring cups for large quantities of dry ingredients, and measuring spoons for small quantities. Fill cups and spoons completely and level off ingredients with a knife for precise measurements.

Mixing Bowls: Not only are mixing bowls essential for mixing; they are also great for organizing ingredients before you start to cook. Buy sets of nesting glass, ceramic, and metal mixing bowls for easy storage.

Muffin Tins: You'll need a 12-cup muffin tin for cupcakes, muffins, and popovers. Paper liners are optional, but most kids like to peel the paper off their cupcakes, so I recommend them.

Parchment Paper: Parchment paper is wonderful for ensuring that your cookies don't stick to the baking sheets. Parchment also makes cleanup easy. Use it for lining the bottoms of cake pans so that your cakes don't stick. Parchment is sold in small rolls at the supermarket. If you bake a lot of cookies, you might want to mail-order a larger quantity of precut parchment sheets.

Pastry Bag and Tips: Entirely optional but fun to have. I use disposable plastic pastry bags because I hate to wash out the canvas ones. I have a whole set of decorating tips but find myself using the plain round ones most often. Pastry bags and tips are available in houseware shops and by mail order (see Mail-Order and Online Resources, page 273).

Pie Pan: All of the pie recipes in this book call for a 9-inch pie pan.

I prefer a glass pan, so I can check on the bottom crust as it browns.

Rolling Pin: Use whatever kind of rolling pin you are comfortable with. I use an untapered wooden rolling pin without handles to roll out my pie dough and cookies.

Spatulas: You'll need a rubber spatula for scraping down the sides of a mixing bowl or food processor and a wide, flexible metal spatula for lifting cookies from a cookie sheet. Use small and large offset spatulas to ice cookies and frost cakes.

Tart Pans with Removable Bottoms: I use 4-, 6-, and 10-inch fluted tart pans to make both pastry- and crumb-crust tarts.

Waffle Iron: Chances are somebody gave you a waffle iron at your wedding shower and it's stowed at the back of your cabinet. If you are in the market for a new waffle iron, look for one that cooks waffles quickly with high heat.

Wire Racks: Important for cooling cookies, cakes, and muffins. It's good to have two or three wire racks for cooling big batches of cookies or multiple cake layers.

Wire Whisk: Use a whisk to break up eggs or thoroughly mix dry ingredients.

BEYOND THE FREEZER CASE:
homemade pancakes and waffles

CLOCKWISE FROM TOP LEFT: Mango-Pecan-Coconut Granola, Baked Apple Pancake, Berry Pancakes

I have been making pancakes and waffles

regularly since my older child started to eat solid food. Plain pancakes are just a step beyond nursery foods: slightly sweet, buttery, and of uniform color, with no scary green parts or seeds. Waffles have a little more texture, it's true, but the fun little squares that hold the syrup more than compensate for this defect. Both pancakes and waffles are great for breakfast, but also for lunch and dinner when someone in your house needs comfort, or if you have completely failed to plan and shop for a real meal.

Basic pancake and waffle recipes have short ingredient lists and can be mixed and cooked in no time. If you have flour, eggs, milk, and butter, you can be eating pancakes in ten minutes. I've seen dozens of recipes that complicate this scenario. Some call for whipping the egg whites for taller pancakes, for making waffles with yeast and letting the batter sit overnight, for using fruit purées (which you have to make yourself) instead of milk. These ideas always intrigue me, and I've tried some of them with tasty results. But since I have two high-maintenance kids who demand breakfast every day as soon as they wake up, I must live in reality. That means using simple recipes without extra ingredients and steps.

I have developed as many variations on the basic recipes as any mom will ever need. Each variation is as simple and pared down as possible. For Oatmeal-Raisin Pancakes I've replaced some of the flour with rolled oats, used brown sugar instead of granulated sugar, and sprinkled the batter with raisins. Just as you'd hope, Ham and Cheese Waffles don't require an all-new, complicated batter recipe. They just have a little less sugar and some ham and cheese stirred in. These simple substitutions and additions make for a completely different taste experience without a lot of hassle.

There's something very satisfying about mixing a big bowl of batter until it's nice and smooth. *Restrain yourself!* If you stir the batter too much, your pancakes and waffles will be tough, not light and fluffy. Lumpy batter makes for better pancakes. So give your mixing arm a rest if you are a pancake perfectionist.

Pancakes should be baked on a griddle or large skillet over medium-high heat. When greasing the cooking surface, I prefer using nonstick cooking spray to butter. Nonstick spray is less likely to burn and leave the later batches of pancakes flecked with icky black stuff. Better still, make pancakes in a nonstick skillet. You won't need any grease at all, and cleanup will be that much easier. Relatively high heat will cook the pancakes quickly, giving them a good rise and nice color. Test the griddle or skillet after a couple of minutes by drizzling a few drops of water onto the cooking surface. If the drips sizzle and evaporate, the surface is hot enough. Do watch the heat carefully, however, and adjust the burner when necessary. I can't tell you how many times I've made a perfect first batch of pancakes only to burn the second batch, not realizing that the pan had gotten too hot.

Waffles should be baked quickly in a very hot waffle iron if they are going to be crunchy on the outside and fluffy on the inside. Four or five minutes is best. If your waffle iron is lukewarm, your waffles will begin to steam and turn rubbery on the inside before they are nice and brown on the outside. I have a wonderful VillaWare waffle iron (see Mail-Order and Online Resources, page 273), which bakes very quickly. If you're in the market for a new waffle iron, check out brands that advertise the high temperatures they are able to achieve. I prefer a waffle iron with a nonstick surface for obvious reasons. Just to be safe, I spray my nonstick iron with cooking spray before cooking the first batch. Further spraying is not necessary. If your waffle iron doesn't have this kind of surface or if the nonstick surface has worn away, spray the surface before cooking each new batch.

In my house we're pretty casual about serving pancakes and waffles. We just dish them out hot from the pan or waffle iron. My husband and I will take turns cooking so that one of us can sit down and supervise the kids as they dig in (we've found that the syrup is more likely to wind up in the hair if no one is watching). If you'd like everyone in your family to sit down and eat at the same time, you may place the pancakes and waffles on a platter, cover them loosely with aluminum foil, and keep them warm in a preheated 200-degree oven until you are finished cooking.

In my opinion, pure maple syrup sets the standard for toppings. There are people who will disagree, preferring cinnamon sugar, powdered sugar, or jam. I've included a few favorite fruit sauce recipes as alternatives. To transform waffles into dessert, top them with ice cream and chocolate sauce.

My own daughter will argue with you for hours about the superiority of Aunt Jemima brand pancake syrup. One day I packed leftover pancakes and a little container of syrup in her lunch box. "Did you eat your pancakes?" I asked when she returned from school. "No," she replied proudly, "but I drank all the syrup!" Ever since this horrifying incident, I have tried to entice her with pancake and waffle recipes that she would actually deem worthy of eating along with the beloved syrup. If your experience is like mine, you'll win some and you'll lose some, but you'll have a lot of good breakfasts on your way to discovering your children's favorites.

basic pancakes

Makes 4 servings, about twelve 4-inch pancakes

Pancake mavens say that the best-tasting pancakes contain buttermilk or yogurt, or that you really should separate the eggs and whip the whites for the fluffiest pancakes. Us moms roll our eyes when we hear this kind of advice. Why complicate something that should be simple? The best everyday pancakes are the ones that can be made from ingredients we always have on hand (my children don't drink buttermilk from a sippy cup) and require just a quick stir before cooking.

Basic pancakes really are so quick and easy that once you make them a couple of times, you'll probably have memorized the ingredients and won't even need the recipe. Serving up from-scratch pancakes on a school day is guaranteed to make you feel like a supermom, and it doesn't take much more time than making hot cereal.

1½ cups unbleached
   all-purpose flour
1½ teaspoons baking powder
¼ teaspoon salt
2 tablespoons sugar
1½ cups whole or lowfat milk
1 large egg
2 tablespoons unsalted butter, melted
   and cooled
Nonstick cooking spray
Pure maple syrup for serving

1. Stir together the flour, baking powder, salt, and sugar in a large mixing bowl.

2. Measure the milk into a large glass measuring cup. Crack the egg into the cup and beat lightly with a fork to break up the egg. Stir in the cooled melted butter.

3. Pour the liquid ingredients into the mixing bowl and stir with a wooden spoon until the dry ingredients are moistened. Don't worry if there are some small lumps.

4. Spray the surface of a griddle or a large skillet with cooking spray. Heat it over medium-high heat. Test the griddle or skillet after a couple of minutes by drizzling a few drops of water onto the cooking surface. If the drops sizzle and evaporate, the surface is hot enough.

5. For each pancake, spoon or ladle about ¼ cup batter onto the surface and cook the pancake until the top begins to bubble and the bottom is golden, 2 to 3 minutes. Check occasionally to make sure the pancakes aren't cooking too quickly and adjust the heat if necessary. Flip each pancake and cook it until it is golden on the second side, an additional minute or two. Serve immediately with maple syrup or keep them warm in a preheated 200-degree oven on a platter loosely covered with aluminum foil. Repeat with the remaining batter, removing the pan from the heat and spraying the cooking surface, if necessary, with more cooking spray before beginning each new batch.

buttermilk pancakes

Makes 4 servings, about twelve 4-inch pancakes

Having rolled my eyes at buttermilk in the previous recipe, I will now admit that I love the tangy flavor that buttermilk lends to pancakes. Buttermilk pancakes aren't so much better than basic pancakes that I'll make a special trip to get this one ingredient, but if I happen to have buttermilk on hand or I'm thinking ahead while I'm at the supermarket, I will use buttermilk instead of milk.

Because buttermilk makes the batter slightly acidic, a little bit of baking soda must be added so that the pancakes will rise properly. *Do not* attempt to substitute more baking powder for baking soda, or your pancakes will be heavy, not fluffy.

1½ cups unbleached
    all-purpose flour
1 teaspoon baking powder
½ teaspoon baking soda
¼ teaspoon salt
2 tablespoons sugar
1¼ cups buttermilk
½ cup milk
1 large egg
2 tablespoons unsalted butter, melted
    and cooled
Nonstick cooking spray
Pure maple syrup for serving

1. Stir together the flour, baking powder, baking soda, salt, and sugar in a large mixing bowl.

2. Measure the buttermilk and milk into a large glass measuring cup. Crack the egg into the cup and beat lightly with a fork to break up the egg. Stir in the cooled melted butter.

3. Pour the liquid ingredients into the mixing bowl and stir with a wooden spoon until the dry ingredients are moistened. Don't worry if there are some small lumps.

4. Spray the surface of a griddle or a large skillet with cooking spray. Heat it over medium-high heat. Test the griddle or skillet after a couple of minutes by drizzling a few drops of water onto the cooking surface. If the drops sizzle and evaporate, the surface is hot enough.

5. Turn the heat down to medium. For each pancake, spoon or ladle about ¼ cup batter onto the surface and cook until the top begins to bubble and the bottom is golden, 2 to 3 minutes. Check occasionally to make sure the pancakes aren't cooking too quickly, and adjust the heat if necessary. Flip each pancake and cook it until it is golden on the second side, an additional 2 minutes. Serve pancakes immediately with maple syrup or keep them warm in a preheated 200-degree oven on a platter loosely covered with aluminum foil. Repeat with the remaining batter, removing the pan from the heat and spraying the cooking surface, if necessary, with more cooking spray before beginning each new batch.

berry pancakes

Makes 4 servings, about twelve 4-inch pancakes

It's best to add berries to pancakes once you've spooned the batter onto the cooking surface. If you add them to the mixing bowl, even a slight stirring may turn your pancakes an unappetizing pink or blue. Fresh berries are great, but I find that frozen berries work just fine. There's no need to defrost frozen berries before adding them to the pancakes. The cold berries will slow down the cooking a little, so turn the heat down to medium and cook the pancakes a minute or two longer than you would if you were using fresh berries. Berry pancakes are nice simply dusted with powdered sugar or drizzled with melted butter and sprinkled with cinnamon sugar.

1½ cups unbleached
   all-purpose flour
1½ teaspoons baking powder
¼ teaspoon salt
3 tablespoons granulated sugar
1½ cups whole or lowfat milk
1 large egg
2 tablespoons unsalted butter, melted and cooled
1½ cups fresh or frozen blueberries or
   raspberries
Nonstick cooking spray
Pure maple syrup, confectioners' sugar,
   or melted butter and Cinnamon Sugar
   (recipe follows) for serving

1. Stir together the flour, baking powder, salt, and granulated sugar in a large mixing bowl.

2. Measure the milk into a large glass measuring cup. Crack the egg into the cup and beat lightly with a fork to break up the egg. Stir in the cooled melted butter.

3. Pour the liquid ingredients into the mixing bowl and stir with a wooden spoon until the dry ingredients are moistened. Don't worry if there are some small lumps.

4. Spray the surface of a griddle or a large skillet with cooking spray. Heat it over medium-high heat. Test the griddle or skillet after a couple of minutes by drizzling a few drops of water onto the cooking surface. If the drops sizzle and evaporate, the surface is hot enough.

Kids Can Help

   I let my five-year-old mix the dry ingredients together. Children ten years and older may be taught the recipe, and after a few tries, will be able to cook pancakes for you.

5. For each pancake, spoon or ladle about ¼ cup batter onto the surface. Sprinkle each pancake with a tablespoonful of berries and press down on the berries lightly with a spatula. Cook each pancake until the top begins to bubble and the bottom is golden, 2 to 3 minutes (3 to 4 minutes if using frozen berries). Check occasionally to make sure the pancakes aren't cooking too quickly, and adjust the heat if necessary. Flip each pancake and cook it until it is golden on the second side, an additional minute or two. Serve the pancakes immediately with maple syrup, powdered sugar, or melted butter and cinnamon sugar or keep them warm in a preheated 200-degree oven on a platter loosely covered with aluminum foil. Repeat with the remaining batter, removing the pan from the heat and spraying the cooking surface with more cooking spray before beginning each new batch.

cinnamon sugar

Makes ½ cup

Mix cinnamon and sugar together in large quantities so you'll always have this topping ready for breakfast.

½ cup sugar
1 teaspoon ground cinnamon

Stir together the sugar and cinnamon until well combined. Store in an airtight container at room temperature until ready to use.

A Good Excuse to Make Pancakes

Pancakes really are so simple that even if you have no cooking or baking experience, you will be able to master this recipe without too much practice. If weekday mornings are too rushed in your house for making basic pancakes, try whipping up a batch for dinner when you've got nothing in the refrigerator but milk and eggs and everyone's craving something comforting.

cranberry-orange pancakes

Makes 4 servings, about twelve 4-inch pancakes

When cranberries start appearing in the produce aisle in the fall, I'll pick up a bag or two to keep in the freezer so that I can make this simple variation on berry pancakes all through the winter. These pancakes are superb with maple syrup.

1½ cups unbleached
    all-purpose flour
1½ teaspoons baking powder
¼ teaspoon salt
3 tablespoons sugar
¼ teaspoon ground cinnamon
1½ cups whole or lowfat milk
1 large egg
2 tablespoons unsalted butter, melted
    and cooled
1½ teaspoons grated orange zest from
    1 large orange
1 cup fresh or frozen cranberries,
    picked over for stems
Nonstick cooking spray
Pure maple syrup for serving

1. Stir together the flour, baking powder, salt, sugar, and cinnamon in a large mixing bowl.

2. Measure the milk into a large glass measuring cup. Crack the egg into the cup and beat lightly with a fork to break up the egg. Stir in the cooled melted butter.

3. Pour the liquid ingredients into the mixing bowl and stir with a wooden spoon until the dry ingredients are moistened. Don't worry if there are some small lumps. Stir in the orange zest and cranberries.

4. Spray the surface of a griddle or a large skillet with cooking spray. Heat it over medium-high heat. Test the griddle or skillet after a couple of minutes by drizzling a few drops of water onto the cooking surface. If the drops sizzle and evaporate, the surface is hot enough.

5. For each pancake, spoon or ladle about ¼ cup batter onto the surface. Cook until the top begins to bubble and the bottom is golden, 2 to 3 minutes (3 to 4 minutes if using frozen cranberries). Check occasionally to make sure the pancakes aren't cooking too quickly, and adjust the heat if necessary. Flip each pancake and cook it until it is golden on the second side, an additional minute or two. Serve the pancakes immediately with maple syrup or keep them warm in a preheated 200-degree oven on a platter loosely covered with aluminum foil. Repeat with the remaining batter, removing the pan from the heat and spraying the cooking surface with more cooking spray before beginning each new batch.

A Good Excuse to Make Cranberry-Orange Pancakes

Buy a 12-ounce bag of cranberries and make up a batch of these pancakes the weekend before Thanksgiving. Then use the leftover berries to make homemade cranberry sauce for your turkey: Cook the rest of the cranberries with 1½ cups sugar and ¾ cup water over medium heat in a medium saucepan until thickened, about 10 minutes, let cool, and refrigerate in an airtight container until Thursday.

chocolate milk pancakes

Makes 4 servings, about twelve 4-inch pancakes

I used to make chocolate pancakes by mixing cocoa powder in with my dry ingredients, but one morning when I opened the refrigerator and saw a quart of chocolate milk a lightbulb went on above my head. Now I just substitute chocolate milk for regular milk in my basic pancake recipe and throw in some chocolate chips for good measure. The chips melt and moisten the pancakes, so no syrup is necessary.

1½ cups unbleached
   all-purpose flour
1½ teaspoons baking powder
¼ teaspoon salt
2 tablespoons sugar
1½ cups chocolate milk
1 large egg
2 tablespoons unsalted butter, melted
   and cooled
¾ cup semisweet chocolate chips
Nonstick cooking spray

1. Stir together the flour, baking powder, salt, and sugar in a large mixing bowl.

2. Measure the chocolate milk into a large glass measuring cup. Crack the egg into the cup and beat lightly with a fork to break up the egg. Stir in the cooled melted butter.

3. Pour the liquid ingredients into the mixing bowl and stir with a wooden spoon until the dry ingredients are moistened. Don't worry if there are some small lumps. Stir in the chocolate chips.

4. Spray the surface of a griddle or a large skillet with cooking spray. Heat it over medium-high heat. Test the griddle or skillet after a couple of minutes by drizzling a few drops of water onto the cooking surface. If the drops sizzle and evaporate, the surface is hot enough.

5. For each pancake, spoon or ladle about ¼ cup batter onto the surface and cook until the top begins to bubble, 2 to 3 minutes. Check occasionally to make sure the pancakes aren't cooking too quickly, and adjust the heat if necessary. Flip each pancake and cook it until it is golden on the second side, an additional minute or two. Serve the pancakes immediately or keep them warm in a preheated 200-degree oven on a platter loosely covered with aluminum foil. Repeat with the remaining batter, removing the pan from the heat and spraying the cooking surface with more cooking spray before beginning each new batch.

A Good Excuse to Make Chocolate Milk Pancakes

If you're a bad mother (like me), you'll make these any time your kids ask for them, and fight with them for the last one. If you have strict rules about healthy breakfasts, save these for birthdays and other special occasions. (The recipe can be doubled for the morning after a slumber party. God help you if you have more than eight kids to feed.)

buckwheat pancakes

Makes 4 servings, about twelve 4-inch pancakes

Buckwheat flour, available in natural foods stores and many supermarkets, gives pancakes an earthy, slightly nutty flavor. Yogurt adds another healthy note. Serve these pancakes with maple syrup, fruit jam, or fresh fruit and honey.

1 cup unbleached
   all-purpose flour
1/2 cup buckwheat flour
1 teaspoon baking powder
1/2 teaspoon baking soda
1/4 teaspoon salt
2 tablespoons sugar
1 cup plain lowfat yogurt
3/4 cup whole or lowfat milk
1 large egg
2 tablespoons unsalted butter, melted
   and cooled
Nonstick cooking spray

1. Stir together the flours, baking powder, baking soda, salt, and sugar in a large mixing bowl.

2. Stir together the yogurt, milk, egg, and cooled melted butter in a large glass measuring cup.

3. Pour the liquid ingredients into the mixing bowl and stir with a wooden spoon until the dry ingredients are moistened. Don't worry if there are some small lumps.

4. Spray the surface of a griddle or a large skillet with cooking spray. Heat it over medium-high heat. Test the griddle or skillet after a couple of minutes by drizzling a few drops of water onto the cooking surface. If the drops sizzle and evaporate, the surface is hot enough.

5. For each pancake, spoon or ladle about 1/4 cup batter onto the surface and cook until the top begins to bubble and the bottom is golden, 2 to 3 minutes. Check occasionally to make sure the pancakes aren't cooking too quickly, and adjust the heat if necessary. Flip each pancake and cook it until it is golden on the second side, an additional minute or two. Serve the pancakes immediately or keep them warm in a preheated 200-degree oven on a platter loosely covered with aluminum foil. Repeat with the remaining batter, removing the pan from the heat and spraying the cooking surface with more cooking spray before beginning each new batch.

cornmeal-cheddar pancakes

Makes 4 servings, about twelve 4-inch pancakes

These slightly crunchy, golden pancakes make a great quick dinner, served with your favorite tomato sauce or salsa. If you are a fan of sweet-and-savory combinations, try them with Apple Cider Syrup (page 37).

¾ cup unbleached
   all-purpose flour
¾ cup yellow cornmeal
2 teaspoons baking powder
½ teaspoon salt
1 tablespoon sugar
1½ cups whole or lowfat milk
1 large egg
2 tablespoons unsalted butter, melted
   and cooled
1 cup grated cheddar cheese
Nonstick cooking spray

1. Stir together the flour, cornmeal, baking powder, salt, and sugar in a large mixing bowl.

2. Measure the milk into a large glass measuring cup. Crack the egg into the cup and beat lightly with a fork to break up the egg. Stir in the cooled melted butter.

3. Pour the liquid ingredients into the mixing bowl and stir with a wooden spoon until the dry ingredients are moistened. Don't worry if there are some small lumps. Stir in the grated cheese.

4. Spray the surface of a griddle or a large skillet with cooking spray. Heat it over medium-high heat. Test the griddle or skillet after a couple of minutes by drizzling a few drops of water onto the cooking surface. If the drops sizzle and evaporate, the surface is hot enough.

5. For each pancake, spoon or ladle about ¼ cup batter onto the surface and cook until the top begins to bubble and the bottom is golden, 2 to 3 minutes. Check occasionally to make sure the pancakes aren't cooking too quickly, and adjust the heat if necessary. Flip each pancake and cook it until it is golden on the second side, an additional minute or two. Serve the pancakes immediately or keep them warm in a preheated 200-degree oven on a platter loosely covered with aluminum foil. Repeat with the remaining batter, removing the pan from the heat and spraying the cooking surface with more cooking spray before beginning each new batch.

oatmeal-raisin pancakes

Makes 4 servings, about twelve 4-inch pancakes

If you are a fan of oatmeal or oatmeal cookies, try these. If your raisins are moist and plump, you can skip the soaking, but if they are hard and dry, they should be rehydrated.

½ cup raisins
¾ cups unbleached all-purpose flour
¾ cups old-fashioned rolled oats (not instant)
1½ teaspoons baking powder
¼ teaspoon salt
¼ cup firmly packed light brown sugar
1½ cups whole or lowfat milk
1 large egg
2 tablespoons unsalted butter, melted and cooled
Nonstick cooking spray
Pure maple syrup for serving

1. Place the raisins in a small heat-proof bowl and cover them with boiling water. Let them soak for 10 minutes, drain them, and pat them dry with paper towels.

2. Stir together the flour, oats, baking powder, salt, and brown sugar in a large mixing bowl.

3. Measure the milk into a large glass measuring cup. Crack the egg into the cup and beat lightly with a fork to break up the egg. Stir in the cooled melted butter.

4. Pour the liquid ingredients into the mixing bowl and stir with a wooden spoon until the dry ingredients are moistened. Don't worry if there are some small lumps. Stir in the drained raisins. Let the batter stand for 15 minutes to thicken and to allow the oats to rehydrate.

5. Spray the surface of a griddle or a large skillet with cooking spray. Heat it over medium-high heat. Test the griddle or skillet after a couple of minutes by drizzling a few drops of water onto the cooking surface. If the drops sizzle and evaporate, the surface is hot enough.

6. For each pancake, spoon or ladle about ¼ cup batter onto the surface and cook until the top begins to bubble and the bottom is golden, 2 to 3 minutes. Check occasionally to make sure the pancakes aren't cooking too quickly, and adjust the heat if necessary. Flip each pancake and cook it until it is golden on the second side, an additional minute or two. Serve the pancakes immediately with maple syrup or keep them warm in a preheated 200-degree oven on a platter loosely covered with aluminum foil. Repeat with the remaining batter, removing the pan from the heat and spraying the cooking surface with more cooking spray before beginning each new batch.

sour cream mini-pancakes

Makes 4 servings, about forty 2-inch pancakes

Every basic cookbook has a variation on this recipe, and for good reason. These silver-dollar-size pancakes are made with an abundance of eggs and sour cream and just a little flour to hold them together. They have a rich, eggy flavor and a lighter-than-air texture. They are delicate, so you must make them small in order to flip them successfully. Serve them with syrup, Warm Blueberry Sauce (page 31), or fresh fruit.

½ cup unbleached all-purpose flour
3 tablespoons sugar
½ teaspoon salt
½ teaspoon baking soda
4 large eggs
2 cups full-fat sour cream
1 teaspoon pure vanilla extract
Nonstick cooking spray

1. Stir together the flour, sugar, salt, and baking soda in a small mixing bowl.

2. Lightly beat the eggs in a large mixing bowl to break them up. Stir in the sour cream and vanilla. With a wooden spoon, stir in the dry ingredients until just combined.

3. Spray the surface of a griddle or a large skillet with cooking spray. Heat it over medium-high heat. Test the griddle or skillet after a couple of minutes by drizzling a few drops of water onto the cooking surface. If the drops sizzle and evaporate, the surface is hot enough.

4. Turn the heat down to medium. For each pancake, spoon about 1 tablespoon of batter onto the surface and cook until the top begins to bubble and the bottom is golden, about 1 minute. Check occasionally to make sure the pancakes aren't cooking too quickly, and adjust the heat if necessary. Flip each pancake and cook it until it is golden on the second side, an additional minute. Serve the pancakes immediately or keep them warm in a preheated 200-degree oven on a platter loosely covered with aluminum foil. Repeat with the remaining batter, removing the pan from the heat and spraying the cooking surface with more cooking spray before beginning each new batch.

A Good Excuse to Make Sour Cream Mini-Pancakes

Because these pancakes have so much fat (why do you think they taste so great?), they really should be reserved for special occasions. Any weekend guest would be impressed with pancakes so light that they seem to float above the plate. I like to eat these in spring or summer with fresh fruit.

lemon-ricotta pancakes

Makes 4 servings, about twelve 4-inch pancakes

These pancakes, made with tart lemon and creamy ricotta, are like warm little cheesecakes. Cottage cheese may be substituted for the ricotta. Sprinkle these pancakes with powdered sugar or serve with Warm Blueberry Sauce (recipe follows). They make a very special brunch dish and may even be served for dessert.

1 cup unbleached
   all-purpose flour
1 teaspoon baking powder
¼ teaspoon baking soda
¼ teaspoon salt
3 tablespoons sugar
¾ cup whole-milk ricotta cheese
¾ cup whole or lowfat milk
¼ cup strained fresh lemon juice
1 large egg
2 tablespoons unsalted butter, melted
   and cooled
1 teaspoon pure vanilla extract
1½ teaspoons grated lemon zest
Nonstick cooking spray

1. Stir together the flour, baking powder, baking soda, salt, and sugar in a small mixing bowl.

2. Combine the ricotta, milk, lemon juice, egg, cooled melted butter, vanilla, and lemon zest in a large mixing bowl. With a wooden spoon, stir in the dry ingredients until just combined.

3. Spray the surface of a griddle or a large skillet with cooking spray. Heat it over medium-high heat. Test the griddle or skillet after a couple of minutes by drizzling a few drops of water onto the cooking surface. If the drops sizzle and evaporate, the surface is hot enough.

4. Turn the heat down to medium. For each pancake, spoon or ladle about ¼ cup

batter onto the surface and cook until the top begins to bubble and the bottom is golden, 2 to 3 minutes. Check occasionally to make sure the pancakes aren't cooking too quickly, and adjust the heat if necessary. Flip each pancake and cook it until it is golden on the second side, an additional 2 minutes. Serve immediately or keep warm in a preheated 200-degree oven on a platter loosely covered with aluminum foil. Repeat with the remaining batter, removing the pan from the heat and spraying the cooking surface with more cooking spray before beginning each new batch.

A Good Excuse to Make Lemon-Ricotta Pancakes

This is one of those recipes I might request for Mother's Day. These pancakes are so simple that any family member can make them perfectly without motherly supervision.

warm blueberry sauce

**Makes 1 cup, enough to top
4 servings of pancakes or waffles**

Blueberry sauce is delicious on a variety of
pancakes and waffles, and it's impossible
to screw up. You may substitute raspberries or hulled and sliced strawberries if
you like.

1 cup fresh or frozen blueberries
¼ cup water
1 tablespoon sugar, or more to taste
1 teaspoon strained fresh lemon juice
1 tablespoon unsalted butter

1. Combine the blueberries, water, sugar,
and lemon juice in a small saucepan. Cook
over medium heat, stirring often, until the
sugar dissolves and the liquid is slightly
thickened, 5 to 8 minutes (frozen blueberries will take longer than fresh ones
will).

2. Remove the pan from the heat and stir
in the butter until it is melted. Serve the
sauce warm or pour it into a tightly
covered container and refrigerate it for
up to 3 days. Reheat it before serving
(but do not boil it, or the butter will
separate out).

The Electric Skillet Option

For some people, an electric skillet is the
cooking implement of choice for cooking
pancakes. It has a nonstick surface, so
cooking spray or any other pan lubricant
is completely unnecessary, and regulat-
ing the pan temperature is as easy as
turning the temperature control on the
skillet to "Pancakes."

baked apple pancake

Makes 4 to 6 servings In a sense, this impressive oven-baked pancake is simpler to make and serve than griddle cakes are. The batter can be mixed in the food processor, and there's no arguing over who gets to eat first—the whole thing comes out of the oven at once. Use an ovenproof skillet with a metal rather than a rubber or plastic handle. Plastic and rubber handles will melt when placed in a hot oven, and the smell will not complement the aroma of the caramelized apples.

¼ cup (½ stick) unsalted butter
1¼ pounds firm, tart apples (about 3 medium), such as Granny Smith, peeled, cored, and cut into ¼-inch-thick slices
¼ cup granulated sugar
¼ teaspoon ground cinnamon
3 large eggs
½ cup whole or lowfat milk
½ cup unbleached all-purpose flour
¼ teaspoon salt
Confectioners' sugar

1. Preheat the oven to 425 degrees. Melt the butter over medium-high heat in an ovenproof 10-inch skillet. Add the apples, granulated sugar, and cinnamon and cook, stirring occasionally, until the apples begin to brown and most of the juices have evaporated, 5 to 7 minutes. Remove the skillet from the heat.

2. Combine the eggs, milk, flour, and salt in a food processor and process until smooth. (This can also be done with an electric mixer or by hand with a whisk.)

3. Spread the browned apples evenly across the bottom of the pan. Pour the batter over the apples. Place the skillet in the oven and bake until the pancake is golden and puffed, 18 to 20 minutes.

4. Remove the pan from the oven and let the pancake rest in the pan for 5 minutes. Sprinkle it with confectioners' sugar, cut into wedges, and serve immediately.

basic waffles

Makes 4 servings

The only difference between this batter and basic pancake batter is the amount of butter. I like to use a little more in waffles to give them some extra richness and crunch.

1½ cups unbleached
   all-purpose flour
1½ teaspoons baking powder
¼ teaspoon salt
2 tablespoons sugar
1½ cups whole or lowfat milk
1 large egg
¼ cup (½ stick) unsalted butter, melted
   and cooled
Nonstick cooking spray
Pure maple syrup for serving

1. Stir together the flour, baking powder, salt, and sugar in a large mixing bowl.

2. Measure the milk into a large glass measuring cup. Crack the egg into the cup and beat lightly with a fork to break up the egg. Stir in the cooled melted butter.

3. Pour the liquid ingredients into the mixing bowl and stir with a wooden spoon until the dry ingredients are moistened. Don't worry if there are some small lumps.

4. Heat the waffle iron. Spray the grids with cooking spray.

5. Pour some batter (how much depends on the size of your waffle iron) onto the grids and spread it to the edges with a spatula. Cook the waffles until they are golden brown, 4 to 7 minutes, depending on your machine. Serve the waffles immediately with maple syrup or keep them warm in a preheated 200-degree oven on a platter loosely covered with aluminum foil. Repeat with the remaining batter, spraying the cooking surface with more cooking spray before beginning each new batch.

buttermilk waffles

Makes 4 servings Tangy and rich, these set the standard for plain waffles.

1½ cups unbleached
    all-purpose flour
1 teaspoon baking powder
¼ teaspoon baking soda
¼ teaspoon salt
2 tablespoons sugar
1¼ cups buttermilk
½ cup whole or lowfat milk
1 large egg
¼ cup (½ stick) unsalted butter, melted
    and cooled
Nonstick cooking spray
Pure maple syrup for serving

1. Stir together the flour, baking powder, baking soda, salt, and sugar in a large mixing bowl.

2. Measure the buttermilk and milk into a large glass measuring cup. Crack the egg into the cup and beat lightly with a fork to break up the egg. Stir in the cooled melted butter.

3. Pour the liquid ingredients into the mixing bowl and stir with a wooden spoon until the dry ingredients are moistened. Don't worry if there are some small lumps.

4. Heat the waffle iron. Spray the grids with cooking spray.

5. Pour some batter (how much depends on the size of your waffle iron) onto the grids and spread it to the edges with a spatula. Cook the waffles until they are golden brown, 4 to 7 minutes, depending on your machine. Serve the waffles immediately with maple syrup or keep them warm in a preheated 200-degree oven on a platter loosely covered with aluminum foil. Repeat with the remaining batter, spraying the cooking surface with more cooking spray before beginning each new batch.

sautéed banana topping

makes 4 servings

Try these delectable bananas as an alternative to maple syrup if you have a little extra time. Sautéed bananas are especially good served over Pecan Waffles, as well as Basic and Buttermilk Pancakes and Waffles.

2 tablespoons unsalted butter
2 medium ripe bananas, peeled and
    sliced into ¼-inch-thick rounds
2 tablespoons firmly packed light brown
    sugar

Heat the butter in a medium skillet over medium heat. When the butter is melted and bubbling, add the bananas and brown sugar and cook, stirring frequently, until the bananas are softened and the sugar is dissolved, 2 to 4 minutes. Remove the pan from the heat. (The bananas can be covered and kept warm for 5 to 10 minutes while the pancakes or waffles cook.) Spoon this topping over pancakes or waffles and serve immediately.

health waffles

Makes 4 servings These waffles contain all things healthy, so serve them without guilt. Rye flakes and flax seeds are available in natural food stores. If you can't find them, substitute rolled oats for the rye and use ½ cup sunflower seeds instead of ¼ cup to make up for not using flax seeds.

**¾ cup unbleached
  all-purpose flour**
½ cup whole wheat flour
¼ cup rye flakes
¼ cup unsalted sunflower seeds
¼ cup flax seeds
1 teaspoon baking powder
½ teaspoon baking soda
¼ teaspoon salt
1½ cups lowfat plain yogurt
1 large egg
2 tablespoons honey
2 tablespoons vegetable oil
Nonstick cooking spray

1. Stir together the flours, rye flakes, sunflower seeds, flax seeds, baking powder, baking soda, and salt in a large mixing bowl.

2. Combine the yogurt, egg, honey, and oil in a medium mixing bowl.

3. Pour the liquid ingredients into the large bowl and stir with a wooden spoon until the dry ingredients are moistened. Don't worry if there are some small lumps.

4. Heat the waffle iron. Spray the grids with cooking spray.

5. Pour some batter (how much depends on the size of your waffle iron) onto the grids and spread it to the edges with a spatula. Cook the waffles until they are golden brown, 4 to 7 minutes, depending on your machine. Serve the waffles immediately or keep them warm in a preheated 200-degree oven on a platter loosely covered with aluminum foil. Repeat with the remaining batter, spraying the cooking surface with more cooking spray before beginning each new batch.

pecan waffles

Makes 4 servings Nuts, brown sugar, and some extra butter make these waffles a sweet treat. Try them drizzled with honey or topped with Sautéed Banana Topping (page 34). They are also great for dessert, with rum-raisin or vanilla ice cream.

1 1/2 cups unbleached all-purpose flour
3/4 cup pecans, finely chopped
1 1/2 teaspoons baking powder
1/4 teaspoon salt
1/4 cup firmly packed light brown sugar
1 1/2 cups whole or lowfat milk
1 large egg
1/4 cup (1/2 stick) unsalted butter, melted and cooled
Nonstick cooking spray
Pure maple syrup, honey, or Sautéed Banana Topping (page 34) for serving

1. Stir together the flour, pecans, baking powder, salt, and brown sugar in a large mixing bowl.

2. Measure the milk into a large glass measuring cup. Crack the egg into the cup and beat lightly with a fork to break up the egg. Stir in the cooled melted butter.

3. Pour the liquid ingredients into the mixing bowl and stir with a wooden spoon until the dry ingredients are moistened. Don't worry if there are some small lumps.

4. Heat the waffle iron. Spray the grids with cooking spray.

5. Pour some batter (how much depends on the size of your waffle iron) onto the grids and spread it to the edges with a spatula. Cook the waffles until they are golden brown, 4 to 7 minutes, depending on your machine. Serve the waffles immediately with maple syrup, honey, or Sautéed Banana Topping or keep them warm in a preheated 200-degree oven on a platter loosely covered with aluminum foil. Repeat with the remaining batter, spraying the cooking surface with more cooking spray before beginning each new batch.

A Good Excuse to Make Pecan Waffles

If you're from the South, celebrate the pecan harvest by making these special waffles. If you're not, pretend to be and make them anyway.

gingerbread waffles

Makes 4 servings These waffles have all the great flavor of gingerbread cake plus something that cake doesn't have—those handy grids that soak up syrup so well.

1½ cups unbleached
   all-purpose flour
1½ teaspoons baking powder
2 tablespoons sugar
¼ teaspoon salt
1½ teaspoons ground ginger
½ teaspoon ground cinnamon
Pinch of ground cloves
1½ cups whole or lowfat milk
1 large egg
¼ cup (½ stick) unsalted butter, melted
   and cooled
2 tablespoons dark (not light or
   blackstrap) molasses
Nonstick cooking spray
Maple syrup or Apple Cider Syrup
   (recipe follows) for serving

1. Stir together the flour, baking powder, sugar, salt, ginger, cinnamon, and cloves in a large mixing bowl.

2. Measure the milk into a large glass measuring cup. Crack the egg into the cup and beat lightly with a fork to break up the egg. Stir in the cooled melted butter and molasses.

3. Pour the liquid ingredients into the mixing bowl and stir with a wooden spoon until the dry ingredients are moistened. Don't worry if there are some small lumps.

4. Heat the waffle iron. Spray the grids with cooking spray.

5. Pour some batter (how much depends on the size of your waffle iron) onto the grids and spread it to the edges with a spatula. Cook the waffles until they are golden brown, 4 to 7 minutes, depending on your machine. Serve the waffles immediately with maple syrup or Apple Cider Syrup or keep them warm in a preheated 200-degree oven on a platter loosely covered with aluminum foil. Repeat with the remaining batter, spraying the cooking surface with more cooking spray before beginning each new batch.

apple cider syrup

Makes about 1 cup, enough to top 4 servings of pancakes or waffles

I especially like this syrup with Oatmeal-Raisin Pancakes (page 28) and Gingerbread Waffles (above).

2 cups apple cider
2 tablespoons honey
2 tablespoons strained fresh lemon
   juice
2 tablespoons unsalted butter

1. Combine the cider, honey, and lemon juice in a small saucepan and bring to a boil. Reduce the heat to medium-low and simmer until mixture is reduced by half.

2. Remove the pan from the heat and stir in the butter. Serve this syrup warm or pour it into a tightly covered container and refrigerate it for up to 1 week. Reheat it before serving (but do not boil it, or the butter will separate out).

ham and cheese waffles

Makes 4 servings I love these waffles because they have the great flavor of a grilled ham-and-cheese sandwich without the grease and mess. Serve them plain or with maple syrup.

1½ cups unbleached all-purpose flour
1½ teaspoons baking powder
¼ teaspoon salt
1 tablespoon sugar
1½ cups whole or lowfat milk
1 large egg
¼ cup (½ stick) unsalted butter, melted and cooled
2 ounces Black Forest ham, thinly sliced and finely chopped
1 cup grated Gruyère cheese
Nonstick cooking spray
Pure maple syrup for serving

1. Stir together the flour, baking powder, salt, and sugar in a large mixing bowl.

2. Measure the milk into a large glass measuring cup. Crack the egg into the cup and beat lightly with a fork to break up the egg. Stir in the cooled melted butter.

3. Pour the liquid ingredients into the mixing bowl and stir with a wooden spoon until the dry ingredients are moistened. Don't worry if there are some small lumps. Stir in the ham and cheese.

4. Heat the waffle iron. Spray the grids with cooking spray.

5. Pour some batter (how much depends on the size of your waffle iron) onto the grids and spread it to the edges with a spatula. Cook the waffles until golden brown, 4 to 7 minutes, depending on your machine. Serve the waffles immediately or keep them warm in a preheated 200-degree oven on a platter loosely covered with aluminum foil. Repeat with the remaining batter, spraying the cooking surface with more cooking spray before beginning each new batch.

pumpkin waffles

Makes 4 servings I like to sweeten moist pumpkin waffles with a little bit of maple syrup instead of sugar since pumpkin and maple have such an affinity for each other.

1½ cups unbleached all-purpose flour
1½ teaspoons baking powder
¼ teaspoon salt
½ teaspoon ground cinnamon
1 cup canned pumpkin purée
1 cup whole or lowfat milk
1 large egg
¼ cup (½ stick) unsalted butter, melted and cooled
¼ cup pure maple syrup plus more for serving
Nonstick cooking spray

1. Stir together the flour, baking powder, salt, and cinnamon in a large mixing bowl.

2. Stir together the pumpkin, milk, egg, butter, and maple syrup in a medium mixing bowl.

3. Stir the wet ingredients into the dry ingredients with a wooden spoon until moistened. Don't worry if there are some small lumps.

4. Heat the waffle iron. Spray the grids with cooking spray.

5. Pour some batter (how much depends on the size of your waffle iron) onto the grids and spread it to the edges with a spatula. Cook the waffles until they are golden brown, 4 to 7 minutes, depending on your machine. Serve the waffles immediately or keep them warm in a preheated 200-degree oven on a platter loosely covered with aluminum foil. Repeat with the remaining batter, spraying the cooking surface with more cooking spray before beginning each new waffle.

bittersweet chocolate waffles

Makes 6 servings   This is my standard dessert waffle, the one I serve with vanilla, strawberry, or coffee ice cream. For really special occasions, top the ice cream and waffles with some Simple Warm Chocolate Sauce (recipe follows).

4 ounces bittersweet chocolate, finely chopped
½ cup (1 stick) unsalted butter, cut into 8 pieces
1 cup unbleached all-purpose flour
1 teaspoon baking powder
¼ teaspoon salt
½ cup plus 2 tablespoons sugar
4 large eggs
2 teaspoons pure vanilla extract
¼ cup whole or lowfat milk
Nonstick cooking spray

1. Put 1 inch of water into the bottom of a double boiler or medium saucepan and bring to a bare simmer. Combine the chocolate and butter in the top of the double boiler, or in a stainless-steel bowl set over a pot of simmering water, making sure that the water doesn't touch the bottom of the bowl. Heat, whisking occasionally, until the chocolate and butter are completely melted. Set aside to let cool slightly.

2. Stir together the flour, baking powder, salt, and sugar in a small mixing bowl.

3. Whisk together the eggs, vanilla, and milk in a large mixing bowl. Whisk in the cooled melted chocolate mixture. Stir in the dry ingredients with a wooden spoon.

4. Heat the waffle iron. Spray the grids with cooking spray.

5. Pour some batter (how much depends on the size of your waffle iron) onto the grids and spread it to the edges with a spatula. Cook the waffles until they are crisp, 3 to 5 minutes, depending on your machine. Serve the waffles immediately or keep them warm in a preheated 200-degree oven on a platter loosely covered with aluminum foil. Repeat with the remaining batter, spraying the cooking surface with more cooking spray before beginning each new batch.

simple warm chocolate sauce

**Makes about ½ cup, enough to top
2 to 4 servings of dessert**

This is the easiest sauce I know. It can be varied by adding 1 tablespoon of orange, hazelnut, or coffee liqueur. For the best results, use a top-quality bittersweet chocolate such as Lindt, Ghirardelli, or Callebaut.

**4 ounces bittersweet chocolate, finely
 chopped**
¼ cup water
1 tablespoon flavored liqueur (optional)

Put 2 inches of water in a medium saucepan and bring to a bare simmer. Combine the chocolate and water in a stainless steel bowl big enough to rest on top of the saucepan and place it on top of the simmering water, making sure that the water doesn't touch the bowl. Heat, whisking occasionally, until the chocolate is completely melted. Turn off the heat. Stir in the liqueur if desired. The sauce may be refrigerated for up to 2 days. Reheat in the microwave for 1½ minutes or over a pot of simmering water.

The Second Time Around

My kids eat like birds, and although they beg for pancakes and waffles, they never finish a whole batch. Leftovers freeze well, and it's great to cook once and have waffles or pancakes on hand for a couple of breakfasts later on. Let pancakes and waffles cool to room temperature, put them in a zipper-lock plastic bag, and freeze them for up to 2 weeks. For the baby, I'll often reheat frozen pancakes in the microwave for thirty seconds to a minute. She's satisfied, but I must admit that I don't like their rubbery texture. If I have a couple of extra minutes (and I'm thinking of eating a few myself), I'll brush frozen pancakes with a little melted butter, place them on a baking sheet, and reheat them in a preheated 200 degree oven for 5 to 8 minutes. Waffles can go directly from the freezer to the toaster.

maple walnut granola

Makes about
6 cups

4 cups old-fashioned rolled oats (not instant)

1 cup chopped walnuts

$\frac{1}{3}$ cup canola oil

$\frac{1}{4}$ cup pure maple syrup

2 teaspoons pure vanilla extract

Nonstick cooking spray (optional)

1 cup raisins

1. Preheat the oven to 325 degrees. Mix the oats, walnuts, oil, maple syrup, and vanilla together in a large mixing bowl. Spray a large baking sheet with cooking spray or line it with parchment paper.

Spread the granola evenly over the baking sheet and bake, tossing twice, until golden, about 15 minutes. Check frequently during the last few minutes to make sure that the granola does not burn.

2. Remove the pan from the oven and let the granola cool completely on the baking sheet placed on a wire rack. Transfer the granola to an airtight container, stir in the raisins, and cover. Store at room temperature.

Homemade Granola

I am a granola freak. After I finished cooking school and was working as a pastry chef, I used to fantasize about opening my own little breakfast place on Main Street in Sag Harbor. I was going to call it The Granola Bar, and I was going to serve only granola. Granola with milk, granola with yogurt, granola muffins, ice cream sprinkled with granola, granola trail mix to go. Ultimately, I was persuaded that this was too narrow a niche for a successful restaurant, but not before I developed some truly great granola recipes.

After putting together all the pancake and waffle recipes in this chapter, I remembered that granola is also a breakfast food that is baked. Why not include my favorite recipes and spread the gospel? Granola is the perfect thing for a modern mom to bake. It's easy, healthy, delicious, and adaptable to any family's tastes. If your kids hate nuts, just leave them out. If you like currants instead of raisins or pumpkin seeds for extra crunch, just substitute or add them. Granola will keep, stored at room temperature in an airtight container, for up to two weeks.

cherry almond granola

Makes about
6 cups

4 cups old-fashioned rolled oats (not instant)

2 teaspoons ground cinnamon

1 cup sliced almonds

1/3 cup canola oil

1/3 cup honey

2 teaspoons pure vanilla extract

Nonstick cooking spray (optional)

1 cup dried sour cherries

1. Preheat the oven to 325 degrees. Mix the oats, cinnamon, almonds, oil, honey, and vanilla together in a large mixing bowl. Spray a large baking sheet with cooking spray or line it with parchment paper. Spread the granola evenly over the baking sheet and bake, tossing twice, until golden, about 15 minutes. Check frequently during the last few minutes to make sure that the granola does not burn.

2. Remove the pan from the oven and let the granola cool completely on the baking sheet placed on a wire rack. Transfer the granola to an airtight container, stir in the cherries, and cover. Store at room temperature.

mango-pecan-coconut granola

Makes about
6 cups

4 cups old-fashioned rolled oats (not instant)

2 teaspoons ground ginger

1 cup chopped pecans

1/2 cup sweetened flaked coconut

1/3 cup canola oil

1/3 cup honey

2 teaspoons pure vanilla extract

Nonstick cooking spray (optional)

1 cup chopped dried mango

1. Preheat the oven to 325 degrees. Mix the oats, ginger, pecans, coconut, oil, honey, and vanilla together in a large mixing bowl. Spray a large baking sheet with cooking spray or line it with parchment paper. Spread the granola evenly over the baking sheet and bake, tossing twice, until golden, about 15 minutes. Check frequently during the last few minutes to make sure that the granola does not burn.

2. Remove the pan from the oven and let the granola cool completely on the baking sheet placed on a wire track. Transfer the granola to an airtight container, stir in the mango, and cover. Store at room temperature.

MOM'S CAFÉ:
muffins, quick breads, biscuits, and scones

TOP TO BOTTOM: Jam-Filled Crumb Muffins, Add-On Scones, Banana Bread

With so many moms and kids hanging out at

upscale coffee bars these days, it's no surprise that muffins and scones have become regular snack fare. Although I enjoy an occasional cup of coffee at the local java hut, I'd rather make my snacks at home. For one thing, you don't have to change out of your bathrobe. For another, homemade muffins and scones, warm from the oven, are much better than even the best commercial baked goods, which tend to be huge, heavy, and always a bit old by the time you buy them. And have you done the math? For the money I spend on two muffins at the café, I bet I could make two dozen at home.

Muffins are among the easiest baked goods you can make. You measure dry ingredients into a bowl. You measure wet ingredients into a bowl. You dump the dry ingredients into the wet ingredients and stir. You don't even need an electric mixer. The batter is loose enough that you can mix it in seconds with a wooden spoon.

Muffins do require one special piece of equipment: a muffin tin. But any muffin tin will do, and if you don't have one, you can buy one at the hardware store or supermarket for less than $5. I bake all my muffins in a standard-size muffin tin; each of its 12 muffin cups holds ½ cup of batter. Bake any of the following batters in any size muffin tin you like. Just fill the cups about two-thirds to three-quarters of the way to the top and adjust the baking time upward or downward, depending on whether you are using larger or smaller cups.

Many people prefer muffins baked directly in greased muffin tins to muffins baked in paper liners. Muffins baked directly in the tins have more crunchy, browned parts than do muffins baked in liners, and they are less messy to eat. But for a lot of people, especially kids, peeling away the paper liner is a large part of the muffin's appeal. I stockpile cute paper liners with hearts, shamrocks, pumpkins, Easter eggs, and anything else I happen to see at my local five-and-dime. You can guess which camp I belong to.

When it comes to muffin ingredients and flavorings, I don't like a whole lot of extras. I've worked hard on my blueberry muffin recipe so that it has just the right balance of sweet cake and juicy berries, with just a touch of lemon zest. I baked many batches of corn muffins before deciding that the ones made with sour cream are the ultimate. These classics, streamlined and perfected, will always satisfy me. I'm not interested in sprinkling streusel topping on my blueberry muffins. It's extra work without much benefit. I might add a chopped chile, a little grated cheese, or some scallions to my corn muffins, but I would never throw all three in. It's too much chopping, and with so many extra ingredients you wouldn't even taste the cornmeal.

As with almost all baked goods, muffins taste better with more rather than less butter. But I have developed a couple of really terrific reduced-fat recipes, both of which replace some of the fat with a nonfat ingredient that helps the muffins retain moisture. Reduced-Fat Apple and Oat Muffins have grated apple instead of a lot of butter. The prune purée in Reduced-Fat Cocoa-Chip Muffins adds wonderful flavor as well as moisture. It is very rare that I will recommend baking without butter, but I urge you to try these muffins even if you are not interested in counting calories or fat grams. They are satisfying by any standard.

I've heard people suggest all kinds of ways to save time when making muffins, but I don't bother with any of them. I am not nearly organized enough to premix and freeze bags of dry ingredients to use at a later date. And, really, how long is it actually going to take you to mix the dry ingredients together? Five minutes? It often takes me that long to find a bag that I've put in the freezer several weeks ago. Making muffin batter and keeping it in the refrigerator for several weeks so that you can make a muffin or two whenever you get the urge is even less appealing to me. I have enough science projects growing in my refrigerator already. I'm content to wrap any leftover muffins in plastic and then aluminum foil and freeze them for up to a month. When I want a muffin, I take one from the freezer, remove the wrapping, and microwave it for 30 seconds. Then I reheat it in a 350-degree oven for 5 minutes to crisp the exterior. All my muffin recipes are quick and easy. Further time-saving tips are really beside the point.

I have included a couple of favorite recipes for quick breads baked in loaf pans. The batters for Banana Bread, Savory Zucchini Bread, and Cranberry-Nut Bread are similar to muffin batter and may, in fact, be baked in muffin tins. But these three breads are especially good sliced and toasted a day or two after baking, so why not bake them in loaf pans and enjoy the leftovers this way?

I bet that most moms have been scared away from making biscuits, thinking that this is a skill you have to be taught by your own Southern mother. I am the living proof that this is not true. The closest my own mom ever got to a biscuit was a bagel. Yet by following a few simple rules (see Techniques for Making Tender Biscuits, page 73), I have been able to overcome my disadvantaged background and make very good biscuits. It may be hard to believe, but the less work you do (the less mixing, less rolling, less rerolling), and the quicker and sloppier you are (just throw the dough out onto the counter and cut the biscuits as quickly as you can; don't worry if your dough looks raggedy, with little bits falling off), the better your biscuits will be.

Scones are really just biscuits with extra butter and sugar. The same tips for making good biscuits apply to preparing scones: Make sure the butter is thoroughly distributed throughout the flour but still solid and chilly, don't overmix the dough or work it too hard or for too long when shaping the scones, and bake them quickly at a high temperature. I like the traditional method for shaping scones: patting the dough into a circle and then cutting the circle into wedges. There is less chance of toughening the dough by rolling over it too much because there are no scraps to reroll. And there is no waste at all.

I've included a few types of scones. The basic recipe can accommodate a variety of added ingredients, from chopped walnuts to crystallized ginger. A lemon-cream version is rich and tender beyond belief. Oatmeal scones made without eggs have the buttery consistency of shortbread. Finally, there is an all-American recipe for chocolate chip scones that probably wouldn't cut it at Harrod's high tea, but these scones are just perfect for a mom's book of baking.

I love the last recipe in this chapter because it embodies the best things about family baking. Popovers are extremely easy to make and can be eaten at breakfast, lunch, and dinner. But beyond ease and utility, popovers demonstrate the magic of combining a few common ingredients and coming up with something absolutely otherworldly. One of the reasons I bake for and with my family is to cultivate a sense of joy in our everyday lives. With a foolproof recipe for popovers, this goal has never been easier to achieve.

best blueberry muffins

Makes 12 muffins

Extra blueberries make these blueberry muffins the best, in my opinion. The balance of fruit and batter is perfect—you feel like you're getting a mouthful of berries with every bite, but there's enough cake so that your muffin holds together when you peel away the paper. I like lemon zest and buttermilk or yogurt in my blueberry muffins to counter the sweetness of the berries and cake.

Nonstick cooking spray (optional)
2 cups unbleached
   all-purpose flour
2 teaspoons baking powder
½ teaspoon baking soda
½ teaspoon salt
½ cup (1 stick) unsalted butter, melted
   and cooled
⅔ cup sugar
2 large eggs
1 teaspoon pure vanilla extract
1 teaspoon grated lemon zest
1 cup buttermilk or lowfat plain yogurt
1¾ cups fresh or frozen blueberries,
   picked over for stems

1. Preheat the oven to 375 degrees. Line a 12-cup muffin tin with paper liners or coat it with cooking spray.

2. Combine the flour, baking powder, baking soda, and salt in a medium mixing bowl.

3. Whisk together the cooled melted butter, sugar, eggs, vanilla, lemon zest, and buttermilk or yogurt in a large mixing bowl. With a wooden spoon, stir in the flour mixture until just combined. Gently stir in the blueberries.

4. Fill each muffin cup about three-quarters full. Bake the muffins until they are golden and a toothpick inserted into the center comes out clean, 22 to 25 minutes. Let them cool in the pan for about 5 minutes, invert them onto a wire rack, and turn them right side up on the rack to cool completely.

Best Blueberry Muffins will keep in an airtight container at room temperature for up to 2 days, or wrap them individually in plastic and then aluminum foil and freeze them for up to 1 month.

cranberry-orange muffins

Makes 12 muffins A muffin shop classic, Cranberry-Orange Muffins are especially good in the fall and winter, when fresh blueberries, strawberries, and raspberries are expensive and hard to find.

Nonstick cooking spray (optional)
**2 cups unbleached
    all-purpose flour**
2 teaspoons baking powder
½ teaspoon baking soda
½ teaspoon salt
**½ cup (1 stick) unsalted butter, melted
    and cooled**
⅔ cup sugar
2 large eggs
1 teaspoon pure vanilla extract
2 teaspoons grated orange zest
1 cup buttermilk or lowfat plain yogurt
**1 cup fresh or frozen cranberries,
    picked over for stems and coarsely
    chopped**

1. Preheat the oven to 375 degrees. Line a 12-cup muffin tin with paper liners or coat it with cooking spray.

2. Combine the flour, baking powder, baking soda, and salt in a medium mixing bowl.

3. Whisk together the cooled melted butter, sugar, eggs, vanilla, orange zest, and buttermilk or yogurt in a large mixing bowl. With a wooden spoon, stir in the flour mixture until just combined. Stir in the cranberries.

4. Fill each muffin cup about three-quarters full. Bake the muffins until they are golden and a toothpick inserted into the center comes out clean, 22 to 25 minutes. Let them cool in the pan for about 5 minutes, invert them onto a wire rack, and then turn them right side up on the rack to cool completely.

Cranberry-Orange Muffins will keep in an airtight container at room temperature for up to 2 days, or wrap them individually in plastic and then aluminum foil and freeze them for up to 1 month.

apricot-almond muffins

Makes 12 muffins

Adding almond extract instead of vanilla to the batter is an easy way to vary the flavor of muffins. I love the combination of apricots and almonds, but other dried fruits, such as cherries, chopped figs, or chopped prunes, may be substituted.

Nonstick cooking spray (optional)
2 cups unbleached all-purpose flour
1 tablespoon baking powder
1/2 teaspoon salt
1/2 cup (1 stick) unsalted butter, melted and cooled
2/3 cup firmly packed light brown sugar
2 large eggs
1 teaspoon pure almond extract
1 cup whole or lowfat milk
1/2 cup blanched whole almonds, coarsely chopped
1 cup dried apricots, finely chopped

1. Preheat the oven to 375 degrees. Line a 12-cup muffin tin with paper liners or coat it with cooking spray.

2. Combine the flour, baking powder, and salt in a medium mixing bowl.

3. Whisk together the cooled melted butter, brown sugar, eggs, almond extract, and milk in a large mixing bowl. With a wooden spoon, stir in the flour mixture until just combined. Stir in the almonds and apricots.

4. Fill each muffin cup about three-quarters full. Bake the muffins until they are golden and a toothpick inserted into the center comes out clean, 22 to 25 minutes. Let them cool in the pan for about 5 minutes, invert them onto a wire rack, and then turn them right side up on the rack to cool completely.

Apricot-Almond Muffins will keep in an airtight container at room temperature for up to 2 days, or wrap them individually in plastic and then aluminum foil and freeze them for up to 1 month.

maple-pecan muffins

Toasting the pecans definitely boosts the flavor in this recipe and is a worthwhile extra step. If you like, you can place a pecan half on top of each muffin before baking as a decorative touch.

Nonstick cooking spray (optional)
1 cup coarsely chopped pecans
2 cups unbleached
   all-purpose flour
2 teaspoons baking powder
½ teaspoon baking soda
½ teaspoon salt
½ cup (1 stick) unsalted butter, melted
   and cooled
½ cup firmly packed
   light brown sugar
¼ cup pure maple syrup
2 large eggs
1 cup buttermilk or lowfat plain yogurt
12 pecan halves (optional)

1. Preheat the oven to 375 degrees. Spread the chopped pecans on a baking sheet and toast them in the oven until they are fragrant, about 5 minutes. Remove the pecans from the oven and let them cool completely. Line a 12-cup muffin tin with paper liners or coat it with cooking spray.

2. Combine the flour, baking powder, baking soda, and salt in a medium mixing bowl.

3. Whisk together the cooled melted butter, brown sugar, maple syrup, eggs, and buttermilk or yogurt in a large mixing bowl. With a wooden spoon, stir in the flour mixture until just combined. Stir in the chopped pecans.

4. Fill each muffin cup about three-quarters full. Place a pecan half on top of each muffin if desired. Bake the muffins until they are golden and a toothpick inserted into the center comes out clean, 22 to 25 minutes. Let them cool in the pan for about 5 minutes, invert them onto a wire rack, and then turn them right side up on the rack to cool completely.

Maple-Pecan Muffins will keep in an airtight container at room temperature for up to 2 days, or wrap them individually in plastic and then aluminum foil and freeze them for up to 1 month.

lemon-ginger muffins

Makes 12 muffins These muffins would be my choice when serving strong tea, hot or iced. Fresh ginger can be found next to the garlic in the produce section of the supermarket. Peel away the tough skin with a vegetable peeler or sharp paring knife. A four- or five-inch piece should yield about ¼ cup chopped ginger. Chop the ginger very fine for the best flavor and texture.

Nonstick cooking spray (optional)
2 cups unbleached
    all-purpose flour
2 teaspoons baking powder
½ teaspoon baking soda
½ teaspoon salt
½ cup (1 stick) unsalted butter, melted
    and cooled
⅔ cup sugar
2 large eggs
1 teaspoon pure vanilla extract
¼ cup peeled and minced fresh ginger
1 tablespoon grated lemon zest
1 cup buttermilk or lowfat plain yogurt

1. Preheat the oven to 375 degrees. Line a 12-cup muffin tin with paper liners or coat it with cooking spray.

2. Combine the flour, baking powder, baking soda, and salt in a medium mixing bowl.

3. Whisk together the cooled melted butter, sugar, eggs, vanilla, ginger, lemon zest, and buttermilk or yogurt in a large mixing bowl. With a wooden spoon, stir in the flour mixture until just combined.

4. Fill each muffin cup about three-quarters full. Bake the muffins until they are golden and a toothpick inserted into the center comes out clean, 22 to 25 minutes. Let the muffins cool in the pan for about 5 minutes, invert them onto a wire rack, and then turn them right side up on the rack to cool completely.

Lemon-Ginger Muffins will keep in an airtight container at room temperature for up to 2 days, or wrap them individually in plastic and then aluminum foil and freeze them for up to 1 month.

pumpkin spice muffins

Makes 18 muffins

Pumpkin purée comes in 15-ounce cans, and, since I hate waste, I designed this recipe to use a whole can. It yields 18 rather than 12 muffins, a good number to bring to school in the autumn when kids are celebrating the harvest. Serve these as a late-morning snack with thermoses of hot chocolate.

Nonstick cooking spray (optional)
1½ cups unbleached
   all-purpose flour
1 teaspoon baking powder
½ teaspoon baking soda
¼ teaspoon salt
½ teaspoon ground cinnamon
½ teaspoon ground ginger
¼ teaspoon ground nutmeg
½ cup (1 stick) unsalted butter, melted
   and cooled
1 cup sugar
2 large eggs
One 15-ounce can pumpkin purée
1 teaspoon pure vanilla extract

1. Preheat the oven to 375 degrees. Line a 12-cup muffin tin and a 6-cup muffin tin with paper liners or coat them with cooking spray.

2. Combine the flour, baking powder, baking soda, salt, cinnamon, ginger, and nutmeg in a medium mixing bowl.

3. Whisk together the cooled melted butter, sugar, eggs, pumpkin purée, and vanilla in a large mixing bowl. With a wooden spoon, stir in the flour mixture until just combined.

4. Fill each muffin cup about three-quarters full. Bake the muffins until they are golden and a toothpick inserted into the center comes out clean, 22 to 25 minutes. Let the muffins cool in the pan for about 5 minutes, invert them onto a wire rack, and then turn them right side up on the rack to cool completely.

Pumpkin Spice Muffins will keep in an airtight container at room temperature for up to 2 days, or wrap them individually in plastic and then aluminum foil and freeze them for up to 1 month.

chocolate chip muffins

Makes 12 muffins These are more like cupcakes than muffins (probably why my five-year-old prefers them to any other variety). The crunchy cinnamon-sugar topping is a nice contrast to the buttery cake.

Nonstick cooking spray (optional)
2 cups unbleached all-purpose flour
1 tablespoon baking powder
½ teaspoon salt
¼ cup granulated sugar
1 teaspoon ground cinnamon
½ cup (1 stick) unsalted butter, melted
  and cooled
⅔ cup firmly packed light brown sugar
2 large eggs
1 teaspoon pure vanilla extract
1 cup whole or lowfat milk
1 cup semisweet chocolate chips

1. Preheat the oven to 375 degrees. Line a 12-cup muffin tin with paper liners or coat it with cooking spray.

2. Combine the flour, baking powder, and salt in a medium mixing bowl. Combine the granulated sugar and cinnamon in a small bowl.

3. Whisk together the cooled melted butter, brown sugar, eggs, vanilla, and milk in a large mixing bowl. With a wooden spoon, stir in the flour mixture until just combined. Stir in the chocolate chips.

4. Fill each muffin cup about three-quarters full. Sprinkle each muffin with about a teaspoon of the cinnamon sugar. Bake the muffins until they are golden and a toothpick inserted into the center comes out clean, 22 to 25 minutes. Let the muffins cool in the pan for about 5 minutes, invert them onto a wire rack, and then turn them right side up on the rack to cool completely.

Chocolate Chip Muffins will keep in an airtight container at room temperature for up to 2 days, or wrap them individually in plastic and then aluminum foil and freeze them for up to 1 month.

jam-filled crumb muffins

Makes 12 muffins These are simple to make, but they do require a couple of extra steps: adding the jam to each muffin and then topping off the muffin with the remaining batter, and making the crumb topping. I think the effort is worth it. Your beautiful, bakery-worthy muffins may even impress jaded teenage coffee bar habitués.

For the muffins

Nonstick cooking spray (optional)
2 cups unbleached all-purpose flour
1 tablespoon baking powder
1/2 teaspoon salt
1/2 cup (1 stick) unsalted butter, melted and cooled
2/3 cup granulated sugar
2 large eggs
1 teaspoon pure vanilla extract
1 cup whole or lowfat milk
1/4 cup best-quality fruit preserves

For the crumb topping

1 cup unbleached all-purpose flour
1/4 cup plus 2 tablespoons firmly packed light brown sugar
1/2 teaspoon ground cinnamon
Pinch of ground nutmeg
6 tablespoons (3/4 stick) unsalted butter, melted

1. Preheat the oven to 375 degrees. Line a 12-cup muffin tin with paper liners or coat it with cooking spray.

2. Make the muffins: Combine the flour, baking powder, and salt in a medium mixing bowl.

3. Whisk together the cooled melted butter, granulated sugar, eggs, vanilla, and milk in a large mixing bowl. With a wooden spoon, stir in the flour mixture until just combined.

4. Fill each cup about half full. Spoon 1 teaspoon of preserves on top of the batter. Cover the preserves with batter so that each muffin cup is about three-quarters full.

5. Make the crumb topping: Combine the flour, brown sugar, cinnamon, and nutmeg in a small mixing bowl. Stir in the melted butter and rub the mixture between your fingers to form coarse crumbs. Scatter the crumbs evenly over the muffins and press on the topping lightly with your fingers so that it will adhere to the muffins.

6. Bake the muffins until they are golden, 22 to 25 minutes. Let the muffins cool in the pan for about 5 minutes, invert them onto a wire rack, and then turn them right side up on the rack to cool completely.

Jam-Filled Crumb Muffins will keep in an airtight container at room temperature for up to 2 days, or wrap them individually in plastic and then aluminum foil and freeze them for up to 1 month.

sour cream corn muffins

Makes 12 muffins

I am a fiend for corn muffins, and these are my favorites. Baked with a cup of sour cream instead of yogurt or buttermilk, they are a down-home indulgence. They're not too sweet (you may add more sugar to taste), but they are rich to the extreme—one is almost a meal in itself. Don't substitute the reduced-fat or nonfat sour cream here. The recipe relies on full-fat sour cream to deliver flavor and moisture. For a more austere cornbread recipe, better suited to accompany a larger meal, see page 69.

Nonstick cooking spray (optional)
1 cup unbleached all-purpose flour
1 cup yellow cornmeal
2 tablespoons sugar
2 teaspoons baking powder
½ teaspoon baking soda
½ teaspoon salt
½ cup (1 stick) unsalted butter, melted and cooled
2 large eggs
1 cup full-fat sour cream

1. Preheat the oven to 375 degrees. Line a 12-cup muffin tin with paper liners or coat it with cooking spray.

2. Combine the flour, cornmeal, sugar, baking powder, baking soda, and salt in a medium mixing bowl.

3. Whisk together the cooled melted butter, eggs, and sour cream in a large mixing bowl. With a wooden spoon, stir in the flour mixture until just combined.

4. Fill each muffin cup about three-quarters full. Bake the muffins until they are golden and a toothpick inserted into the center comes out clean, 22 to 25 minutes. Let the muffins cool in the pan for about 5 minutes, invert them onto a wire rack, and then turn them right side up on the rack to cool completely.

Sour Cream Corn Muffins will keep in an airtight container at room temperature for up to 2 days, or wrap them individually in plastic and then aluminum foil and freeze them for up to 1 month.

raspberry-cornmeal muffins

Make these corn muffins, sweetened with some brown sugar and studded with raspberries, when you want to add some color to your muffin basket. They are sweet, tart, and crunchy at the same time.

Nonstick cooking spray (optional)
1 cup unbleached
   all-purpose flour
1 cup yellow cornmeal
2 teaspoons baking powder
1/2 teaspoon baking soda
1/2 teaspoon salt
1/2 cup (1 stick) unsalted butter, melted
   and cooled
1/2 cup firmly packed
   light brown sugar
2 large eggs
1 teaspoon pure vanilla extract
1 cup buttermilk or lowfat plain yogurt
1 3/4 cups fresh or frozen raspberries

1. Preheat the oven to 375 degrees. Line a 12-cup muffin tin with paper liners or coat it with cooking spray.

2. Combine the flour, cornmeal, baking powder, baking soda, and salt in a medium mixing bowl.

3. Whisk together the cooled melted butter, brown sugar, eggs, vanilla, and buttermilk or yogurt in a large mixing bowl. With a wooden spoon, stir in the flour mixture until just combined. Gently stir in the raspberries.

4. Fill each muffin cup about three-quarters full. Bake the muffins until they are golden and a toothpick inserted into the center comes out clean, 22 to 25 minutes. Let the muffins cool in the pan for about 5 minutes, invert them onto a wire rack, and then turn them right side up on the rack to cool completely.

Raspberry-Cornmeal Muffins will keep in an airtight container at room temperature for up to 2 days, or wrap them individually in plastic and then aluminum foil and freeze them for up to 1 month.

cornmeal and cheddar cheese muffins

Cheddar cheese and cornmeal muffins are wonderful with hot apple cider on chilly mornings.

Nonstick cooking spray (optional)
1 cup unbleached
   all-purpose flour
1 cup yellow cornmeal
1 tablespoon sugar
1 tablespoon baking powder
1 teaspoon salt
½ cup (1 stick) unsalted butter, melted
   and cooled
2 large eggs
¾ cup whole or lowfat milk
1½ cups coarsely grated sharp cheddar
   cheese (about 4 ounces)

1. Preheat the oven to 375 degrees. Line a 12-cup muffin tin with paper liners or coat it with cooking spray.

2. Combine the flour, cornmeal, sugar, baking powder, and salt in a medium mixing bowl.

3. Whisk together the cooled melted butter, eggs, and milk in a large mixing bowl. With a wooden spoon, stir in the flour mixture until just combined. Stir in the grated cheese.

4. Fill each muffin cup about three-quarters full. Bake the muffins until they are golden and a toothpick inserted into the center comes out clean, 22 to 25 minutes. Let the muffins cool in the pan for about 5 minutes, invert them onto a wire rack, and then turn them right side up on the rack to cool completely.

Cornmeal and Cheddar Muffins will keep in an airtight container at room temperature for up to 2 days, or wrap them individually in plastic and then aluminum foil and freeze them for up to 1 month.

fresh corn and cornmeal muffins

Makes 12 muffins   Although they generally refuse vegetables, my children make an exception for corn. I'm happy to indulge them during the height of the corn season with these muffins.

Nonstick cooking spray (optional)
1 cup unbleached all-purpose flour
1 cup yellow cornmeal
1 tablespoon sugar
2 teaspoons baking powder
½ teaspoon baking soda
½ teaspoon salt
½ cup (1 stick) unsalted butter, melted and cooled
2 large eggs
1 cup buttermilk or lowfat plain yogurt
1½ cups fresh corn kernels from about 2 medium ears of corn

1. Preheat the oven to 375 degrees. Line a 12-cup muffin tin with paper liners or coat it with cooking spray.

2. Combine the flour, cornmeal, sugar, baking powder, baking soda, and salt in a medium mixing bowl.

3. Whisk together the cooled melted butter, eggs, and buttermilk or yogurt in a large mixing bowl. With a wooden spoon, stir in the flour mixture until just combined. Stir in the corn.

4. Fill each muffin cup about three-quarters full. Bake the muffins until they are golden and a toothpick inserted into the center comes out clean, 22 to 25 minutes. Let the muffins cool in the pan for about 5 minutes, invert them onto a wire rack, and then turn them right side up on the rack to cool completely.

Fresh Corn and Cornmeal Muffins will keep in an airtight container at room temperature for up to 2 days, or wrap them individually in plastic and then aluminum foil and freeze them for up to 1 month.

Kids Can Help

Shucking two ears of corn is a good job for any kid five or older. It's only two ears, after all, so your little one won't get bored before he or she finishes the task. And it will save you a few extra minutes of preparation time.

reduced-fat cocoa-chip muffins

These are definitely my favorite lowfat muffins. Prune purée replaces the butter; its flavor complements that of the cocoa and adds great moisture. In fact, these muffins will stay moist for a day or two longer than muffins made with butter. A handful of chocolate chips gives the muffins a fudgy flavor and texture, but if you are a real ascetic you may leave them out; the muffins will still be chocolatey. I use mini chips because with tinier chips the relatively small amount of chocolate is distributed more evenly throughout the batter.

Nonstick cooking spray (optional)
1 cup (about 6 ounces) pitted prunes
1 cup unbleached
   all-purpose flour
½ cup unsweetened Dutch-process
   cocoa powder, sifted
¾ cup sugar
1¼ teaspoons baking powder
½ teaspoon baking soda
¼ teaspoon salt
2 large eggs
1 teaspoon pure vanilla extract
1½ cups nonfat buttermilk or lowfat
   plain yogurt
⅓ cup miniature semisweet chocolate
   chips

1. Preheat the oven to 375 degrees. Line a 12-cup muffin tin with paper liners or coat it with cooking spray.

2. Place the prunes in a small saucepan and cover them with water. Bring the water to a boil, remove the pan from the heat, and let them stand for 5 minutes. Transfer the prunes to a food processor and process them until smooth, scraping down the sides of the bowl once or twice as necessary. Transfer the prune purée to a small bowl and let it cool to room temperature.

3. Combine the flour, cocoa powder, sugar, baking powder, baking soda, and salt in a medium mixing bowl.

4. Whisk together the eggs, vanilla, buttermilk or yogurt, and prune purée in a large mixing bowl. With a wooden spoon, stir in the flour mixture until all the ingredients are moistened. Stir in the chocolate chips if you are using them.

5. Fill each muffin cup about two-thirds full. Bake the muffin until a toothpick inserted into the center comes out clean, 20 to 22 minutes. Let the muffins cool in the pan for about 5 minutes, invert them onto a wire rack, and then turn them right side up on the rack to cool completely.

Reduced-Fat Cocoa-Chip Muffins will keep in an airtight container at room temperature for up to 3 days, or wrap them individually in plastic and then aluminum foil and freeze them for up to 1 month.

reduced-fat apple and oat muffins

Makes 10 muffins

Oats, apples, and cinnamon give these muffins great flavor. The batter doesn't rise much, but don't be alarmed. The muffins have a light, fluffy texture that will surprise you.

Nonstick cooking spray (optional)
3 medium apples (about 1½ pounds)
¾ cup unbleached all-purpose flour
¼ cup whole wheat flour
1¼ teaspoons baking powder
½ teaspoon baking soda
½ teaspoon salt
⅛ teaspoon ground cinnamon
⅔ cup firmly packed light brown sugar
¼ cup vegetable oil
1 large egg
1 teaspoon pure vanilla extract
1 cup nonfat buttermilk or nonfat plain yogurt
1 cup old-fashioned rolled oats (not instant)

1. Preheat the oven to 375 degrees. Line a 12-cup muffin tin with paper liners or coat it with cooking spray.

2. Peel the apples and grate them using the large holes of a box grater, making sure to stop before you hit seeds. Squeeze the grated apples over the sink to remove excess moisture. Set the grated apple aside.

3. Combine the flours, baking powder, baking soda, salt, cinnamon, and brown sugar in a large mixing bowl. Add the oil, egg, vanilla, and buttermilk or yogurt.

With a wooden spoon, stir until all the ingredients are moistened. Stir in the grated apples and oats.

4. Fill each muffin cup about two-thirds full. Bake the muffins until they are golden and a toothpick inserted into the center comes out clean, 20 to 22 minutes. Let the muffins cool in the pan for about 5 minutes, invert them onto a wire rack, and then turn them right side up on the rack to cool completely.

Reduced-Fat Apple and Oat Muffins will keep in an airtight container at room temperature for up to 2 days, or wrap them individually in plastic and then aluminum foil and freeze them for up to 1 month.

A Good Excuse to Make Reduced-Fat Apple and Oat Muffins

Bake these and take them along on a family hike or other athletic outing some morning when you want to feel very virtuous and healthy.

seeded raisin-bran muffins

Makes 12 muffins

I get nostalgic about back-of-the-box recipes because they were the first recipes I ever followed as a kid. But when I revisited one sentimental favorite, muffins made from bran cereal, I was disappointed. Making muffins with wheat bran makes all the difference. I love seeds as well as raisins in my muffins, but you may leave them out if you don't have them on hand or your children hate them.

Nonstick cooking spray (optional)
¾ cup unbleached
   all-purpose flour
¼ cup whole wheat flour
1 cup wheat bran
1 ¼ teaspoons baking powder
½ teaspoon baking soda
½ teaspoon salt
⅓ cup firmly packed light brown sugar
5 tablespoons vegetable oil
¼ cup unsulphured molasses
2 large eggs
1 teaspoon pure vanilla extract
1 cup buttermilk or lowfat plain yogurt
¾ cup raisins
½ cup unsalted raw sunflower, pumpkin,
   or flax seeds (optional)

1. Preheat the oven to 375 degrees. Line a 12-cup muffin tin with paper liners or coat it with cooking spray.

2. Combine the flours, bran, baking powder, baking soda, salt, and brown sugar in a large mixing bowl. Add the oil, molasses, eggs, vanilla, and buttermilk or yogurt. With a wooden spoon, stir until all the ingredients are moistened. Stir in the raisins and seeds if you are using them.

3. Fill each muffin cup about two-thirds full. Bake the muffins until a toothpick inserted into the center comes out clean, 20 to 22 minutes. Let the muffins cool in the pan for about 5 minutes, invert them onto a wire rack, and then turn them right side up on the rack to cool completely.

Seeded Raisin-Bran Muffins will keep in an airtight container at room temperature for up to 2 days, or wrap them individually in plastic and then aluminum foil and freeze them for up to 1 month.

Muffin Baskets

Muffins are a good answer when you are wondering what to serve a crowd for breakfast. They suit a variety of occasions—parent/teacher coffee meetings, soccer breakfasts, Girl Scout get-togethers. Homemade muffins require a little more effort than picking up a bag of bagels and a tub of cream cheese, but they are a lot easier than cooking pancakes or eggs for the masses.

You can bake muffins ahead of time, freeze them, defrost what you need at room temperature, and rewarm them for 5 minutes in a pre-heated 350-degree oven. Muffins will defrost quickly. Loosen the plastic wrap and spread the muffins out on the counter for half an hour to 45 minutes. Or you can measure out your dry ingredients the night before your big breakfast, get up a little early, and mix and bake a few batches just before breakfast time. Serve muffins with milk, juice or fruit, and hot coffee for the grown-ups.

Here are my favorite muffin trios:

The Classic
* Best Blueberry Muffins (page 49)
* Sour Cream Corn Muffins (page 57)
* Seeded Raisin-Bran Muffins (page 63)

Autumn Sampler
* Cranberry-Orange Muffins (page 50)
* Maple-Pecan Muffins (page 52)
* Pumpkin Spice Muffins (page 54)

Summer Muffin Fun
* Best Blueberry Muffins (page 49)
* Raspberry-Cornmeal Muffins (page 58)
* Lemon-Ginger Muffins (page 53)

Healthy Muffins for Anxious Mothers
* Fresh Corn and Cornmeal Muffins (page 60)
* Reduced-Fat Cocoa-Chip Muffins (page 61)
* Reduced-Fat Apple and Oat Muffins (page 62)

Dessert Masquerading as Breakfast
* Apricot-Almond Muffins (page 51)
* Chocolate Chip Muffins (page 55)
* Jam-Filled Crumb Muffins (page 56)

banana bread

**Makes one
9-inch loaf**

The key to good banana bread is overripe bananas (my daughter calls them rotten—you've probably had this argument with your own children). If the bananas aren't ripe enough—if they aren't soft and almost completely brown—the bread will not be moist and sweet. If you are thrifty and organized, you may peel and freeze overripe bananas in a zipper-lock plastic bag until you have enough for a recipe or two of banana bread. If you are like me, however, you are sure to have overripe bananas lying around on the counter all the time just begging to be baked into bread rather than thrown in the garbage. For a change, you may add ½ cup of sweetened, flaked coconut with the nuts, or ½ cup semisweet chocolate chips.

**Nonstick cooking spray
2 cups unbleached all-purpose flour
2 teaspoons baking powder
½ teaspoon salt
½ cup (1 stick) unsalted butter,
    softened
¾ cup sugar
2 large eggs
3 very ripe bananas, peeled and mashed
    (about 1½ cups)
1 teaspoon pure vanilla extract
1 cup chopped walnuts or pecans**

1. Preheat the oven to 350 degrees. Coat the inside of a 9 x 5-inch loaf pan with cooking spray.

2. Combine the flour, baking powder, and salt in a medium mixing bowl.

3. Combine the butter and sugar in a large bowl. With an electric mixer, on medium-high speed, cream them together until fluffy, 2 to 3 minutes. Add the eggs, bananas, and vanilla and beat until smooth. With a wooden spoon, stir in the flour mixture until just combined. Stir in the nuts.

4. Scrape the batter into the prepared pan. Bake the loaf until it is golden, and a toothpick inserted into the center comes out clean, 50 to 55 minutes. Let the bread cool in the pan for about 5 minutes, invert it onto a wire rack, and then turn it right side up on the rack to cool completely.

Banana Bread will keep, wrapped in plastic, at room temperature for up to 2 days, or wrap it in plastic and then aluminum foil and freeze it for up to 1 month. To freeze individual servings, slice the bread once it has cooled completely. Place a slice or two in a plastic sandwich bag, and then wrap each portion in aluminum foil before storing it in the freezer. To serve, pop the frozen bread in the toaster oven.

savory zucchini bread

The idea of using zucchini in a sweet bread just didn't appeal to me while I was working on this book, probably because I occasionally craved something savory while I was eating so many sweets. This bread is good with bowls of tomato soup. Don't be alarmed at the large quantity of baking powder called for in the recipe. The rather wet batter requires a lot to lighten and lift it.

Nonstick cooking spray
1 cup peeled and grated zucchini (use the large holes of a box grater)
3 cups unbleached all-purpose flour
1 tablespoon plus
1 teaspoon baking powder
½ teaspoon salt
1 large egg
¼ cup olive oil
1¼ cups whole or lowfat milk
1½ cups grated Pecorino Romano or Parmesan cheese
⅓ cup pitted and coarsely chopped Kalamata olives
¼ cup finely chopped fresh parsley leaves

1. Preheat the oven to 350 degrees. Coat the inside of a 9 x 5-inch loaf pan with cooking spray. Squeeze the grated zucchini over the sink to remove excess moisture. Set it aside.

2. Combine the flour, baking powder, and salt in a large mixing bowl. Add the egg, oil, and milk. With a wooden spoon, stir until all the ingredients are moistened. Stir in the zucchini, cheese, olives, and parsley.

3. Scrape the batter into the prepared pan. Bake the loaf until it is golden and a toothpick inserted into the center comes out clean, 60 to 65 minutes. Let the bread cool in the pan for about 5 minutes, invert it onto a wire rack, and then turn it right side up on the rack to cool completely.

Savory Zucchini Bread will keep, wrapped in plastic, at room temperature for up to 2 days, or wrap it in plastic and then aluminum foil and freeze it for up to 1 month. To freeze individual servings, slice the bread once it has cooled completely. Place a slice or two in a plastic sandwich bag, and then wrap each portion in aluminum foil before storing it in the freezer. To serve, pop the frozen bread in the toaster oven.

A Good Excuse to Make Savory Zucchini Bread

I won't say anything trite about what to do with a huge zucchini harvest. I don't grow zucchini myself. But you might try this recipe to serve with those cans of tomato soup that have been sitting in your pantry since the last time you moved. And this bread is so good that if you try it once you won't need an excuse to try it again.

cranberry-nut bread

Makes one
9-inch loaf

This bread is a tradition at my husband's holiday table and toasted for breakfast the next day. (In *my* mother's house we always have rye bread and pickles, but you'll have to ask her about that.)

Nonstick cooking spray
2 cups unbleached all-purpose flour
1½ teaspoons baking powder
½ teaspoon baking soda
½ teaspoon salt
6 tablespoons (¾ stick) unsalted butter, softened
⅔ cup firmly packed light brown sugar
2 large eggs
¼ cup whole or lowfat milk
¼ cup orange juice
1 tablespoon grated orange zest
1½ cups fresh or frozen cranberries, picked over for stems and coarsely chopped
1 cup chopped walnuts or pecans

1. Preheat the oven to 350 degrees. Coat the inside of a 9 x 5-inch loaf pan with cooking spray.

2. Combine the flour, baking powder, baking soda, and salt in a medium mixing bowl.

3. Place the butter and brown sugar in a large mixing bowl. With an electric mixer, cream them together on medium-high speed until fluffy, 2 to 3 minutes. Add the eggs one at a time and beat each in until smooth, scraping down the sides of the bowl once or twice as necessary. With a wooden spoon, stir in the milk, orange juice, and zest. Stir in the flour mixture until just combined. Fold in the cranberries and nuts.

4. Scrape the batter into the prepared loaf pan. Bake the bread until it is golden and a toothpick inserted into the center comes out clean, 50 to 55 minutes. Let the bread cool in the pan for about 5 minutes, invert it onto a wire rack, and then turn it right side up on the rack to cool completely.

Cranberry-Nut Bread will keep, wrapped in plastic, at room temperature for up to 2 days, or wrap it in plastic and then aluminum foil and freeze it for up to 1 month. To freeze individual servings, slice the bread once it has cooled completely. Place a slice or two in a plastic sandwich bag, and then wrap each portion in aluminum foil before storing it in the freezer. To serve, pop the frozen bread in the toaster oven.

Quick Breads into Muffins

The batters for Banana Bread, Savory Zucchini Bread, and Cranberry-Nut Bread can all be baked in muffin tins. Each recipe will make 12 muffins. Reduce the baking time; between 22 and 25 minutes should do it. Bake the muffins until they are golden and a toothpick inserted into the center comes out clean. You can wrap leftovers in plastic and freeze them for up to 1 month.

A Good Excuse to Make Savory Cornbread

Here's a simple recipe for Cornbread Stuffing. It makes about 6 cups, enough to stuff a 12- to 15-pound turkey.

1 recipe Savory Cornbread (opposite)
1 cup chicken stock or canned chicken broth
1 large egg, lightly beaten
½ cup pecans, coarsely chopped
¼ cup finely chopped fresh parsley leaves
1½ teaspoons salt
Ground black pepper
1 tablespoon olive oil
½ pound sweet sausage, removed from casing and crumbled
2 medium onions, coarsely chopped
2 celery stalks, coarsely chopped
½ cup white wine
1 teaspoon dried thyme

1. Combine the cornbread, chicken stock, egg, pecans, parsley, salt, and pepper to taste in a large mixing bowl.
2. Heat the oil over medium heat in a large skillet and add the sausage. Cook it, breaking it into small pieces, until it loses its color, about 5 minutes. Transfer the sausage to the bowl of stuffing.
3. Add the onions and celery to the skillet and cook, stirring, until softened, 8 to 10 minutes. Add the wine and thyme, turn the heat to high, and boil until the wine has evaporated, 2 to 3 minutes. Add the onion-and-celery mixture to the bowl of stuffing and mix well.
4. Loosely stuff and truss the turkey. Cook the turkey until both the breast and the stuffing register 165 degrees on an instant-read thermometer. Alternatively, bake the stuffing outside the bird: Place it in a shallow, buttered baking dish and moisten it with ½ cup of chicken broth. Bake the stuffing for about 40 minutes in a 350-degree oven until it is heated through and the top is golden.

savory cornbread

Makes 16 cornbread squares

This is the cornbread I make to serve with chili or spicy black bean soup. It's less rich and sweet than my Sour Cream Corn Muffins (page 57), more suited for dinner than for breakfast. I also use this recipe when I need cornbread to stuff my Thanksgiving turkey.

Nonstick cooking spray
½ cup unbleached all-purpose flour
1½ cups yellow cornmeal
1 tablespoon sugar
2 teaspoons baking powder
1 teaspoon salt
¼ cup (½ stick) unsalted butter, melted and cooled
1 large egg
1¼ cups whole or lowfat milk

1. Preheat the oven to 375 degrees. Coat the inside of an 8-inch square baking pan with cooking spray.

2. Combine the flour, cornmeal, sugar, baking powder, and salt in a medium bowl.

3. Whisk together the cooled melted butter, egg, and milk in a large mixing bowl. With a wooden spoon, stir the flour mixture until just combined.

4. Pour the batter into the prepared pan. Bake the cornbread until it is golden and a toothpick inserted into the center comes out clean, about 30 minutes. Let the cornbread cool for 5 minutes in the pan and serve it warm.

Savory Cornbread is best eaten the day it is baked.

irish soda bread

Makes 1 round loaf

I make this simple bread once or twice a year to accompany corned beef and cabbage, but I make it many more times just as an afternoon snack.

Nonstick cooking spray (optional)
¼ cup (½ stick) unsalted butter, chilled
3 cups unbleached all-purpose flour
2 tablespoons firmly packed light brown sugar
1½ teaspoons baking powder
1½ teaspoons baking soda
½ teaspoon salt
1 cup golden raisins
1 tablespoon caraway seeds
1 large egg, lightly beaten
1 cup plus 2 tablespoons buttermilk

1. Preheat the oven to 350 degrees. Coat a baking sheet with cooking spray or line it with parchment paper. Cut the butter into ¼-inch dice. Place the butter in a small bowl and set it in the freezer while you gather together the rest of the ingredients.

2. Combine the flour, brown sugar, baking powder, baking soda, and salt in a large mixing bowl. Add the chilled butter pieces and mix with an electric mixer on low speed until the mixture resembles coarse meal. Stir in the raisins and caraway seeds.

3. Stir in the egg and buttermilk on low speed until the dry ingredients are just moistened. Do not overmix.

4. Turn the dough out onto a lightly floured work surface and shape it into a high, round ball. Place the ball on the prepared baking sheet. With a sharp knife, make 2 cuts on top, about 4 inches long and ½ inch deep, in a cross shape. Bake the bread until it is golden and a wooden or metal skewer inserted into the center comes out clean, 50 to 55 minutes. Let the loaf cool for 15 minutes and serve it warm, or let it cool completely.

Irish Soda Bread is best eaten the day it is baked.

baking powder biscuits

Makes about ten
2-inch biscuits

Baking Powder Biscuits can always be conjured at the spur of the moment, since they contain ingredients you're sure to have on hand. I'm not from the South; I'm from New Jersey. Maybe that is why I prefer butter to shortening (or lard) in my biscuits. I just think that whatever you lose in flakiness, you gain in flavor with butter. Substitute shortening for some or all of the butter if you like.

Nonstick cooking spray
6 tablespoons (¾ stick) unsalted butter,
**   chilled**
2 cups unbleached all-purpose flour
1 tablespoon baking powder
1 teaspoon sugar
½ teaspoon salt
¾ cup whole milk, plus
**   1 or 2 tablespoons more if necessary**

1. Preheat the oven to 500 degrees. Coat a baking sheet with cooking spray or line it with parchment paper. Cut the butter into ¼-inch dice. Place it in a small bowl and set it in the freezer while you gather together the rest of the ingredients.

2. Combine the flour, baking powder, sugar, and salt in a large mixing bowl. Add the chilled butter pieces and, with an electric mixer, mix on low speed until the mixture resembles coarse meal. With a wooden spoon, stir in the milk by hand until the mixture starts to form clumps. Add a tablespoon or two more of milk if the mixture is too dry.

3. Turn the clumps out onto a lightly floured work surface and gently knead once or twice until the dough comes together. With one or two passes of a lightly floured rolling pin, gently roll the dough out ½ inch thick. Dip a 2-inch biscuit cutter in some flour and cut as many biscuits as you can from the dough. Transfer the biscuits to the prepared baking sheet. Gently pat the scraps together and repeat with the remaining dough.

4. Bake the biscuits until they have risen and are light golden, 10 to 12 minutes. Serve them warm or let them cool completely on a wire rack, wrap them in plastic and then aluminum foil, and freeze them for up to 1 month. Thaw and warm the biscuits for 3 minutes in a preheated 500-degree oven before serving.

buttermilk biscuits

**Makes about ten
2-inch biscuits**

When I know ahead of time that I'm going to be making biscuits, I go out of my way to buy buttermilk. I'm not sure why, but I always get a better rise and flakier crumb when I use buttermilk in my biscuits.

Nonstick cooking spray (optional)
6 tablespoons (¾ stick) unsalted butter, chilled
2 cups unbleached all-purpose flour
2 teaspoons baking powder
½ teaspoon baking soda
1 teaspoon sugar
½ teaspoon salt
¾ cup buttermilk, plus
   1 or 2 tablespoons more if necessary

1. Preheat the oven to 500 degrees. Coat a baking sheet with cooking spray or line it with parchment paper. Cut the butter into ¼-inch dice. Place the butter in a small bowl and set it in the freezer while you gather together the rest of the ingredients.

2. Combine the flour, baking powder, baking soda, sugar, and salt in a large mixing bowl. Add the chilled butter pieces and, with an electric mixer, mix on low speed until the mixture resembles coarse meal. Stir in the buttermilk with a wooden spoon until the mixture starts to form clumps. Add a tablespoon or two more of buttermilk if the mixture is too dry.

3. Turn the clumps out onto a lightly floured work surface and gently knead once or twice until the dough comes together. With one or two passes of a lightly floured rolling pin, gently roll the dough out ½ inch thick. Dip a 2-inch biscuit cutter in some flour and cut as many biscuits as you can from the dough. Transfer the biscuits to the prepared baking sheet. Gently pat the scraps together and cut out more biscuits with the remaining dough.

4. Bake the biscuits until they have risen and are light golden, 10 to 12 minutes. Serve them warm or let them cool completely on a wire rack, wrap them in plastic and then aluminum foil, and freeze them for up to 1 month. Thaw the biscuits and warm them for 3 minutes in a preheated 500-degree oven before serving.

Techniques for Making Tender Biscuits

Biscuits hold an almost mythical place in the American culinary imagination—so much so that a lot of home bakers are too intimidated to even try them. In reality, biscuits are easy. Literally: The less you work on them, the better they will be.

Mixing and rolling encourage the formation of gluten, strands of protein that make baked goods tough. So if you barely mix the dough and roll it out with just one or two passes of the rolling pin, you'll have tender biscuits, no sweat. Beat the dough too much with a mixer or a wooden spoon and roll it out again and again, putting lots of pressure on your rolling pin, and you will have hockey pucks.

In addition to using a light touch, here are a few more hints for producing great biscuits:

* Beware of time-saving appliances. I like to cut the butter into the flour with the paddle of my electric mixer, but I stir the milk or buttermilk in by hand. A few stirs too many in the mixer and the dough becomes an elastic ball that bakes up rubbery. I avoid the food processor altogether because such a powerful machine can ruin biscuit dough in a millisecond. I find a rolling pin helps me to flatten the dough efficiently, but some cooks simply pat the dough out to a ½-inch thickness. If you tend to wield a rolling pin like a club, patting is the way to go.

* Chill the butter, and don't work it into the flour with warm fingers. A good rise depends on air pockets created when the water trapped in cold, solid bits of butter evaporates as the biscuits bake. If the butter is already halfway melted and the liquid has already begun to escape from the fat, your biscuits won't rise well.

* Substitute some cake flour for the all-purpose flour. Cake flour contains less protein than all-purpose flour, and in general it produces softer baked goods. Substitute 1 cup of cake flour for the all-purpose flour in either Baking Powder Biscuits (page 71) or Buttermilk Biscuits (page 72) for extra-tender biscuits.

* Add some flavor and spice. Added ingredients won't make your biscuits flakier or more tender, but they will add flavor if you want some. Depending on what I'm serving with my biscuits, I may stir in ¼ cup chopped fresh parsley leaves, 1 cup freshly grated Parmesan cheese, or ¼ cup finely chopped ham or prosciutto.

cornmeal biscuits

**Makes about ten
2-inch biscuits**

A cup of cornmeal in place of some of the flour makes a really great biscuit. Serve these biscuits as an alternative to cornbread with oven-fried chicken, barbecued ribs, or beef brisket.

Nonfat cooking spray (optional)
6 tablespoons (¾ stick) unsalted butter, chilled
1 cup unbleached all-purpose flour
1 cup yellow cornmeal
2 teaspoons baking powder
½ teaspoon baking soda
1 teaspoon sugar
½ teaspoon salt
¾ cup buttermilk, plus
  1 or 2 tablespoons more if necessary

1. Preheat the oven to 500 degrees. Coat a baking sheet with cooking spray or line it with parchment paper. Cut the butter into ¼-inch dice. Place the butter in a small bowl and set it in the freezer while you gather together the rest of the ingredients.

2. Combine the flour, cornmeal, baking powder, baking soda, sugar, and salt in a large mixing bowl. Add the chilled butter pieces and, with an electric mixer, mix on low speed until the mixture resembles coarse meal. Stir in the buttermilk with a wooden spoon until the mixture starts to form clumps. Add a tablespoon or two more of buttermilk if the mixture is too dry.

3. Turn the clumps out onto a lightly floured work surface and gently knead once or twice until the dough comes together. With one or two passes of a lightly floured rolling pin, gently roll the dough out ½ inch thick. Dip a 2-inch biscuit cutter in some flour and cut as many biscuits as you can from the dough. Transfer the biscuits to the prepared baking sheet. Gently pat the scraps together and cut out more biscuits with the remaining dough.

4. Bake the biscuits until they have risen and are light golden, 10 to 12 minutes. Serve them warm or let them cool completely on a wire rack, wrap them in plastic and then aluminum foil, and freeze them for up to 1 month. Thaw and warm the biscuits for 3 minutes in a preheated 500-degree oven before serving.

A Good Excuse to Make Strawberry Shortcake

Strawberry shortcakes can be made with any of the three biscuit recipes. Of course, other ripe summer fruit—blueberries or raspberries, peeled and sliced peaches, plums, apricots, or mangoes—may be substituted for the strawberries according to taste and availability.

add-on scones

Makes 12 scones

There are a couple of tricks to making light, tender scones: Use very cold butter, don't overwork the dough, bake scones in a very hot oven, and don't overbake them or you'll risk drying them out. This basic scone recipe can accommodate a variety of add-ons.

Nonstick cooking spray (optional)
6 tablespoons (¾ stick) unsalted butter, chilled
3 cups unbleached all-purpose flour
⅓ cup sugar
1 tablespoon baking powder
½ teaspoon salt
Add-on ingredients (see page 77)
2 large eggs, lightly beaten, plus 1 large egg, lightly beaten, for brushing the tops
¾ cup whole or lowfat milk

1. Preheat the oven to 450 degrees. Coat a baking sheet with cooking spray or line it with parchment paper. Cut the butter into ¼-inch dice. Place the batter in a small bowl and set it in the freezer while you gather together the rest of the ingredients.

2. Combine the flour, sugar, baking powder, and salt in a large mixing bowl. Add the chilled butter pieces and, with an electric mixer, mix on low speed until the mixture resembles coarse meal. Stir in the add-on ingredients, if you are using them.

3. Stir in 2 eggs and the milk and mix on low speed until the dry ingredients are just moistened. Do not overmix.

4. Turn the dough onto a lightly floured work surface and divide it in half. Shape each half into a 6-inch disk. With a sharp chef's knife, cut each disk into 6 wedges. Place the wedges ½ inch apart on the prepared baking sheet. Brush them with the remaining beaten egg. Bake the scones until they are golden, about 15 minutes. Let them cool for 5 minutes and serve them warm, or let them cool completely.

Add-On Scones are best eaten on the day they are baked.

oatmeal scones

Makes 12 scones

These oatmeal scones are made with just butter, no egg, and have a rich and crumbly shortbreadlike texture.

Nonstick cooking spray (optional)
½ cup (1 stick) unsalted butter, chilled
⅓ cup plus 2 tablespoons sugar
¼ teaspoon ground cinnamon
1½ cups unbleached all-purpose flour
1 tablespoon baking powder
½ teaspoon salt
1½ cups old-fashioned rolled oats (not instant)
¾ cup raisins or dried currants, cranberries, or cherries (optional)
1 cup whole or lowfat milk
1 large egg, lightly beaten

1. Preheat the oven to 475 degrees. Coat a baking sheet with cooking spray or line it with parchment paper. Cut the butter into ¼-inch dice. Place it in a small bowl and set it in the freezer while you gather together the rest of the ingredients.

2. Combine 2 tablespoons of the sugar and the cinnamon in a small bowl and set aside. Combine the flour, baking powder, salt, and the remaining ⅓ cup sugar in a large mixing bowl. Add the chilled butter pieces and, with an electric mixer, mix on low speed until the mixture resembles coarse meal. Stir in the oats and dried fruit if desired.

3. Stir in the milk on low speed until the dry ingredients are just moistened. Do not overmix.

4. Turn the dough onto a lightly floured work surface and divide it in half. Shape each half into a 6-inch disk. With a sharp chef's knife, cut each disk into 6 wedges. Place the wedges ½ inch apart on the prepared baking sheet. Brush the scones with the beaten egg and sprinkle them with the cinnamon sugar. Bake the scones until they are golden, about 15 minutes. Let them cool for 5 minutes and serve them warm, or let them cool completely.

Oatmeal Scones are best eaten on the day they are baked.

A Good Excuse to Make Oatmeal Scones

Bought a one-year supply of oatmeal at your warehouse club and now no one in the family wants to eat it for breakfast? Here is one recipe that will help you make a dent in it before its expiration date rolls around.

lemon cream scones

Makes 12 scones

If you want to go for broke and make the lightest, richest scones, follow this recipe. Cake flour gives them a very tender texture. A little lemon zest adds a hint of lemon flavor, but not so much that you can't taste the cream before the pastry melts in your mouth.

Nonstick cooking spray (optional)
2 cups unbleached all-purpose flour
1 cup cake flour (not self-rising)
1/2 cup sugar, plus more for sprinkling on the scones
1 tablespoon plus 1 teaspoon baking powder
1/2 teaspoon salt
1 large egg, lightly beaten
1 cup heavy cream, plus more for brushing on top of scones
1 teaspoon grated lemon zest

1. Preheat the oven to 450 degrees. Spray a baking sheet with cooking spray or line it with parchment paper.

2. Combine the flours, sugar, baking powder, and salt in a large mixing bowl.

3. Stir in the egg, heavy cream, and lemon zest with a wooden spoon until the dry ingredients are just moistened. Do not overmix.

4. Turn the dough onto a lightly floured work surface and divide it in half. Shape each half into a 6-inch disk. With a sharp chef's knife, cut each disk into 6 wedges. Place the wedges 1/2 inch apart on the prepared baking sheet. Brush the scones with cream and sprinkle them with sugar. Bake the scones until they are golden, 12 to 15 minutes. Let them cool for 5 minutes and serve them warm, or let them cool completely.

Lemon Cream Scones are best eaten on the day they are baked.

Mom's Favorite Scone Add-Ons

I love scones with any of the following ingredients mixed in. Choose from my list, or use it as a starting point for compiling your own scone add-on list:

* 3/4 cup raisins or dried currants
* 3/4 cup chopped pitted prunes, dried apricots, dried figs, dried apples, or dried pears
* 3/4 cup chopped walnuts or pecans
* 1 cup fresh or frozen blueberries and 1/4 teaspoon ground cinnamon
* 3/4 cup dried cranberries, 3/4 cup chopped walnuts, and 2 teaspoons grated orange zest
* 1/3 cup finely chopped crystallized ginger and 1 teaspoon grated lemon zest

chocolate chip scones

According to my children, I haven't explored a category of baked goods completely if I have not developed at least one recipe that relies on chocolate chips. (Grudgingly, they make an exception for pizza.) If your family loves chocolate chip cookies above all others, they will definitely go for these scones.

Nonstick cooking spray (optional)
6 tablespoons (¾ stick) unsalted butter, chilled
2 tablespoons granulated sugar
¼ teaspoon ground cinnamon
3 cups unbleached all-purpose flour
⅓ cup firmly packed light brown sugar
1 tablespoon baking powder
½ teaspoon salt
1 cup semisweet chocolate chips
¾ cup chopped walnuts or pecans
2 large eggs, lightly beaten
¾ cup whole or lowfat milk
1 teaspoon pure vanilla extract

1. Preheat the oven to 450 degrees. Coat a baking sheet with cooking spray or line it with parchment paper. Cut the butter into ¼-inch dice. Place the butter in a small bowl and set it in the freezer while you gather together the rest of the ingredients.

2. Combine the granulated sugar and cinnamon in a small bowl and set it aside. Combine the flour, brown sugar, baking powder, and salt in a large mixing bowl.

Add the chilled butter pieces and, with an electric mixer, mix on low speed until the mixture resembles coarse meal. Stir in the chocolate chips and nuts.

3. Stir in the eggs, milk, and vanilla on low speed until the dry ingredients are just moistened. Do not overmix.

4. Turn the dough onto a lightly floured work surface and divide in half. Shape each half into a 6-inch disk. With a sharp chef's knife, cut each disk into 6 wedges. Place the wedges ½ inch apart on the prepared baking sheet. Sprinkle the scones with the cinnamon sugar. Bake them until they are golden, about 15 minutes.

Chocolate Chip Scones are best eaten on the day they are baked.

popovers

Makes 12 popovers

When I was a kid at sleepaway camp, on visiting day my parents used to take me to a restaurant that was famous for its popovers. Those popovers made a big impression on me then; my children were equally impressed when I made these at home. At that restaurant, I used to tear open a steaming popover and slather it with butter, and I encourage my kids to do the same. Popovers are also good for breakfast with jam. If you have a special popover pan, go ahead and use it, but these come out just great in a regular old muffin tin.

Nonstick cooking spray
1 cup unbleached all-purpose flour
½ teaspoon salt
3 large eggs
1 cup whole milk
2 tablespoons unsalted butter, melted and cooled

1. Preheat the oven to 450 degrees. Coat a 12-cup muffin tin with cooking spray.

2. Combine the flour, salt, eggs, milk, and cooled melted butter in a food processor or blender and process until smooth.

3. Divide the batter evenly among the muffin cups, filling each cup about halfway full. Bake the popovers for 15 minutes, turn the oven temperature down to 350 degrees, and continue to bake them until they are well browned, 18 to 20 minutes. Turn the popovers out of the pan and serve them immediately.

A Good Excuse to Make Popovers

With so few ingredients and such a simple technique, do you really need an excuse? Use this recipe when you want to make something fun and fast for your family for breakfast (with butter and jam), for lunch (with soup), or for dinner (popovers go well with roast chicken and gravy, juicy flank steak, or pot roast).

THE COOKIE JAR:
old-fashioned cookies mom's way

CLOCKWISE FROM TOP: Sprinkle Cookies, Thin and Chewy Oatmeal Chocolate Chip Cookies, Chocolate Sandwich Cookies

Over the years, both as a professional baker and as a mom, I've learned a few things about making great cookies. I've decided, after trying a whole spectrum of recipes—from the recipe on the back of the chocolate chip bag to the fantasy cookies pictured in food magazines—that ho-hum cookies are not worth the calories. At the same time, I don't like to work too hard to produce real showstoppers. Cookie baking is fun. Cookie art is stressful.

Since this is a baking book for moms, I've kept the focus on cookies that are extrasimple to make, that have potential as rainy-day or holiday projects, and that kids will enjoy eating. In general, I've gathered together the standard cookie recipes, thought about ways to make them easier, better-tasting, or both, and presented my results. Since I started using melted butter, I think my chocolate chip cookies turn out better than the back-of-the-bag variety. Melting rather than creaming the butter is quicker, too. By using all-natural peanut butter and a whole cup of chopped salted peanuts, I've jammed more real peanut flavor into the peanut butter cookies recipe found underneath the lid of a mass-market-brand peanut butter jar.

There are all kinds of cookies here, and particular advice can be found in individual recipes. I do have a few tips about equipment, storing, and freezing that will make your life easier and your cookies better.

If there is one item that will change your cookie-baking life, it is parchment paper. Available in cookware shops, by mail order, and in most supermarkets, parchment paper transforms any baking sheet into a nonstick surface. You can buy it in rolls, but I prefer to order it already cut into baking sheet–size pieces. It is not necessary to bake all cookies on parchment (I've specified in particular recipes where parchment is a must), but using it does make cookie baking that much easier. Using parchment eliminates any chance that your cookies will stick. And you will save on cleanup time. Just toss the paper away, let the cookie sheets cool off, and put them back in the cabinet. In a pinch, you can line your baking sheets with aluminum foil, but the cookies won't slide off the foil quite so effortlessly. They may have to be peeled away once they've cooled for a few minutes.

I always use insulated baking sheets, which brown but don't burn the bottoms of the cookies. Cookies should be baked in the middle of the oven. If baked near the bottom, the undersides will cook too quickly. If baked near the top, the cookies will be pale, not appetizingly golden.

If necessary, I will cream softened butter for cookie dough, but whenever possible I use melted butter, since it's quicker and in general I prefer the results. Dough made with melted butter needs to rest and firm up a bit in the refrigerator for about ten minutes before baking, and you can leave the dough in your refrigerator for up to six hours if you like.

While testing cookie recipes for this book, I often found myself up to my ears in irresistible cookies. Although most cookies will keep in an airtight container at room temperature for a couple of days, they never seem to last that long in my house. No matter how big the batch, my husband and I found ourselves gorging on them until they were all gone (our children have much more self-restraint). I don't really like to freeze cookies that have already been baked. When they thaw out they are a little bit soggy, and it's a pain to reheat them just to crisp them up. I started to freeze balls of unbaked cookie dough and was much happier with this solution. Anytime one of us felt like a cookie or two, I'd just go to the freezer, remove a few balls of dough, and bake them up fresh. Try it! You can have cookies warm from the oven every night if you like, with no danger of overdoing it.

One of the most entertaining tasks I set for myself when working on these cookies was to come up with homemade versions of store-bought favorites. Graham crackers, chocolate sandwich cookies, vanilla wafers, and fig bars are all simple to make at home, and the ones you make will be far better than the boxed versions. I'm not one of those militant mothers who refuses to buy packaged cookies (sometimes I even let my kids watch commercial television, which is probably where they got their desire for store-bought cookies in the first place). It's just fun every once in a while to make the cookies yourself, especially when the results are so delicious.

All the kids who have come through my house have enjoyed ice-cream sandwiches made from homemade chocolate chip cookies. Cookie pops have also been a big hit. But given their choice of cookie projects, most kids will go for the ones involving sprinkles. You might want to invest in a variety pack of sprinkles from the King Arthur catalogue (see Mail-Order and Online Resources, page 273). If you find yourself buying lots of tiny containers of sprinkles at the supermarket, you will probably save money in the long run by buying in bulk. Since I began ordering sprinkles from King Arthur, I've become completely addicted. For every holiday, King Arthur offers special packages of colors and decorations. This is the place where you can also get tiny sugar flowers, dinosaurs, or dump trucks to sprinkle on your cookies.

The chapter ends with some recipes that I reserve for holiday baking. Although I make rolled vanilla and chocolate cookies throughout the year, I only do gingerbread just before Christmas. Stained-Glass Cookies, Chocolate-Cherry Rugelach, and Anise-Flavored Butter Cookies are also holiday specialties in our house. If these choices don't excite you, you might think about setting aside some of your own favorites just for special times of the year. That way you can build a sense of tradition through baking, and provide your kids with some wonderful sense memories that they'll have forever.

I will never forget the apple pie my mother served only on Thanksgiving. Or the chocolate frosting I used to request for my birthday cake every year when I was a kid. I was allowed to spread the leftover frosting on saltine crackers as a snack on the afternoon of my birthday dinner, and I'll remember that unlikely but wonderful combination until I'm an old lady. I don't think I'll mind, twenty years from now, if I hear my two kids reminiscing about how I used to tear open a box of Oreos for them in the supermarket so that I could get my shopping done in peace…so long as they remember the superb rugelach I baked for the first night of Chanukah!

mom's chocolate chip cookies

Makes about 36 large cookies

I remember myself as a college student, desperate for Toll House cookies and frustrated that I had to wait for my butter to soften rather than just melting it. I only worked up the courage years later to actually try melting the butter, and, what do you know, it works just fine. In fact, I think that chocolate chip cookies made with melted butter have a better texture. They don't bake up flat and rather hard, as do Toll House cookies, but are thick, soft, and chewy. I like my cookies big, but you may make these any size you like.

2¼ cups unbleached all-purpose flour
1 teaspoon baking soda
1 teaspoon salt
1 cup (2 sticks) unsalted butter, melted and cooled slightly
1 cup firmly packed light brown sugar
½ cup granulated sugar
2 large eggs
1 teaspoon pure vanilla extract
2 cups semisweet chocolate chips
1½ cups chopped walnuts or pecans (optional)

1. Preheat the oven to 375 degrees.

2. Combine the flour, baking soda, and salt in a medium mixing bowl.

3. Cream the cooled melted butter and sugars together in a large mixing bowl with a wooden spoon until smooth. Add the eggs and vanilla and beat until smooth. Stir in the flour mixture until just incorporated. Stir in the chocolate chips and nuts, if you are using them. Place the bowl in the refrigerator for 10 minutes (or for up to 6 hours) to let the dough firm up.

4. Drop the batter by heaping tablespoonfuls onto ungreased baking sheets, leaving about 3 inches between each cookie. (Balls of dough may be placed next to each other on parchment-lined baking sheets, frozen, transferred to zipper-lock plastic freezer bags, and stored in the freezer for up to 1 month. Frozen cookies may be placed in the oven directly from the freezer and baked as directed.) Bake the cookies until golden around the edges but still soft on top, about 10 minutes (a minute or two longer for frozen dough). Let the cookies stand on the baking sheet for 5 minutes and then remove them with a metal spatula to a wire rack to cool completely.

Mom's Chocolate Chip Cookies will keep in an airtight container for 2 to 3 days.

Chocolate Chip Cookie Ice-Cream Sandwiches

Makes 4 ice cream tsandwiches

My large chocolate chip cookies are just the right size for making home-made ice cream sandwiches. It's simple. Just take a pint of ice cream, cut it into 4 rounds, and sandwich the rounds between cookies. Of course, you can double, triple, or quadruple the recipe, depending on how many sandwiches you need. Make sure your ice cream is frozen solid, so that it's easy to make clean cuts. It's better to make these ice-cream sandwiches just before serving. Freezing the sandwiches will make the cookies tough and dry.

These are great for casual entertaining. I serve them when I invite another family with kids over for a summertime barbecue.

1 pint vanilla, chocolate, or coffee ice cream, frozen very hard

8 Mom's Chocolate Chip Cookies (page 85)

1. Place the pint of ice cream on its side on a cutting board. With a sharp chef's knife, cutting right through the cardboard container, slice the ice cream into four ¾-inch-thick disks.
2. Peel away and discard the cardboard. (You may place the ice cream disks on a baking sheet, wrap the sheet in plastic, and freeze the disks for up to 1 day before using them.) Place each ice cream disk between 2 cookies and serve immediately.

chocolate chip cookies without the chocolate chips

Makes about 36 large cookies

There were so many times that I wanted to bake chocolate chip cookies but didn't have any chocolate chips in my pantry that one day I just decided to make a batch of cookie dough without the chips to see if the chipless cookies would satisfy my craving. Extra nuts more than compensate for the chips. Although this recipe was developed out of desperation, it's really one of my favorites.

2¼ cups unbleached all-purpose flour
1 teaspoon baking soda
1 teaspoon salt
1 cup (2 sticks) unsalted butter, melted and cooled
1 cup firmly packed light brown sugar
½ cup granulated sugar
2 large eggs
1 teaspoon pure vanilla extract
4 cups chopped walnuts or pecans

1. Preheat the oven to 375 degrees.

2. Combine the flour, baking soda, and salt in a medium mixing bowl.

3. Cream the cooled melted butter and sugars together in a large mixing bowl with a wooden spoon until smooth. Add the eggs and vanilla and beat until smooth. Stir in the flour mixture until just incorporated. Stir in the nuts. Place the bowl in the refrigerator for 10 minutes (or for up to 6 hours) to let the dough firm up.

4. Drop the batter by heaping tablespoonfuls onto ungreased baking sheets, leaving about 3 inches between each cookie. (Balls of dough may be placed next to each other on parchment-lined baking sheets, frozen, transferred to zipper-lock plastic freezer bags, and stored in the freezer for up to 1 month. Frozen cookies may be placed in the oven directly from the freezer and baked as directed.) Bake the cookies until golden around the edges but still soft on top, 10 to 12 minutes (a minute or two longer for frozen dough). Let them stand on the baking sheet for 5 minutes and then remove them with a metal spatula to a wire rack to cool completely.

Chocolate Chip Cookies Without the Chocolate Chips will keep in an airtight container for 2 to 3 days.

my favorite chocolate chocolate chip cookies

Makes about 32 large cookies

Unsweetened and semisweet chocolate in the batter make these chocolate chocolate chip cookies trufflelike. They are so chocolatey because there's just a little flour binding them together. This makes the dough very loose. If you want to freeze the unbaked cookies, refrigerate the dough for at least half an hour before spooning it out and preparing to freeze it. Also let the cookies cool completely before removing them from the parchment; when warm, they tend to fall apart.

4 ounces unsweetened chocolate, finely chopped
2½ cups semisweet chocolate chips
½ cup (1 stick) unsalted butter, cut into 8 pieces
½ cup unbleached all-purpose flour
½ teaspoon baking powder
½ teaspoon salt
4 large eggs
1½ cups sugar
2 teaspoons pure vanilla extract

1. Preheat the oven to 350 degrees.

2. Put 1 inch of water in the bottom of a double boiler or medium saucepan and bring to a bare simmer. Combine the unsweetened chocolate, 1½ cups of the chocolate chips, and the butter in the top of the double boiler or in a stainless-steel bowl set on top of the simmering water, making sure that the water doesn't touch the bottom of the bowl. Heat, whisking occasionally, until the chocolate and butter are completely melted. Set aside to cool slightly.

3. Combine the flour, baking powder, and salt in a small bowl.

4. Combine the eggs and sugar in a large mixing bowl and, with an electric mixer, beat on high speed until they are thick and pale, about 5 minutes. Stir in the chocolate mixture and vanilla on low speed until smooth. Stir in the flour mixture until just combined. Stir in the remaining 1 cup chocolate chips. Place the bowl in the refrigerator for 15 minutes (or up to 6 hours) to let the dough firm up.

5. Drop the batter by heaping tablespoonfuls onto parchment-lined baking sheets, leaving about 3 inches between each cookie. (If you plan on freezing the unbaked cookies, let the batter stand in the refrigerator for at least half an hour or it will be too loose to spoon out for the freezer. Balls of dough may be placed next to each other on parchment-lined baking sheets, frozen, transferred to zipper-lock plastic freezer bags, and stored in the freezer for up to 1 month. Frozen cookies may be placed in the oven directly from the freezer and baked as directed.) Bake the cookies until the tops are cracked and shiny, 10 to 12 minutes (a minute or two longer for frozen dough). Carefully slide the entire parchment sheet with the cookies from the pan to a wire rack and let the cookies cool completely.

My Favorite Chocolate Chip Cookies will keep in an airtight container for 2 to 3 days.

thin and chewy oatmeal chocolate chip cookies

Makes about 32 large cookies

Over the years I've seen a number of chocolate chip cookie recipes that use ground oats in place of some of the flour, claiming that this is the secret ingredient in the best chocolate chip cookies. Here's my version of the recipe, which bakes up thin and chewy, more candylike than regular chocolate chip cookies.

1 cup old-fashioned rolled oats (not instant)
1¼ cup unbleached all-purpose flour
1 teaspoon baking soda
1 teaspoon salt
1 cup (2 sticks) unsalted butter, melted and cooled
1 cup firmly packed dark brown sugar
½ cup granulated sugar
2 large eggs
1 teaspoon pure vanilla extract
2 cups semisweet chocolate chips
1½ cups chopped walnuts or pecans (optional)

1. Preheat the oven to 375 degrees.

2. Place the oats in a food processor and grind them fine. Combine the oats, flour, baking soda, and salt in a medium mixing bowl.

3. Cream the cooled melted butter and sugars together in a large mixing bowl with a wooden spoon until smooth. Add the eggs and vanilla and beat until smooth. Stir in the oat-and-flour mixture until just combined. Stir in the chocolate chips and nuts, if you are using them. Place the bowl in the refrigerator for 10 minutes (or up to 6 hours) to let the dough firm up.

4. Drop the batter by heaping tablespoon-fuls onto ungreased baking sheets, leaving about 3 inches between each cookie. (Balls of dough may be placed next to each other on parchment-lined baking sheets, frozen, transferred to zipper-lock plastic freezer bags, and stored in the freezer for up to 1 month. Frozen cookies may be placed in the oven directly from the freezer and baked as directed.) Bake the cookies until golden around the edges but still soft on top, about 10 minutes (a minute or two longer for frozen dough). Let them stand on the baking sheet for 5 minutes and then remove them with a metal spatula to a wire rack to cool completely.

Thin and Chewy Oatmeal Chocolate Chip Cookies will keep in an airtight container for 2 to 3 days.

Measuring Chocolate Chips

Because I use so many chocolate chips, I buy them in economy-size bags at my local warehouse club. When I need them, I measure them by the cup out of this big bag. But I realize that most people buy either 6-ounce or 12-ounce bags at the supermarket, and you might like to know that 1 cup of chocolate chips (the amount you'll need to make Chocolate Chip Muffins, page 55) weighs about 6 ounces, and 2 cups (the amount called for in Mom's Chocolate Chip Cookies, page 85) weigh 12 ounces.

sprinkle cookies

5 excellent

add 1/4 cup more flour

Makes about
24 large cookies

This is my five-year-old's favorite cookie. She says that these taste like cupcakes, and that Chocolate Sprinkle Cookies (page 93) taste like brownies.

2½ cups unbleached all-purpose flour
1 teaspoon baking powder
½ teaspoon salt
1 cup (2 sticks) unsalted butter, softened
1 cup sugar
2 large eggs
2 teaspoons pure vanilla extract
½ cup multicolor sprinkles

1. Preheat the oven to 375 degrees.

2. Combine the flour, baking powder, and salt in a medium mixing bowl.

3. Combine the butter and sugar in a large mixing bowl with an electric mixer on medium-high speed until fluffy, 2 to 3 minutes. Add the eggs and vanilla and beat until smooth. Stir in the flour mixture until just combined.

4. Place the sprinkles in a small bowl. Scoop up a heaping tablespoon of dough and roll it between your palms to form a ball. Roll the top half of each ball in the sprinkles. Place the balls, sprinkle side up, on an ungreased baking sheet, leaving about 3 inches between each cookie.

(Cookies may be placed next to each other on parchment-lined baking sheets, frozen, transferred to zipper-lock plastic freezer bags, and stored in the freezer for up to 1 month. Frozen cookies may be placed in the oven directly from the freezer and baked as directed.) Bake the cookies until they are pale golden around the edges but still soft on top, about 10 minutes (a minute or two longer for frozen dough). Let them stand on the baking sheet for 5 minutes and then remove them with a metal spatula to a wire rack to cool completely.

Sprinkle Cookies will keep in an airtight container for 2 to 3 days.

Kids Can Help

Kids love to dip dough balls in the sprinkles. Place bowls of sprinkles on a rimmed baking sheet and the cookie dough balls on another. When the excess sprinkles fall off the cookies, they will end up on one or the other of the sheets rather than the floor.

slice and bake butter cookies

Makes about
60 cookies

Keep this dough in the freezer for a rainy day.

2 cups unbleached all-purpose flour
$\frac{1}{2}$ teaspoon baking powder
$\frac{1}{2}$ teaspoon salt
**1 cup (2 sticks) unsalted butter,
   softened**
$\frac{3}{4}$ cup sugar
1 large egg
2 teaspoons pure vanilla extract

1. Combine the flour, baking powder, and salt in a medium mixing bowl.

2. Combine the butter and sugar in a large mixing bowl and cream together with an electric mixer on medium-high speed until fluffy, 2 to 3 minutes. Add the egg and vanilla and beat until smooth. Stir in the flour mixture until just incorporated.

3. Divide the dough into two portions. Turn one portion onto a piece of wax paper and shape it, rolling it inside the paper, into a log about 10 inches long and $1\frac{1}{2}$ inches in diameter. Wrap the dough in plastic and refrigerate it for at least 2 hours or for up to 24 hours. Repeat with the remaining dough. (Dough logs may be wrapped in plastic and frozen for up to 1 month. Defrost the dough in the refrigerator overnight and slice it.)

4. Preheat the oven to 350 degrees.

5. Slice the dough into $\frac{1}{3}$-inch-thick rounds. Place the cookies on ungreased baking sheets at least 2 inches apart. Bake them until they are pale golden around the edges but still soft on top, 13 to 15 minutes. Let them stand on the baking sheet for 5 minutes and then remove them with a metal spatula to a wire rack to cool completely.

Slice and Bake Butter Cookies will keep in an airtight container for 2 to 3 days.

chocolate–peanut butter cups

**Makes about
24 cookies**

As a fan of the peanut butter cup, I wondered what would happen if I baked chocolate and peanut butter chip cookie dough in mini-muffin cups. You can just drop the batter on cookie sheets if you don't have the muffin cups around or prefer the cookie shape.

1 cup unbleached all-purpose flour
6 tablespoons unsweetened
   Dutch-process cocoa powder, sifted
1/2 teaspoon baking soda
1/2 teaspoon salt
10 tablespoons (1 1/4 sticks) unsalted
   butter, softened
1 cup sugar
1 large egg
1 teaspoon pure vanilla extract
1 1/2 cups peanut butter chips

1. Preheat the oven to 350 degrees.

2. Combine the flour, cocoa powder, baking soda, and salt in a medium mixing bowl.

3. Cream the butter and sugar together in a large mixing bowl with an electric mixer on medium-high speed until fluffy, 2 to 3 minutes. Add the egg and vanilla and beat until smooth. Stir in the flour mixture until just combined. Stir in the peanut butter chips.

4. Scoop up a tablespoon of dough and roll it between your palms to form a ball. Place the balls in paper-lined mini-muffin tins or on a parchment-lined baking sheet, leaving about 3 inches between each cookie. (Dough balls may be placed next to each other on parchment-lined baking sheets, frozen, transferred to zipper-lock plastic freezer bags, and stored in the freezer for up to 1 month. Put the frozen dough balls on parchment-lined baking sheets or in paper-lined mini-muffin tins and bake as directed.) Bake the peanut butter cups until they are dry on top, 8 to 10 minutes (a minute or two longer for frozen dough). Let them stand in the muffin tins or on the baking sheet for 5 minutes and then carefully remove them from the tins or slide the entire parchment sheet with the peanut butter cups from the pan to a wire rack and let them cool completely.

Chocolate–Peanut Butter Cups will keep in an airtight container for 2 to 3 days.

chocolate sprinkle cookies

Makes about 24 cookies

These cookies are surprisingly rich considering that they are flavored with cocoa powder rather than with chocolate. Use a good-quality cocoa (I like Pernigotti, available through Williams-Sonoma) for the best flavor. I love this recipe not only because the cookies are great, but also because I almost always have the ingredients on hand.

1 cup unbleached all-purpose flour
6 tablespoons unsweetened
   Dutch-process cocoa powder, sifted
½ teaspoon baking soda
½ teaspoon salt
10 tablespoons (1¼ sticks) unsalted
   butter, softened
1 cup sugar
1 large egg
1 teaspoon pure vanilla extract
⅓ cup chocolate sprinkles

1. Preheat the oven to 350 degrees.

2. Combine the flour, cocoa powder, baking soda, and salt in a medium mixing bowl.

3. Cream the butter and sugar together in a large mixing bowl with an electric mixer on medium-high speed until fluffy, 2 to 3 minutes. Add the egg and vanilla and beat until smooth. Stir in the flour mixture until just combined.

4. Place the sprinkles in a small bowl. Scoop up a tablespoon of dough and roll it between your palms to form a ball. Roll the top half of each ball in the sprinkles. Place the balls, sprinkle side up, on a parchment-lined baking sheet, leaving about 3 inches between each cookie. (Cookies may be placed next to each other on parchment-lined baking sheets, frozen, transferred to zipper-lock plastic freezer bags, and stored in the freezer for up to 1 month. Frozen cookies may be placed in the oven directly from the freezer and baked as directed.) Bake the cookies until they are dry on top, 8 to 10 minutes (a minute or two longer for frozen dough). Let them stand on the baking sheet for 5 minutes and then carefully slide the entire parchment sheet with the cookies from the pan to a wire rack and let the cookies cool completely.

Chocolate Sprinkle Cookies will keep in an airtight container for 2 to 3 days.

A Good Excuse to Make Chocolate Sprinkle Cookies

King Arthur carries chocolate sprinkles that are actually made out of chocolate. Order some (see Mail-Order and Online Resources, page 273) and make the ultimate version of these cookies.

snickerdoodles

**Makes about
32 large cookies**

These really homey, comforting cookies couldn't be easier to make. Supposedly, the cream of tartar gives them a slightly tangy flavor, but it was too subtle for my five-year-old to detect. This is a good starter cookie for younger children, since it's delicious but rather plain.

2¼ cups unbleached all-purpose flour
2 teaspoons cream of tartar
1 teaspoon baking soda
½ teaspoon salt
1 cup (2 sticks) unsalted butter, softened
1¾ cups sugar
2 large eggs
2 teaspoons ground cinnamon

1. Preheat the oven to 400 degrees.

2. Combine the flour, cream of tartar, baking soda, and salt in a medium mixing bowl.

3. Cream the butter and 1½ cups of the sugar together in a large mixing bowl with an electric mixer on medium-high speed until fluffy, 2 to 3 minutes. Add the eggs and beat until smooth. Stir in the flour mixture until just combined.

4. Combine the cinnamon and the remaining ¼ cup sugar in a small bowl. Scoop up a heaping tablespoon of dough and roll it between your palms to form a ball. Roll each ball in the cinnamon sugar to coat it completely. Place the balls on a parchment-lined baking sheet, leaving about 3 inches between each cookie. (Cookies may be placed next to each other on parchment-lined baking sheets, frozen, transferred to zipper-lock plastic freezer bags, and stored in the freezer for up to 1 month. Frozen cookies may be placed in the oven directly from the freezer and baked as directed.) Bake the cookies until they are pale golden around the edges but still soft on top, about 10 minutes (a minute or two longer for frozen dough). Let them stand on the baking sheet for 5 minutes and then carefully slide the entire parchment with the cookies from the pan to a wire rack to cool completely.

Snickerdoodles will keep in an airtight container for 2 to 3 days.

molasses cookies

Makes about
24 large cookies

If stranded on a desert island, I couldn't live without these chewy, spicy cookies. I got the recipe from a college roommate's mom, so it has the perfect pedigree for this book.

2 cups unbleached all-purpose flour
1 teaspoon ground ginger
1 teaspoon ground cinnamon
½ teaspoon ground cloves
½ teaspoon salt
½ teaspoon baking soda
¾ cup (1½ sticks) unsalted butter, softened
1 cup sugar
¼ cup dark (not light or blackstrap) molasses
2 large eggs

1. Preheat the oven to 350 degrees.

2. Combine the flour, ginger, cinnamon, cloves, salt, and baking soda in a medium mixing bowl.

3. Cream the butter, sugar, and molasses together in a large mixing bowl with an electric mixer on medium speed until smooth. Add the eggs and beat until smooth. Stir in the flour mixture until just combined. Place the bowl in the refrigerator for 10 minutes (or for up to 6 hours) to let the dough firm up.

4. Drop the batter by heaping tablespoonfuls onto parchment-lined baking sheets, leaving about 3 inches between each cookie. (Balls of dough may be placed next to each other on parchment-lined baking sheets, frozen, transferred to zipper-lock plastic freezer bags, and stored in the freezer for up to 1 month. Frozen cookies may be placed in the oven directly from the freezer and baked as directed.) Bake the cookies until the edges are firm but the tops are still soft, 10 to 12 minutes. Let them stand on the baking sheet for 5 minutes and then carefully slide the entire parchment with the cookies from the pan to a wire rack and let them cool completely.

Molasses Cookies will keep in an airtight container for 2 to 3 days.

oatmeal cookies

The only way my older daughter will eat raisins is if they are baked in oatmeal cookies. I like oatmeal cookies better with dried cherries or cranberries and a lot of chopped walnuts to cut the sweetness of the dough. Choose add-ons according to your taste. As with chocolate chip cookies, I prefer melting the butter to creaming it with the sugar. The cookies are softer and chewier this way.

1½ cups unbleached all-purpose flour
1 teaspoon baking soda
½ teaspoon salt
¼ teaspoon ground nutmeg
1 cup (2 sticks) unsalted butter, melted and cooled slightly
1 cup firmly packed light brown sugar
½ cup granulated sugar
2 large eggs
1 teaspoon pure vanilla extract
3 cups old-fashioned rolled oats (not instant)
1 cup raisins or dried cherries or cranberries (optional)
1 cup chopped walnuts (optional)

1. Preheat the oven to 350 degrees.

2. Combine the flour, baking soda, salt, and nutmeg in a medium mixing bowl.

3. Cream the cooled melted butter and sugars together in a large mixing bowl with an electric mixer on medium speed until smooth. Add the eggs and vanilla and beat until smooth. Stir in the flour mixture until just combined. Stir in the oats, dried fruit, and walnuts, if you are using them. Place the bowl in the refrigerator for 10 minutes (or up to 6 hours) to let the dough firm up.

4. Drop the batter by heaping tablespoonfuls onto ungreased baking sheets, leaving about 3 inches between each cookie. (Balls of dough may be placed next to each other on parchment-lined baking sheets, frozen, transferred to zipper-lock plastic freezer bags, and stored in the freezer for up to 1 month. Frozen cookies may be placed in the oven directly from the freezer and baked as directed.) Bake the cookies until they are golden around the edges but still soft on top, 15 to 17 minutes (a minute or two longer for frozen dough). Let them stand on the baking sheet for 5 minutes and then remove them with a metal spatula to a wire rack to cool completely.

Oatmeal Cookies will keep in an airtight container for 2 to 3 days.

oatmeal lace cookies

Makes about 24 large cookies

Oatmeal Lace Cookies are a little on the elegant side for this book, but kids love them because of their candylike texture.

1½ **cups old-fashioned rolled oats (not instant)**
¾ **cup sugar**
2 **tablespoons unbleached all-purpose flour**
½ **teaspoon salt**
1 **teaspoon pure vanilla extract**
¾ **cup (1½ sticks) unsalted butter, melted and cooled slightly**
1 **large egg, lightly beaten**

1. Preheat the oven to 325 degrees.

2. Combine the oats, sugar, flour, and salt in a large mixing bowl. With a wooden spoon, stir in the vanilla and cooled melted butter until combined. Stir in the egg until combined.

3. Drop the batter by scant tablespoonfuls onto parchment-lined baking sheets, leaving about 3 inches between each cookie. Bake the cookies until they are golden around the edges, 12 to 13 minutes. Carefully slide the entire parchment with the cookies from the pan to a wire rack and let them cool completely.

Oatmeal Lace Cookies will keep in an airtight container for 2 to 3 days.

peanut butter cookies

**Makes about
40 cookies**

Most peanut butter cookies are just not peanutty enough. Adding chopped roasted peanuts to the dough gives these cookies the necessary flavor boost. Be careful not to overprocess the peanuts or you'll wind up with peanut butter rather than chopped nuts.

1 cup roasted salted peanuts
2 cups unbleached all-purpose flour
½ teaspoon baking soda
½ teaspoon baking powder
½ teaspoon salt
1 cup (2 sticks) unsalted butter, melted
    and cooled slightly
1 cup firmly packed light brown sugar
1 cup granulated sugar
2 large eggs
1 teaspoon pure vanilla extract
1 cup natural chunky peanut butter

1. Preheat the oven to 350 degrees.

2. Place the nuts in a food processor and chop fine. Combine the flour, baking soda, baking powder, and salt in a medium bowl.

3. Cream the cooled melted butter and sugars together in a large mixing bowl with an electric mixer on medium speed until smooth. Add the eggs, vanilla, and peanut butter and beat until smooth. Stir in the flour mixture until just combined. Stir in the chopped peanuts. Place the bowl in the refrigerator for 10 minutes (or up to 6 hours) to let the dough firm up.

4. Scoop up a heaping tablespoon of dough and roll it between your palms to form a ball. Place the balls on a parchment-lined baking sheet, leaving about 3 inches between each cookie. Press each cookie with the back of a fork twice, in opposite directions, to make a criss-cross pattern. (Balls of dough may be placed next to each other on parchment-lined baking sheets, frozen, transferred to zipper-lock plastic freezer bags, and stored in the freezer for up to 1 month. Frozen cookies may be placed in the oven directly from the freezer and baked as directed.) Bake the cookies until they are lightly colored, about 15 minutes (a minute or two longer for frozen dough). Let them stand on the baking sheet for 5 minutes and then carefully slide the entire parchment with the cookies from the pan to a wire rack and let them cool completely.

Peanut Butter Cookies will keep in an airtight container for 2 to 3 days.

peanut butter thumbprints with jelly filling

Makes about
40 cookies

You can certainly fill these cookies using a small measuring spoon, but to keep your fingers clean and do the job more quickly, try using a pastry bag. In fact, this is the perfect opportunity to try out this piece of equipment and practice piping. It's actually lots of fun and makes you feel like a real pro. See "Pastry Bag Basics," page 224, to learn how to fill, hold, and squeeze a pastry bag.

**1 recipe Peanut Butter Cookie dough
   (opposite)**
**½ cup best-quality raspberry or
   strawberry jam**

1. Preheat the oven to 350 degrees.

2. Scoop up a heaping tablespoon of dough and roll it between your palms to form a ball. Place the balls on a parchment-lined baking sheet, leaving about 3 inches between each cookie. Press each cookie with the back of a small measuring spoon (I use my round half teaspoon, and it works perfectly) to make a well or "thumbprint." (Shaped cookies may be placed next to each other on parchment-lined baking sheets, frozen, transferred to zipper-lock plastic freezer bags, and stored in the freezer for up to 1 month. Frozen cookies may be placed in the oven directly from the freezer and baked as directed.) Bake the cookies until they are lightly colored, about 15 minutes (a minute or two longer for frozen dough). Let them

stand on the baking sheet for 5 minutes and then carefully slide the entire parchment with the cookies from the pan to a wire rack and let them cool completely.

3. Carefully fill each cookie indentation with about 1 teaspoon jam, using a small measuring spoon. Alternatively, place the jam in a pastry bag and pipe some jam into each indentation.

Peanut Butter Thumbprints with Jelly Filling will keep in an airtight container for 2 to 3 days.

Filling Thumbprints

Jelly is only one of the possible fillings for Peanut Butter Thumbprints with Jelly Filling. I have tried Hershey Kisses, miniature Reese's Peanut Butter Cups, chocolate-covered raisins, halved marshmallows, jelly beans, and gumdrops.

almond thumbprints

Makes about 24 large cookies

A more refined version of Peanut Butter Thumbprints with Jelly Filling (page 99)—I wouldn't use jelly beans or gumdrops here. Use best-quality jam instead, for a bakery-style treat. Or pipe a little Milk Chocolate Ganache (page 227) into the centers of completely cooled cookies.

1½ cups blanched whole almonds
2 cups unbleached all-purpose flour
½ teaspoon salt
1 cup (2 sticks) unsalted butter, melted and cooled slightly
½ cup firmly packed light brown sugar
6 tablespoons granulated sugar
1 large egg
1 teaspoon pure almond extract
½ cup best-quality apricot or raspberry jam

1. Preheat the oven to 325 degrees.

2. Place the nuts in a food processor and chop fine. Don't overprocess; the nuts should look dry, not oily. Combine the flour, salt, and ground nuts in a medium mixing bowl.

3. Cream the cooled melted butter and sugars together in a large mixing bowl with an electric mixer on medium speed until smooth. Add the egg and almond extract and beat until smooth. Stir in the flour-and-nut mixture until just combined.

4. Scoop up a heaping tablespoonful of dough and roll it between your palms to form a ball. Place the balls on a parchment-lined baking sheet, leaving about 3 inches between each cookie. Press each cookie with the back of a small measuring spoon (I use my round half-teaspoon, and it works perfectly) to make a well or "thumbprint." If the edges crack when you make the thumbprint, just press them back together. (Shaped cookies may be placed next to each other on parchment-lined baking sheets, frozen, transferred to zipper-lock plastic freezer bags, and stored in the freezer for up to 1 month. Frozen cookies may be placed in the oven directly from the freezer and baked as directed.) Bake the cookies until they are lightly colored, 20 to 22 minutes. Let them stand on the baking sheet for 5 minutes and then carefully slide the entire parchment with the cookies from the pan to a wire rack and let them cool completely.

5. Carefully fill each cookie indentation with about 1 teaspoon jam. Alternatively, place the jam in a pastry bag and pipe some jam into each indentation.

Almond Thumbprints will keep in an airtight container for 2 to 3 days.

Kids Can Help

My older daughter is fascinated by the pastry bag, and filling thumbprints is a not-too-messy way to let her use one. If you and your kids have never tried to pipe anything, this is a good introduction.

mexican wedding cakes

Makes about
24 cookies

These unbelievably tender cookie classics are simple to make. Kids are intensely attracted to them because of their powdered sugar coating.

1½ cups pecan halves
2¼ cups unbleached
   all-purpose flour
1 teaspoon salt
1 cup (2 sticks) unsalted butter,
   softened
½ cup granulated sugar
1½ teaspoons water
1½ teaspoons pure vanilla extract
6 tablespoons confectioners' sugar

1. Preheat the oven to 325 degrees.

2. Place the pecans in a food processor and process until they are finely chopped. Combine the chopped nuts, flour, and salt in a medium mixing bowl and set aside.

3. Cream the butter and granulated sugar together in a large mixing bowl with an electric mixer on medium-high speed until fluffy, 2 to 3 minutes. Beat the water and vanilla into the butter mixture. Stir in the nut-and-flour mixture until just combined.

4. Scoop up a rounded tablespoonful of dough and roll it between your palms to form a ball. Place the balls on an ungreased baking sheet, leaving 1½ inches between each cookie. Bake the cookies until they are cooked through but not dry, about 20 minutes. Remove the cookies with a metal spatula to a wire rack to cool.

5. Place the confectioners' sugar in a shallow bowl. When the cookies are completely cooled, roll each one in the sugar to coat.

Mexican Wedding Cakes will keep in an airtight container for 2 to 3 days.

cranberry-walnut hermits

Hermits are old-fashioned cookies made with fruit, nuts, and spices. Many recipes call for molasses to give them their characteristic dark color and rich flavor, but I already had a molasses cookie recipe that I adored. So when it was time to develop my ideal hermit, I didn't want it to taste too similar to the cookies. Intrigued by a couple of recipes that used strong brewed coffee, I decided to try it. I loved the result. So did the mothers at my daughter's last birthday party. They devoured these hermits before moving on to the chocolate chip and peanut butter cookies. These hermits don't have a recognizable coffee flavor—just a hint of the coffee's bitterness to cut the sweetness of the sugar and fruit.

2 cups unbleached all-purpose flour
¾ teaspoon baking soda
¼ teaspoon salt
½ teaspoon ground cinnamon
½ teaspoon ground ginger
¼ teaspoon ground nutmeg
½ cup (1 stick) unsalted butter, softened
1 cup firmly packed light brown sugar
1 large egg
¼ cup strong brewed coffee or espresso, cooled
1 cup dried cranberries
1 cup chopped walnuts
1 recipe Basic White Glaze (optional; recipe follows)

Kids Can Help

If you think your kids are old enough to wave forks dripping with cookie glaze over the cookies without splattering the walls, let them ice the cookies.

1. Preheat the oven to 375 degrees.

2. Combine the flour, baking soda, salt, cinnamon, ginger, and nutmeg in a medium mixing bowl.

3. Cream the butter and sugar together in a large mixing bowl with an electric mixer on medium speed until fluffy, 2 to 3 minutes. Add the egg and coffee and beat until smooth. Stir in the flour mixture until just combined. Stir in the cranberries and walnuts.

4. Drop the batter by heaping tablespoon-fuls onto parchment-lined baking sheets, leaving about 3 inches between each cookie. (Balls of dough may be placed next to each other on parchment-lined baking sheets, frozen, transferred to zipper-lock plastic freezer bags, and stored in the freezer for up to 1 month. Frozen cookies may be placed in the oven directly from the freezer and baked as directed.) Bake the cookies until they are golden around the edges but still soft on top, about 10 minutes (a minute or two longer for frozen dough). Let them stand on the baking sheet for 5 minutes, then carefully slide the entire parchment with the cookies from the pan to a wire rack and let them cool completely.

5. To glaze, if desired, place the cooled cookies on a foil- or parchment-lined baking sheet. Dip a fork into the glaze and wave it over each cookie, re-dipping the fork in the glaze as necessary, to create a pattern of lines. Let the glaze harden, about 10 minutes, before serving.

Cranberry-Walnut Hermits will keep in an airtight container for 2 to 3 days.

basic white glaze

Makes about 1½ cups

Here's the simplest recipe for the sugary white icing that kids just love. I drizzle it over Oatmeal Cookies (page 96), Molasses Cookies (page 95), and Cranberry-Walnut Hermits (opposite). I also use it as a coating for Molasses Cookie Pop Faces (page 128). Don't try to skip sifting the sugar before whisking in the milk. If you do, your icing will be lumpy, not smooth.

1½ cups confectioners' sugar, sifted
¼ cup whole or lowfat milk

1. Combine the confectioners' sugar and milk in a medium mixing bowl and whisk until smooth. Use immediately, or cover the surface of the glaze with plastic wrap and store it for up to 6 hours at room temperature, re-whisking before using.

2. To apply the glaze, dip a fork in it and drizzle it over the cookies by waving the fork in a back-and-forth motion. Or spread the glaze on the cookies with a small offset spatula or craft stick.

homemade honey graham crackers

**Makes about
16 cookies**

Don't get annoyed at the idea of making your own graham crackers until you've tried these. I, too, was skeptical about improving on the factory-made rectangles. But while I was making these cookies, I actually got into it—pricking the tops with a fork and sometimes even scoring them down the center with a sharp paring knife to make them look like the kind you buy in the supermarket. They're actually nothing like store-bought graham crackers. They are less sweet and have a more distinct whole-wheat flavor that moms love.

1½ **cups unbleached all-purpose flour**

½ **cup whole wheat flour**

½ **teaspoon baking powder**

¼ **teaspoon baking soda**

Pinch of salt

¼ **cup (½ stick) unsalted butter, melted and cooled**

¼ **cup firmly packed light brown sugar**

2 **tablespoons honey**

1 **teaspoon pure vanilla extract**

¼ **cup whole or lowfat milk**

1 **tablespoon granulated sugar**

¼ **teaspoon ground cinnamon**

1. Combine the flours, baking powder, baking soda, and salt in a medium mixing bowl.

2. Cream the butter and brown sugar together in a large mixing bowl with an electric mixer on medium speed until smooth. Add the honey, vanilla, and milk and beat until smooth. Add the flour mixture and stir until the dough comes together.

3. Divide the dough into two 4-inch squares, wrap in plastic, and refrigerate for at least 2 hours or for up to 2 days.

4. Preheat the oven to 350 degrees.

5. Combine the granulated sugar and cinnamon in a small bowl. On a lightly floured work surface with a lightly floured rolling pin, roll one portion of the chilled dough out into a ⅛-inch-thick-square. Using a ruler or a straightedge, cut the dough into 3-inch squares. Repeat with the remaining portion of dough. Reroll the scraps to make more squares. Transfer the squares to a parchment-lined baking sheet. Prick the tops of the cookies with a fork. Sprinkle them with the cinnamon sugar. Bake them until they are lightly colored, about 10 minutes. Let them stand on the baking sheet for 5 minutes, then carefully slide the entire parchment with the cookies from the pan to a wire rack and let them cool completely.

Homemade Honey Graham Crackers will keep for up to 1 week, stored at room temperature in an airtight container.

Five Fun Things to Do with
Homemade Honey Graham Crackers

Plain homemade graham crackers cry out for embellishment. Here are a few things I like to do with mine once they've cooled:

1. Make a sandwich with a jelly filling.
2. Make a sandwich with peanut butter and thin slices of banana.
3. Make a sandwich with Marshmallow Fluff.
4. Skip the cinnamon sugar and drizzle or cover them with Chocolate Glaze (page 151).
5. Make S'mores. If you've already decided to try the Homemade Honey Graham Cracker recipe (opposite), you might go all the way and use your graham crackers to make S'mores. Here's how:

8 Homemade Honey Graham Crackers
Two 1.55-ounce Hershey or other chocolate bars, broken in half
4 marshmallows

Lay 4 graham crackers, cinnamon side down, on a platter. Place half a chocolate bar on top of each of the crackers. Toast the marshmallows over a charcoal fire, gas grill, or cooktop flame. Place one toasted marshmallow on top of each chocolate bar half. Top with the remaining graham cracker, placing the cinnamon side up, then smush the cookies together and devour.

chocolate sandwich cookies

These are so much better than store-bought cookies that I just scream in frustration when my brand-conscious five-year-old insists that she prefers Oreos. Letting her lick the icing bowl goes a little way toward persuading her to at least try my version. And she never actually refuses to eat the finished product. I prefer butter in the filling for its flavor, but if you use butter you'll have to eat the cookies right away. Filling made with vegetable shortening will last for several days.

For the cookies

1 cup unbleached all-purpose flour
6 tablespoons unsweetened
   Dutch-process cocoa powder, sifted
½ teaspoon baking soda
½ teaspoon salt
10 tablespoons (1¼ sticks) unsalted
   butter, softened
1 cup granulated sugar
1 large egg
1 teaspoon pure vanilla extract

For the filling

½ cup (1 stick) unsalted butter,
   softened, or vegetable shortening
2½ cups confectioners' sugar
1 teaspoon pure vanilla extract
Pinch of salt
1½ teaspoons water

1. Make the cookies: Combine the flour, cocoa powder, baking soda, and salt in a medium mixing bowl.

2. Cream the butter and granulated sugar together in a large mixing bowl with an electric mixer on medium speed until fluffy, 2 to 3 minutes. Add the egg and vanilla and beat until smooth. Stir in the flour mixture until just combined.

3. Divide the dough into 2 portions. Shape each portion into a log about 9 inches long and 1½ inches in diameter. Wrap in plastic and refrigerate for at least 2 hours or for up to 24 hours. (Dough logs may be wrapped in plastic and frozen for up to 1 month. Defrost the dough on the counter for 15 minutes before proceeding.)

4. Preheat the oven to 350 degrees.

5. Slice the dough into ¼-inch-thick rounds and place the cookies on an ungreased baking sheet, leaving about 2 inches between each cookie. Bake the cookies until they are dry on top, 6 to 8 minutes (a minute or two longer for partially frozen dough). Let them stand on the baking sheet for 5 minutes and then remove them from the sheet with a metal spatula to a wire rack and let them cool completely.

6. Make the filling: Cream the butter or vegetable shortening and confectioners' sugar together in a large mixing bowl with an electric mixer on low speed until combined. Stir in the vanilla and salt. Add the water and beat on high until light and fluffy, about 5 minutes. Use the filling immediately, or cover the surface of the filling with plastic wrap. If using butter, store the filling in the refrigerator for up to 1 day and re-whip it before using. If using vegetable shortening, store the filling at room temperature for up to several days and re-whip it before using.

7. Spoon 1 teaspoon of the filling onto the flat side of a cookie. Sandwich with another cookie. Repeat with the remaining cookies.

Chocolate Sandwich Cookies are best eaten on the day they are made. Store in an airtight container at room temperature.

A Lot of Good Excuses to Make Chocolate Sandwich Cookies

It's easy enough to tint chocolate sandwich cookie filling by stirring in a drop or two of food coloring. Invest in one of those decorator food coloring sets and you'll be able to celebrate any holiday, suit any mood, or coordinate any outfit with matching cookies. Obviously, green would be good for St. Patrick's Day, orange would brighten up Halloween, and red and pink would be sweet on Valentine's Day. Here are a few more ideas:

* **For the Fourth of July,** divide the filling into three portions. Tint one portion red, one blue, and leave one white.

* **Choose a couple of pastels for Easter:** pale yellow, violet, rose, robin's egg blue. Go easy on the food coloring, adding just a little at a time, or you'll have neon before you know it.

* **Nothing too sacred to be celebrated with homemade Oreos?** Try red and green for Christmas; blue and white for Chanukah; or red, green, and yellow for Kwanzaa.

* **If Barbie is big in your house,** go with hot pink. Purple and green are fun for Barney-loving preschoolers. Try bright blue and magenta for fans of *Blue's Clues.*

homemade vanilla wafers

Makes about 32 small cookies

These are extratender because of the cake flour and extrarich from the egg yolks and butter. Drop rounded teaspoonfuls onto parchment paper for cookies that closely resemble commercial vanilla wafers but taste much better.

¾ cup unbleached all-purpose flour
½ cup cake flour (not self-rising)
1 teaspoon baking powder
¼ teaspoon salt
½ cup (1 stick) unsalted butter, softened
¾ cup sugar
1 large egg plus 2 large egg yolks
2 tablespoons pure vanilla extract

1. Preheat the oven to 400 degrees. Combine the flours, baking powder, and salt in a medium mixing bowl.

2. Cream the butter and sugar together in a large mixing bowl with an electric mixer on medium speed until fluffy, 2 to 3 minutes. Add the whole egg, yolks, and vanilla and beat until smooth. Stir in the flour mixture until just combined.

3. Place the bowl in the refrigerator for 10 minutes (or up to 6 hours) to let the dough firm up.

4. Drop the batter by rounded teaspoonfuls onto parchment-lined baking sheets, leaving about 2 inches between each cookie. (Cookies may be placed next to each other on parchment-lined baking sheets, frozen, transferred to zipper-lock plastic freezer bags, and stored in the freezer for up to 1 month. Frozen cookies may be placed in the oven directly from the freezer and baked as directed.) Bake until the edges have browned and the tops of the cookies are set, 6 to 8 minutes. Remove the sheet from the oven and let the cookies firm up on the baking sheet for 2 minutes. With a metal spatula, transfer the cookies to a wire rack to cool completely.

Homemade Vanilla Wafers will keep in an airtight container for 2 to 3 days.

no-bake natural foods store nut butter buttons

Makes about 30 cookies

I've always wanted to try some of those vintage 1960s recipes for no-bake cookies made with peanut butter and rice cereal, but my Inner Pastry Chef always stopped me. But when I began developing recipes for this book, I thought an updated version would be perfect for modern moms—it's quick, kid friendly, and I shop for the ingredients at my natural foods store, although you may buy your supplies at the supermarket. I cover the cookies with chocolate (you can buy organic chocolate, you know), but you can leave them plain if you like.

1 cup natural peanut butter, hazelnut butter, almond butter, or cashew butter

½ cup honey

3 cups all-natural rice cereal

8 ounces bittersweet chocolate (optional)

2 tablespoons vegetable oil (optional)

1. In a large mixing bowl, stir together the nut butter and honey with a wooden spoon until blended. Stir in the rice cereal and mix until all the cereal is evenly coated with the nut butter mixture. Drop rounded tablespoonfuls onto a wax-paper-lined baking sheet and refrigerate until firm, 2 to 3 hours.

2. To glaze, if you want, put 1 inch of water in the bottom of a double boiler or medium saucepan and bring to a bare simmer. Combine the chocolate and oil in the top of the double boiler, or in a stainless-steel bowl set on top of the simmering water, making sure that the water doesn't touch the bottom of the bowl. Heat, whisking occasionally, until the chocolate and oil are completely melted.

3. Using a fork, spear a cookie and dip it into the glaze. Allow excess glaze to drip off the cookie and back into the bowl or pan. Place the glazed ball back on the baking sheet and repeat with remaining balls. Let the cookies stand at room temperature until the chocolate is firm, about 2 hours.

No-Bake Natural Foods Store Nut Butter Buttons will keep in an airtight container at room temperature for up to 3 days.

homemade fig cookies

If they're used to the supermarket version, your kids may not recognize the flavor of real figs. They may be confused and disbelieving when you explain that the fig is actually a kind of fruit that grows on trees before it is processed at the factory. Unbelievable!

8 ounces dried figs
1 cup water
1 1/2 cups unbleached all-purpose flour
1/2 teaspoon baking powder
1/4 teaspoon salt
1/8 teaspoon ground nutmeg
1/2 cup (1 stick) unsalted butter, softened
1/2 cup sugar
1 large egg
1 teaspoon pure vanilla extract
1 large egg white

1. Trim the tough stems from the figs. Combine the figs and water in a medium saucepan and bring to a boil. Reduce the heat to low and simmer, uncovered, until the figs are soft and have absorbed most of the liquid, about 20 minutes. Place the figs in a food processor and process until smooth. Set them aside to cool completely.

2. Combine the flour, baking powder, salt, and nutmeg in a medium mixing bowl.

3. Cream the butter and sugar together in a large mixing bowl with an electric mixer on medium speed until fluffy, 2 to 3 minutes. Add the whole egg and vanilla and beat until smooth. Stir in the flour mixture until just combined. Divide the dough in half, wrap it in plastic, and refrigerate it for at least 2 hours or up to 24 hours. (The dough may be wrapped in plastic and frozen for up to 1 month.)

4. Preheat the oven to 350 degrees.

5. Remove one piece of the dough from the refrigerator. On a lightly floured work surface with a lightly floured rolling pin, roll the dough into a 12-by-6-inch rectangle. Spoon half of the fig mixture down the middle of the rectangle in a 2-inch-wide strip. Fold the sides of the dough over the filling so that there is a 1/2-inch overlap. Carefully lift the fig roll from the work surface and place it on a parchment-lined baking sheet, seam side down. Repeat with the remaining dough and filling and place the second roll alongside the first roll on the baking sheet. Put the rolls in the refrigerator to chill for 15 minutes.

6. Brush each roll with the egg white and bake until the edges of the rolls are golden, 23 to 25 minutes. Slide the entire parchment with the cookies onto a wire rack and let the rolls cool completely. Slice each roll into 12 cookies.

Homemade Fig Cookies will keep for 2 to 3 days, stored at room temperature in an airtight container.

scottish shortbread buttons

Makes 24 cookies

Shortbread is usually baked in a round pan and cut into wedges. But the dough makes a great icebox cookie, too. Nothing is easier than slicing and baking, so this is the way I usually go. Since shortbread circles are rather plain, I pierce them with four small holes to make them look like giant buttons. The simple flavor and cute "decoration" delight small children.

1 cup (2 sticks) unsalted butter, chilled, cut into 16 pieces

½ cup sugar

2 cups unbleached all-purpose flour

1. Cream the butter and sugar together in a large mixing bowl with an electric mixer on medium speed until fluffy, 3 to 4 minutes. Stir in the flour on low speed until the dough just comes together.

2. Turn the dough onto a sheet of wax paper and shape it, rolling it inside the paper, into a log about 10 inches long and 2 inches in diameter. Wrap the dough in plastic and refrigerate it for at least 2 hours or for up to 24 hours. (Dough logs may be wrapped in plastic and frozen for up to 1 month. Defrost the dough in the refrigerator overnight before proceeding with the recipe.)

3. Preheat the oven to 250 degrees.

4. Slice the dough into ⅓-inch-thick rounds and place them on an ungreased baking sheet, leaving an inch between each cookie. Using a metal skewer, pierce each cookie with 4 holes in the center so that it looks like a button. Bake the cookies until they are dry and firm but have not changed color, about 45 minutes. Let them stand on the baking sheet for 5 minutes, then remove them with a metal spatula to a wire rack and let them cool completely.

Scottish Shortbread Buttons will keep for 3 to 4 days, stored at room temperature in an airtight container.

Cookies and Milk

Although it may not be recommended by the American Board of Pediatrics, one surefire way to get your kids to drink milk is to offer it with cookies and encourage dunking. Although almost any cookie can be dunked in milk, some kinds just cry out for dunking. Here are my top ten choices, in alphabetical order:

1. Chocolate Biscotti (page 116)
2. Chocolate Sandwich Cookies (page 106)
3. Dad's Italian Biscotti (page 114)
4. Homemade Honey Graham Crackers (page 104)
5. Homemade Vanilla Wafers (page 108)
6. Mocha Shortbreads (opposite)
7. Mom's Chocolate Chip Cookies (page 85)
8. Molasses Cookies (page 95)
9. Oatmeal Cookies (page 96)
10. Peanut Butter Cookies (page 98)

mocha shortbreads

These cookies have just enough coffee flavor to keep adults interested, but not so much that they taste too grown-up for kids. They are good for dunking (see the previous page for my top-ten list of dunkers).

Nonstick cooking spray
1½ cups unbleached all-purpose flour
½ cup unsweetened Dutch-process cocoa powder
¼ teaspoon salt
1 tablespoon instant espresso powder
1 cup (2 sticks) unsalted butter, softened
1 cup firmly packed light brown sugar

1. Preheat the oven to 325 degrees. Coat the inside of a 9-inch tart pan with cooking spray.

2. Sift together the flour, cocoa powder, salt, and espresso powder into a medium mixing bowl.

3. Cream the butter and brown sugar together in a large mixing bowl with an electric mixer on medium speed until fluffy, 2 to 3 minutes. Add the flour mixture and beat on low speed until the dough just comes together. Do not overmix.

4. Turn the dough into the pan and press it to the edges with your fingertips. Bake until the shortbread is firm at the edges but still soft in the center, 40 to 45 minutes. Let the shortbread cool completely on a wire rack and then cut it into 16 wedges with a sharp paring knife.

Mocha Shortbreads will keep for 2 to 3 days, stored in an airtight container at room temperature.

dad's italian biscotti

Biscotti in a mom's baking book? Of course. Nowadays, most kids have cut their teeth on them at the local espresso bar. This recipe makes the best biscotti I've had. It was developed by noted Italian cooking expert Jack Bishop, who also happens to be my husband and the father of my children. Jack likes to mix them by hand, the way he imagines old Italian grandmothers do, but I think they taste just as good mixed in my KitchenAid mixer.

1 cup whole almonds with skins
2 cups unbleached all-purpose flour
1 cup sugar
½ teaspoon baking powder
Pinch of salt
3 large eggs
2 large egg yolks
1 teaspoon pure vanilla extract

1. Preheat the oven to 350 degrees.

2. Spread the almonds on a large baking sheet and toast them until fragrant, 6 to 8 minutes. Set them aside to cool. When they are cool, coarsely chop them. Line another large baking sheet with parchment paper.

3. Combine the flour, sugar, baking powder, and salt in a large mixing bowl. Add 2 of the whole eggs, the egg yolks, and vanilla and mix together with an electric mixer on low speed until just combined. Mix in the almonds.

4. Turn the dough out onto a lightly floured work surface and divide it in half. Shape each half into a flat log about 12 inches long and 2½ inches wide. Place the logs on the prepared baking sheet several inches apart.

5. Beat the remaining whole egg and brush it over the dough. Bake the logs until they are firm to the touch, about 35 minutes. Remove them from the oven and allow them to cool completely.

6. Reduce the oven temperature to 325 degrees. Transfer the logs to a cutting board and cut them into 1-inch-thick slices. Lay the slices cut side down on the baking sheet and return them to the oven. Bake them until they are crisp, about 10 minutes. Transfer sliced cookies to wire racks and let them cool completely.

Dad's Italian Biscotti will keep in an airtight container for 1 to 2 weeks.

cornmeal-raisin biscotti

Makes about 24 large biscotti

You can find one hundred variations on the basic almond biscotti recipe, but this is one of the best. Cornmeal and raisins give the cookies wholesome crunch and sweetness. Cinnamon and brown sugar make them all-American in spite of their Italian shape.

1 cup whole almonds with skins
1 cup unbleached all-purpose flour
1 cup yellow cornmeal
1 cup firmly packed light brown sugar
½ teaspoon baking powder
½ teaspoon ground cinnamon
Pinch of salt
3 large eggs
2 large egg yolks
1 teaspoon pure vanilla extract
½ cup raisins

1. Preheat the oven to 350 degrees.

2. Spread the almonds on a large baking sheet and toast them until they are fragrant, 6 to 8 minutes. Set them aside to cool. When cool, coarsely chop them. Line another large baking sheet with parchment paper.

3. Combine the flour, cornmeal, brown sugar, baking powder, cinnamon, and salt in a large mixing bowl. Add 2 of the whole eggs, the egg yolks, and vanilla and mix with an electric mixer on low speed until just combined. Mix in the almonds and raisins on low speed.

4. Turn the dough out onto a lightly floured work surface and divide in half. Shape each half into a flat log about 12 inches long and 2½ inches wide. Place the logs on the prepared baking sheet several inches apart.

5. Beat the remaining whole egg and brush it over the dough. Bake the logs until they are firm to the touch, about 35 minutes. Remove them from the oven and allow them to cool completely.

6. Reduce the oven temperature to 325 degrees. Transfer the logs to a cutting board and cut them into 1-inch-thick slices. Lay the slices cut side down on the baking sheet and return them to the oven. Bake the cookies until they are crisp, about 10 minutes. Transfer the cookies to wire racks and let them cool completely.

Cornmeal-Raisin Biscotti will keep in an airtight container for 1 to 2 weeks.

chocolate biscotti

**Makes about
24 large biscotti**

For the darkest, most chocolatey biscotti, I use an extrarich Dutch-process cocoa such as Pernigotti (see Mail-Order and Online Resources, page 273). The dough spreads quite a bit during baking, so make sure to use a large baking sheet and space the logs at least 3 inches apart.

⅔ cup whole almonds with skins
1⅔ cups unbleached all-purpose flour
⅓ cup unsweetened Dutch-process
   cocoa powder
1 teaspoon baking soda
½ teaspoon salt
1 cup sugar
3 large eggs
2 large egg yolks
1 teaspoon pure vanilla extract
1 cup semisweet chocolate chips

1. Preheat the oven to 350 degrees.

2. Spread the almonds on a large baking sheet and toast them until fragrant, 6 to 8 minutes. Set them aside to cool. When they are cool, coarsely chop them. Line another large baking sheet with parchment paper.

3. Sift together the flour, cocoa powder, baking soda, and salt in a large mixing bowl. Stir in the sugar. Add 2 of the whole eggs, the egg yolks, and vanilla and mix with an electric mixer on low speed until just combined. Mix in the almonds and chocolate chips on low speed.

4. Turn the dough out onto a lightly floured work surface and divide it in half. Shape each half into a flat log about 12 inches long and 2½ inches wide. Place the logs on the prepared baking sheet several inches apart.

5. Beat the remaining whole egg and brush it over the dough. Bake the logs until they are firm to the touch, about 35 minutes. Remove them from the oven and allow them to cool completely.

6. Reduce the oven temperature to 325 degrees. Transfer the logs to a cutting board and cut them into 1-inch-thick slices. Lay the slices cut side down on the baking sheet and return the cookies to the oven. Bake them until they are crisp, about 10 minutes. Transfer the cookies to wire racks and let them cool completely.

Chocolate Biscotti will keep in an airtight container for 1 to 2 weeks.

Playing Around
with Chocolate Biscotti

For some reason, looking at a bowl of chocolate biscotti dough makes me want to improvise. Here are a few of my favorite things to do:

* Glazed Biscotti: Dip half of each cookie in Chocolate Glaze (page 151). Place the dipped cookies on sheets of wax paper and let the glaze harden for at least 2 hours before storing the cookies in an airtight container.
* Polka Dot Biscotti: Substitute 1 cup white chocolate chips for the semi-sweet chocolate chips.
* Chocolate-Ginger Biscotti: Add ⅓ cup finely chopped crystallized ginger to the dough along with the chocolate chips.
* Gianduia Biscotti: Substitute hazelnuts for the almonds.
* Mocha Biscotti: Add 1 tablespoon instant espresso powder to the flour mixture.
* Chocolate-Orange Biscotti: Add 1 teaspoon grated orange zest to the dough along with the vanilla.

meringues

Makes about
24 large cookies

Speaking as the mother of a child who subsists on a diet of cream of wheat, white bread (crusts removed), plain pasta, French fries, yogurt, and vanilla ice cream, I believe that a baking book with any hope of pleasing kids should contain plenty of all-white recipes. The meringue is the ultimate cookie for kids who refuse food with any specks. These cookies are snowy white and supremely simple, with only three ingredients. Bake them at a low temperature to dry the batter but keep the cookies from browning.

4 large egg whites
1 cup sugar
1 teaspoon pure vanilla extract

1. Position one oven rack in the top third of the oven and the other rack on the bottom third of the oven. Preheat the oven to 225 degrees. Line 2 baking sheets with parchment paper.

2. Put 1 inch of water in the bottom of a double boiler or medium saucepan and bring the water to a bare simmer. Combine the egg whites and sugar in a large mixing bowl and place it on top of the simmering water, making sure that the water doesn't touch the bottom of the bowl. Whisk the mixture constantly until the egg whites are warm and the sugar has dissolved, about 5 minutes. To test the consistency, dip a finger into the mixture; when it feels smooth, not grainy, remove the bowl from the heat.

3. Fit an electric mixer with the whisk attachment. Add the vanilla to the bowl of sugar and egg whites and whisk on high speed until the mixture is cool and the egg whites hold stiff peaks, about 5 minutes.

4. Drop heaping tablespoonfuls of the meringue batter onto the prepared baking sheets, leaving about 1 ½ inches between each cookie. Bake the meringues until they are completely dry, about 2 hours. Let them cool completely on wire racks and then carefully peel them off the parchment paper.

Meringues will keep in an airtight container at room temperature for up to 1 week.

cinnamon toast meringues

Makes about
24 large cookies

These child-friendly meringues remind me of cinnamon toast, but they get their crunch from ground pecans rather than from toasted white bread.

¾ cup pecans
1 cup sugar
½ teaspoon ground cinnamon
3 large egg whites
1 teaspoon pure vanilla extract

1. Position one oven rack in the top third of the oven and the other rack on the bottom third of the oven. Preheat the oven to 275 degrees. Line 2 baking sheets with parchment paper.

2. Combine the pecans, ¼ cup of the sugar, and the cinnamon in a food processor and grind until fine. Be careful not to overprocess the pecans or they will release their oil.

3. Place the egg whites in a large mixing bowl with an electric mixer fitted with the whisk attachment. Beat them on medium speed until the egg whites are frothy, about 30 seconds. Turn the speed to high and pour the remaining ¾ cup sugar into the bowl in a slow, steady stream. Continue to beat until the egg whites are stiff and shiny. Fold in the nut mixture and vanilla with a rubber spatula, being careful not to deflate the meringue.

4. Drop heaping tablespoonfuls of the meringue batter onto the prepared baking sheets, leaving about 1½ inches between each cookie. Bake the meringues until they are completely dry, about 40 minutes. Let them cool completely on wire racks and then carefully peel them off the parchment paper.

Cinnamon Toast Meringues will keep for several days in an airtight container.

chocolate chip meringues

Makes about
24 large cookies

These meringues have the same appeal for chocolate lovers that plain white meringues have for vanilla fans.

3 large egg whites
1 cup sugar
2 tablespoons unsweetened
   Dutch-process cocoa powder
One 6-ounce bag miniature semisweet
   chocolate chips

1. Position one oven rack in the top third of the oven and the other rack on the bottom third of the oven.

2. Preheat the oven to 275 degrees. Line 2 baking sheets with parchment paper. Place the egg whites in a large mixing bowl. With an electric mixer fitted with the whisk attachment, beat the egg whites on medium speed until they are frothy, about 30 seconds. Turn the speed to high and pour the sugar into the bowl in a slow, steady stream. Continue to beat until the egg whites are stiff and shiny.

3. Hold a small fine-mesh strainer over the bowl and sift the cocoa powder into the bowl. Pour the chocolate chips into the bowl. Fold the ingredients together with a rubber spatula, being careful not to deflate the meringue.

4. Drop heaping tablespoonfuls of the meringue onto the prepared baking sheets, leaving about 1 1/2 inches between each cookie. Bake the meringues until they are firm on the outside but still soft on the inside, about 30 minutes. Let them cool on wire racks for 5 minutes, and then carefully peel them off the parchment paper.

Chocolate Chip Meringues will keep for several days in an airtight container.

coconut macaroons

Makes about
24 cookies

As a kid, I always hated coconut macaroons. They were too sticky and sweet for me. These are different. They are made with unsweetened coconut (available at natural foods stores), rather than sweetened flaked coconut. They have a light, fluffy texture, great coconut flavor, and are just sweet enough. These are the cookies I make for Passover, along with Chocolate Chip Meringues, and no one seems to miss the store-bought versions.

¾ cup sugar
2½ cups unsweetened shredded
   coconut
2 large egg whites
1 teaspoon pure vanilla extract
⅛ teaspoon salt

1. Preheat the oven to 375 degrees. Line 2 baking sheets with parchment paper.

2. Combine the sugar, coconut, egg whites, and vanilla in a medium mixing bowl and mix with a rubber spatula.

3. Drop the batter by heaping tablespoonfuls onto the prepared baking sheets, leaving about 1½ inches between each cookie.

4. Bake until golden, 10 to 12 minutes. Slide the parchment onto a wire rack and let the cookies cool completely. Carefully peel them off the parchment paper.

Coconut Macaroons will keep in an airtight container at room temperature for up to 1 week.

rolled sugar cookies

Makes about
80 small cut-out
cookies

This dough rolls out beautifully and is my choice when I'm making cookies for decorating. It bakes up golden and crisp but not fragile—perfect for slathering with Royal Icing (opposite) and coating with sprinkles.

1 cup (2 sticks) unsalted butter,
   softened
½ cup sugar
1 large egg yolk
1 teaspoon pure vanilla extract
2¼ cups unbleached all-purpose flour

1. Cream the butter and sugar together in a large mixing bowl with an electric mixer on medium-high speed until fluffy. Add the egg yolk and vanilla and beat until incorporated, scraping down the sides of the bowl as necessary. Add the flour and mix on low speed until the dough comes together in a ball.

2. Divide the dough into 3 equal balls. Wrap each ball in plastic and refrigerate it for at least 2 hours and for up to 2 days. (The dough can be frozen for up to 1 month; defrost it in the refrigerator before use.)

3. Preheat the oven to 375 degrees. Line a baking sheet with parchment paper.

4. Remove one ball from the refrigerator and knead it 4 or 5 times on a lightly floured work surface to soften it. With a lightly floured rolling pin, roll out the dough ⅛ inch thick. Cut it into the desired shapes and place it on the prepared baking sheet. Refrigerate the scraps.

5. Bake the cookies until they are firm and golden around the edges, about 8 minutes. Slide the entire parchment sheet with the cookies onto a wire rack and let the cookies cool completely. Repeat with the remaining balls of dough and then with the chilled scraps, using fresh parchment paper. Decorate the cookies as desired.

Rolled Sugar Cookies will keep in an airtight container for several days.

Rolled Chocolate Sugar Cookies: Add ¼ cup unsweetened Dutch-process cocoa powder, sifted, along with the flour. I like these cookies with all chocolate decorations—Chocolate Glaze (page 151) and chocolate sprinkles.

Kids Can Help

Kids eight and older will enjoy rolling dough and cutting out cookie shapes. Give younger kids dough you've rolled out and choose cookie cutters with edges that aren't dangerously sharp.

royal icing

**Makes about 3 cups, enough to decorate
1 batch of rolled cookies**

In an effort to simplify this, I've tried every recipe for royal icing that doesn't contain meringue powder (a mixture of sugar and dried egg whites), but I don't like any of them as much as the one that contains this ingredient for smooth, shiny, easy-to-work-with icing. Most supermarkets stock this item in the baking aisle, but if you have trouble finding it, you can mail-order it (see Mail-Order and Online Resources, page 273). Meringue powder keeps forever in the pantry, and one 10-ounce container has taken me through about 10 batches of cookies.

2 tablespoons meringue powder
¼ cup water
2 cups confectioners' sugar, sifted
Food coloring (optional)

1. Combine the meringue powder and water in a medium mixing bowl. With an electric mixer fitted with the whisk attachment, beat the mixture on high speed until soft peaks form. Add the confectioners' sugar and beat until the icing is shiny and smooth, about 3 to 5 minutes.

2. Divide the icing among small bowls and stir in a drop or two of food coloring in each bowl, if desired. Use immediately, or cover the surface of each bowl of icing with plastic wrap (otherwise the icing will begin to harden) and refrigerate it until you are ready to use it, up to 1 day. Spread the icing on the cookies with a small offset spatula or craft stick.

rolled gingerbread cookies

Makes about 40 medium gingerbread people

These cookies are mildly spiced, for kids. If you like your gingerbread men a little hotter, use 1 tablespoon each of ground cinnamon and ginger instead of 2 teaspoons. The dough can be cut into gingerbread people, of course, and decorated with raisins, red hots, and chocolate chips before being baked. Or cut the dough into any shape and decorate the cookies with Royal Icing (page 123).

3 cups unbleached all-purpose flour
1 teaspoon baking soda
$1/2$ teaspoon salt
2 teaspoons ground ginger
2 teaspoons ground cinnamon
$1/2$ teaspoon ground cloves
1 cup (2 sticks) unsalted butter, softened
$3/4$ cup firmly packed light brown sugar
1 large egg
$1/2$ cup dark (not light or blackstrap) molasses
1 tablespoon water

1. Whisk together the flour, baking soda, salt, ginger, cinnamon, and cloves in a medium mixing bowl.

2. Cream the butter and brown sugar together in a large mixing bowl with an electric mixer on medium-high speed until fluffy. Add the egg, molasses, and water and beat until incorporated, scraping down the sides of the bowl as necessary. Add the flour mixture all at once and mix on low speed until the dough comes together in a ball.

3. Divide the dough into 3 equal balls. Wrap each ball in plastic and refrigerate it for at least 2 hours and for up to 2 days. (The dough can be frozen for up to 1 month; defrost it in the refrigerator before use.)

4. Preheat the oven to 350 degrees. Line a baking sheet with parchment paper.

5. With a lightly floured rolling pin, roll out a ball of dough $1/8$ inch thick on a lightly floured work surface. Cut the dough into gingerbread people or any other desired shapes and place the cookies on the prepared baking sheet. If making gingerbread people, make eyes, nose, mouth, and buttons with raisins, red hots, small gumdrops, and/or chocolate chips. Refrigerate the scraps.

6. Bake the cookies until they are firm, about 8 minutes. Slide the entire parchment sheet with the cookies onto a wire rack and let the cookies cool completely. Repeat with the remaining balls and then with the chilled scraps, using fresh parchment paper. Decorate with Royal Icing as desired.

Rolled Gingerbread Cookies will keep in an airtight container for several days.

Kids Can Help

If your kids are too young to roll dough, let them strategically place the raisins and other decorations on the rolled gingerbread people (or three-eyed alien people, as they are often called in our house).

Kids Can Help—
Cookie Decorating Parties

I'm not one of those bakers who labors over each cookie, creating masterpieces that are ready to be photographed for *Pastry Chef Magazine*. But I do love to mail-order sprinkles, sanding sugars, dragées, and unusual shades of food coloring. I usually just put these goodies plus chopped nuts, currants, mini chocolate chips, and whatever else I have around into little bowls and let my daughter and her friends go wild, spreading the icing on with craft sticks and sprinkling on decorations.

I've organized many cookie decorating parties for the schoolroom and in my own kitchen. All you need is a lot of icing, craft sticks, a good selection of stuff to sprinkle on the iced cookies, and a broom to sweep up afterward. The icing hardens quickly once it is spread thin, so by the time everyone is finished decorating, the cookies will be ready to eat. Alternatively, I've decorated cookies with the kids at school on one day, packed them in an airtight container, and served them the next day as part of a holiday party (Halloween, Christmas/Chanukah/Kwanzaa, Valentine's Day, or Easter). To me, cookies decorated by kids look just amazing and perfect when set out all together on a platter, even if individually they look a little sloppy.

Here are a few tips for making good-looking cookies with kids:

1. Collect sets of holiday cookie cutters. For about $5 at your local housewares store, you can get a box of five or six themed cutters (my Halloween box contains a pumpkin, ghost, witch, cat, and spider web) that you will use over and over again.

2. Tint the icing with pastels. Bright colors are less appetizing and harder to clean off hands, clothes, and furniture than are pale shades.

3. Have enough little cups of icing and decorations so that the kids don't have to reach over each other (or fight with each other) to get to the stuff. Use very small paper cups, and fill them only a quarter of the way up. You'll be surprised at how far a small amount of sprinkles goes. You'll also be surprised at how much decorating material winds up on the floor if you are too generous.

4. Get creative with decorating materials. Check out the bins of candy and treats at the supermarket and natural foods store. Set out small bowls of nonpareils, snippets of shoestring licorice, shredded coconut, and yogurt-covered peanuts as well as the usual sprinkles and sanding sugar.

5. Set out a large sheet of parchment or wax paper on a separate counter or table for the finished cookies and place them there to dry. It's wonderful to see the colorful cookies accumulate as the kids work.

6. Don't forget to photograph the kids and their finished cookies before you start to eat.

stained-glass butter cookies

Makes about 42 cookies

Melted bits of hard candy in the center of these cookies look like stained glass. For the prettiest cookies, use a fluted cutter. Red and green hard candies are traditional, but I also like the way butterscotch looks and tastes with the buttery cookie. A sprinkling of sugar gives the cookies a sparkly holiday look.

1 cup (2 sticks) unsalted butter, softened
¾ cup sugar
1 large egg yolk
1 teaspoon pure vanilla extract
2¼ cups unbleached all-purpose flour
¾ cup (about 6 ounces) red or green hard candies or butterscotch candies

1. Cream the butter and ½ cup of the sugar together in a large mixing bowl with an electric mixer on medium-high speed until fluffy. Add the egg yolk and vanilla and beat until incorporated, scraping down the sides of the bowl as necessary. Add the flour and mix on low speed until the dough comes together in a ball.

2. Divide the dough into 3 equal balls. Wrap each ball in plastic and refrigerate it for at least 2 hours and up to 2 days. (The dough can be frozen for up to 1 month; defrost it in the refrigerator before use.)

3. Preheat the oven to 375 degrees. Line a large baking sheet with parchment paper.

4. Place the hard candies in a food processor fitted with a metal blade and process until they are finely ground. Transfer the ground candy to a small bowl.

5. Remove one ball of dough from the refrigerator and knead it 4 or 5 times on a lightly floured work surface to soften it. With a lightly floured rolling pin, roll out the dough to ⅛ inch thick. Using a small glass or biscuit cutter, cut the dough into 3-inch circles. Using small cookie cutters or a sharp paring knife, make decorative cuts in the center of each cookie, leaving a cutout area to fill with candy. Transfer the cookies to the prepared baking sheet. Using a very small measuring spoon, carefully fill each cutout with the candy so that the candy is resting on the parchment paper and is level with the dough. Sprinkle the cookies with some of the remaining ¼ cup sugar. Refrigerate the scraps.

6. Bake the cookies until they are firm and golden around the edges, about 8 minutes. Let them cool completely on the baking sheet. Repeat with the remaining dough balls and then the chilled scraps, using fresh parchment paper.

Stained-Glass Butter Cookies will keep in an airtight container for several days.

chocolate-peppermint stained-glass cookies

Makes about 48 cookies

These cookies are pretty and taste great too.

1 ounce (1 square) unsweetened chocolate
2¼ cups unbleached all-purpose flour
¼ cup unsweetened Dutch-process cocoa powder
½ teaspoon salt
1 cup (2 sticks) unsalted butter, softened
1 cup sugar
1 large egg plus 1 large egg yolk
1 teaspoon pure vanilla extract
½ cup (about 4 ounces) peppermint candies

1. Melt the chocolate in the top of a double boiler set over simmering water or in the microwave on high for 20 seconds to 1 minute depending on how powerful your microwave oven is. Set it aside to cool.

2. Sift together the flour, cocoa powder, and salt in a medium mixing bowl.

3. Cream the butter and sugar together in a large mixing bowl with an electric mixer on medium speed until fluffy. Add the melted chocolate and beat to combine. Add the whole egg, egg yolk, and vanilla. Add the flour and cocoa mixture and beat until incorporated, scraping down the sides of the bowl as necessary.

4. Divide the dough into 2 equal pieces and shape each piece into a 6-inch disk. Wrap each disk in plastic and refrigerate it for at least 2 hours and for up to 2 days.

(The dough can be frozen for up to 1 month; defrost it in the refrigerator before use.)

5. Preheat the oven to 375 degrees. Line a large baking sheet with parchment paper.

6. Place the peppermints in a food processor and process until finely ground. Transfer the ground candy to a small bowl.

7. Remove one dough disk from the refrigerator and with a lightly floured rolling pin, roll out the dough ⅛ inch thick on a lightly floured work surface. Using a small glass or biscuit cutter, cut the dough into 3-inch circles. Using small cookie cutters or a sharp paring knife, make decorative cuts in the center of each cookie, leaving a cutout area to fill with candy. Transfer the cookies to the prepared baking sheet. Using a very small measuring spoon, carefully fill each cutout with peppermint candy so that the candy is resting on the parchment paper and is level with the dough. Refrigerate the scraps.

8. Bake the cookies until they are firm, 6 to 8 minutes. Let them cool completely on the baking sheet. Repeat with the remaining dough balls and then the chilled scraps, using fresh parchment paper.

Chocolate-Peppermint Stained-Glass Cookies will keep in an airtight container for up to 2 weeks.

Cookie Pops

Before I was a mother, I wouldn't even have known where to buy craft sticks. Now I have them spilling out of every cabinet in my kitchen. In addition to making great picture frames and miniature cabins, they come in handy for making cookies on a stick. Make your cookies extra large. Insert a craft stick into the center of each ball of dough (you'll have to arrange the dough in alternating rows of 2 and 3 cookies or 3 and 4 cookies so that there's room for the sticks). Bake the cookies as directed. I like to keep the decorations simple, and I choose glazes and decorations for taste as much as for looks. I would never decorate a chocolate chip cookie with jelly beans, for example, but I do like certain jelly beans on peanut butter cookies. Here are some of my favorite cookie pops, with decorating suggestions to get you going.

* **Sprinkle Cookie Pops:** These are the easiest. Just insert craft sticks halfway into double-size balls of Sprinkle Cookie (page 90) dough and roll the balls in sprinkles. Bake a minute or two longer than smaller sprinkle cookies.

* **Molasses Cookie Pop Faces:** Put double-size molasses cookies into the oven to bake for 2 or 3 minutes. Then insert the craft sticks. Spread Basic White Glaze (page 103) over the top of each cooled cookie to cover. Place the cookies on wax paper, glazed side up. Use dried blueberries for the eyes, dried cranberries for the mouth, and raisins for hair. Allow the glaze to set completely, at least 30 minutes, before serving.

* **Chocolate Chip Cookie Pops:** Bake large balls of chocolate chip cookie dough for 2 to 3 minutes before inserting the craft sticks. Dip the cooled cookies into Chocolate Glaze (page 151) to cover. Place the cookies on wax paper and let stand until the glaze is hard, about 2 hours. If you want to go further, sprinkle the cookies with ground nuts or shredded coconut before the glaze has set.

* **Peanut Butter Cookie Pops:** Bake large balls of peanut butter cookie dough for 2 to 3 minutes before inserting the craft sticks. (Leave the balls unmarked; no cross-hatches or thumbprints.) Dip the fronts of the cooled cookies into Chocolate Glaze (page 151) to cover. Place on wax paper, glazed side up. Decorate with whole or chopped peanuts, or make polka-dot cookies with peanut butter chips or jelly beans.

anise-flavored butter cookies

Ground nuts add extra richness to these pleasingly simple, unusually flavored holiday cookies.

Nonstick cooking spray
¾ cup walnuts
½ cup (1 stick) unsalted butter, softened
1 cup sugar
2 large eggs
2¼ cups unbleached all-purpose flour
2 teaspoons anise seeds
1 teaspoon baking powder
½ teaspoon salt

1. Preheat the oven to 350 degrees. Coat 2 large baking sheets with cooking spray.

2. Place the walnuts in a food processor and process until finely ground. Be careful not to overprocess them or the walnuts will release their oil.

3. Cream together the butter and ¾ cup of the sugar in a large mixing bowl with an electric mixer on medium-high speed until fluffy. Add the eggs and beat, scrap-ing down the sides of the bowl once or twice, until well combined. Mix in the flour, anise seeds, chopped walnuts, baking powder, and salt on low speed until just combined.

4. Place the remaining ¼ cup sugar in a small bowl. With floured hands, roll rounded tablespoonfuls of the dough into balls. Dip the tops of the balls in the sugar and place, sugar side up, on the prepared baking sheets, leaving 2 inches between each cookie. Flatten each ball slightly with the palm of your hand. Bake until the bottoms of the cookies are golden, about 20 minutes. Transfer the cookies to a wire rack with a metal spatula to cool.

Anise-Flavored Butter Cookies will keep in an airtight container for 2 to 3 days.

chocolate-currant rugelach

Makes 32 rugelach Freezing the rugelach before baking ensures that the rich, flaky dough holds its shape. It also makes this recipe super-convenient. Make the cookies whenever you have time, and bake them just in time for Chanukah.

For the cream cheese dough

2 cups unbleached all-purpose flour
1½ tablespoons sugar
¼ teaspoon salt
One 8-ounce package chilled cream cheese, cut into 8 pieces
1 cup (2 sticks) chilled unsalted butter, cut into 16 pieces

For the chocolate-currant filling

½ cup sugar
1 teaspoon ground cinnamon
1 cup walnuts
⅔ cup raspberry preserves
1 cup miniature semisweet chocolate chips
⅔ cup (about 4 ounces) dried currants

For the glaze

⅓ cup heavy cream

1. Make the dough: Combine the flour, sugar, and salt in a food processor and pulse to combine. Add the cream cheese and butter and pulse until the mixture resembles coarse meal (do not overprocess).

2. Turn the mixture out onto a lightly floured work surface and press it into a ball. Divide the ball into 4 equal pieces and shape each piece into a 4-inch disk. Wrap each disk in plastic and refrigerate it for at least 2 hours and for up to 2 days.

(The dough can be frozen for up to 1 month; defrost it in the refrigerator before use.)

3. Preheat the oven to 375 degrees. Line 2 baking sheets with parchment paper.

4. Make the filling: Combine the sugar and cinnamon in a small bowl. Place the walnuts in a food processor and process until finely chopped. Transfer the chopped walnuts to a medium mixing bowl. Place the preserves in the food processor and process until any large chunks are broken up. Transfer to a small bowl.

5. Remove one dough disk from the refrigerator and with a lightly floured rolling pin, roll out the dough into a 9-inch circle on a lightly floured work surface. Using a 9-inch plate or pie plate as a guide, trim the edges to make a neat circle. Spread 2½ tablespoons of the preserves over the dough. Sprinkle with 2½ tablespoons of the currants and ¼ cup of the chocolate chips. Sprinkle with 2 tablespoons of the cinnamon sugar. Sprinkle with ¼ cup of the walnuts. Pat the filling firmly with your fingertips to secure it to the dough. Cut the dough circle into 8 wedges. Roll each wedge into

Rugelach Fillings

Rugelach dough may be filled with any number of combinations of nuts and dried fruits according to your taste. If your dried fruit is very dry, place it in a heatproof bowl, cover it with boiling water, and let it stand for 5 minutes. Drain and pat the fruit dry with paper towels before proceeding. Here are some of the fillings I use when I want to vary the recipe.

cinnamon-raisin rugelach

1/2 cup sugar
1 teaspoon ground cinnamon
1 1/4 cups finely chopped walnuts
2/3 cup raspberry preserves
1 1/4 cups raisins

cherry and white chocolate rugelach

1/2 cup sugar
1/2 teaspoon ground cinnamon
1 cup finely chopped walnuts
2/3 cup cherry preserves
6 ounces best-quality white chocolate, finely chopped
2/3 cup (about 4 ounces) dried cherries

apricot and almond rugelach

1/2 cup sugar
1/2 teaspoon ground cinnamon
1/4 teaspoon ground ginger
1 1/4 cups finely chopped almonds
2/3 cup apricot preserves
1 1/4 cups finely chopped dried apricots

fig and chocolate rugelach

1/2 cup sugar
1/2 teaspoon ground cinnamon
1 cup finely chopped pecans
2/3 cup fig jam
1 cup finely chopped dried figs
1 cup semisweet chocolate chips

a crescent and place it on the prepared baking sheet. Place the baking sheet in the freezer for at least 30 minutes. Repeat with the remaining dough disks. (Rolled rugelach can be wrapped in plastic and frozen for up to 1 month. Place the rugelach in the oven directly from the freezer.)

6. Brush the frozen rugelach with the heavy cream and bake them until they are golden, 24 to 26 minutes. Transfer them to wire racks with a metal spatula and let them cool completely.

Rugelach will keep in an airtight container for 2 to 3 days.

EASY-BAKE OVEN: keeping it simple with brownies and bars

CLOCKWISE FROM TOP MIDDLE: Blueberry-Cornmeal Crumb Squares, Apricot Linzer Bars, Four-Layer Bars, Caramel Swirl Brownies

When I want a sweet treat without any fuss,
I immediately think of brownies and bars. As simple to mix as cookie dough, they are even simpler to bake, since the batter is just scraped into the pan rather than portioned into cookie shapes. There is a brownie or bar to please any kid. Even if your kids don't like chocolate, nuts, raisins, or peanut butter, there's hope. Try Lemon Squares. If all else fails, try Marshmallow Treats.

Volumes have been written making brownies and bars more difficult. I've seen brownie recipes that call for three kinds of nuts and marshmallow frosting. I've seen recipes for bar cookies with pastry crusts, complicated fruit fillings, and fussy streusel toppings. My feeling is, if bars are going to take this much effort, why not just skip it and make a pie?

I want simple, intense flavor with no distractions. It's true that some brownies and bars benefit from a little extra work. Peanut Butter Blondies, for example, would seem naked without a chocolate glaze. Whole Wheat Blondies, on the other hand, are perfect as is. Why distract from their wholesome flavor and texture by covering them with coconut glop?

There are different types of brownies, and each type has its fans. For minimalists like me, there are Best Basic Brownies, which deliver pure chocolate flavor and nothing else. There is no fancy technique here, just a simple substitution of cake flour for unbleached all-purpose flour that gives them an ethereal texture.

For people who like brownies with *stuff*, I've developed Add-On Brownies, with a sturdy batter that can handle whatever you throw into it. Just choose the combination of nuts, dried fruit, and/or chocolate chips that you like best.

For people who want their brownies when they want them, I've even developed a fantastic recipe for Microwave Brownies. With this recipe, you can mix, bake, and eat your brownies in under fifteen minutes.

The blondie is the natural companion to the brownie in any mom's baking repertoire. I like to bake a batch of each and pile a platter on one side with brownies and on the other with blondies for a black-and-white effect. While staying true to the butterscotch essence of basic blondies, I've had some fun with the recipe when cooking up variations. I stick to combinations that make good flavor sense. Blondie batter is the perfect medium for classic pairings such as coconut and ginger or maple and walnut. My granola bars are a distant relative of these blondies. Like blondies, they get their rich molasses flavor from brown sugar. A generous quantity of oats, nuts, seeds, and dried fruit sets them apart.

When you want something that is more like a confection than a cookie, try Layer Bars and S'mores Bars. These bars have a buttery graham cracker crust topped with all kinds of good, sweet stuff. In keeping with my philosophy that less is more, these bars are relatively restrained. Instead of the traditional seven layers, my Layer Bars have just a few premium ingredients. And although they taste decadent, S'mores bars are positively spare when it comes to ingredients—just five, and that includes a pinch of salt. Speaking of confections, what would a mom's baking book be without a recipe for marshmallow treats? I've tinkered only a little bit with the classic, replacing the vegetable oil with butter and adding vanilla for flavor.

Occasionally I do venture into the territory of bars with pastry crusts, but I try my hardest to keep it simple. The shortbread like crust that forms the base for Lemon Squares, Caramel Nut Squares, and Raspberry Cheesecake Bars doesn't have to be rolled. Simply pat the crumbly mixture into the bottom of the pan and cover it with the topping of your choice.

I've also developed two crumb bar recipes that look a lot more difficult to make than they actually are. For both Blueberry-Cornmeal Crumb Squares and Apricot Linzer Bars, the crust and crumb are made from the same mixture. The difference is in the way you put the crust and crumb in the pan. First you pat half the mixture into the pan so it forms a solid pastry base. You top that with the fruit. Then you sprinkle the remaining crust mixture on top so it forms loose crumbs. So simple, so modern!

How Not to Overbake Your Brownies and Bars

Take care not to overbake your brownies and bars. The batter near the edges of the pan will cook more quickly than the batter in the center, so if you wait for the center to bake through completely before removing your pan from the oven, the outside bars will be intolerably dry. Using a toothpick to judge the doneness of baked goods has always confounded me. Yes, I can see when the toothpick is covered with liquid batter, but I'm never sure what it means if a few crumbs stick to the toothpick. Will the brownies be underdone at this stage? If I wait until the toothpick comes out clean, will they be overdone? I don't even bother with a toothpick when it comes to brownies and bars; I just try to take them from the oven as soon as the center is set and doesn't jiggle when I shake the pan. This way I know they will be ultra-moist in the center and pleasantly cakey on the outside.

best basic brownies

Makes 16 brownies

The debate about the best brownies (cakey versus fudgy; nuts versus no nuts) will no doubt rage on, but in my opinion these are it. Cake flour gives them a tender crumb. Whipping the eggs and sugar together gives the brownies a crackly, flaky surface that contrasts with the moist, fudgy brownie below. Unbleached all-purpose flour may be substituted, but your brownies won't be as delicate and delicious.

½ cup (1 stick) unsalted butter
2 ounces (2 squares) unsweetened chocolate
⅔ cup cake flour (not self-rising)
¼ teaspoon salt
1 cup sugar
2 large eggs
1 teaspoon pure vanilla extract

1. Preheat the oven to 350 degrees. Line an 8-inch square baking pan with heavy-duty aluminum foil, making sure that the foil is tucked into all the corners and that there is at least 1 inch overhanging the top of the pan on all sides.

2. Put 1 inch of water in the bottom of a double boiler or medium saucepan and bring to a bare simmer. Combine the butter and chocolate in the top of the double boiler or in a stainless-steel bowl and set on top of the simmering water, making sure that the water doesn't touch the bottom of the bowl. Heat, whisking occasionally, until the chocolate and butter are completely melted. Set aside to cool slightly.

3. Combine the flour and salt in a small mixing bowl.

4. Combine the sugar and eggs in a large mixing bowl. With an electric mixer, beat on high speed until the mixture is thick and pale, about 5 minutes. Stir in the chocolate mixture and vanilla on low speed until smooth. Stir in the flour mixture until just incorporated.

5. Pour the batter into the prepared baking pan. Bake the brownies until they are just set in the center, 20 to 22 minutes. Let them cool completely on a wire rack.

6. Grasping the overhanging foil on either side of the pan, lift out the brownies and place them on a cutting board. Cut them into 16 squares.

Best Basic Brownies will keep at room temperature in an airtight container for up to 3 days.

mocha brownies

Makes 16 brownies

Espresso powder and chocolate chips added to the Best Basic Brownie recipe ratchet up the richness level. These aren't exactly adult; they're brownies, after all. But the coffee gives them a little bit of an edge that's tempered beautifully by a glass of milk.

½ cup (1 stick) unsalted butter

2 ounces (2 squares) unsweetened chocolate

⅔ cup cake flour (not self-rising)

¼ teaspoon salt

2 tablespoons instant espresso powder

1 cup sugar

2 large eggs

2 teaspoons pure vanilla extract

½ cup semisweet chocolate chips

1. Preheat the oven to 350 degrees. Line an 8-inch square baking pan with heavy-duty aluminum foil, making sure that the foil is tucked into all the corners and that there is at least 1 inch overhanging the top of the pan on all sides.

2. Put 1 inch of water in the bottom of a double boiler or medium saucepan and bring to a bare simmer. Combine the butter and chocolate in the top of the double boiler or in a stainless-steel bowl set on top of the simmering water, making sure that the water doesn't touch the bottom of the bowl. Heat, whisking occasionally, until the chocolate and butter are completely melted. Set aside to cool slightly.

3. Combine the flour, salt, and espresso powder in a small mixing bowl.

4. Combine the sugar and eggs in a large mixing bowl. With an electric mixer, beat on high speed until the mixture is thick and pale, about 5 minutes. Stir in the chocolate mixture and vanilla on low speed until smooth. Stir in the flour mixture until just incorporated. With a wooden spoon, stir in the chocolate chips.

5. Pour the batter into the prepared baking pan. Bake the brownies until they are just set in the center, 20 to 22 minutes. Let them cool completely on a wire rack.

6. Grasping the overhanging foil on either side of the pan, lift out the brownies and place them on a cutting board. Cut them into 16 squares.

Mocha Brownies will keep at room temperature in an airtight container for up to 3 days.

orange brownies

Makes 16 brownies This is one of my favorite variations on Best Basic Brownies. It's simple but dramatic. Orange zest and almonds give these brownies an almost Mediterranean flavor.

¹/₂ cup (1 stick) unsalted butter
**2 ounces (2 squares) unsweetened
  chocolate**
²/₃ cup cake flour (not self-rising)
¹/₄ teaspoon salt
1 cup sugar
2 large eggs
1 teaspoon pure vanilla extract
**2 tablespoons Grand Marnier or other
  orange liqueur**
1 teaspoon grated orange zest
¹/₂ cup chopped almonds

1. Preheat the oven to 350 degrees. Line an 8-inch square baking pan with heavy-duty aluminum foil, making sure that the foil is tucked into all the corners and that there is at least 1 inch overhanging the top of the pan on all sides.

2. Put 1 inch of water in the bottom of a double boiler or a medium saucepan and bring to a bare simmer. Combine the butter and chocolate in the top of the double boiler or in a stainless-steel bowl and set on top of the simmering water, making sure that the water doesn't touch the bottom of the bowl. Heat, whisking occasionally, until the chocolate and butter are completely melted. Set aside to cool slightly.

3. Combine the flour and salt in a small mixing bowl.

4. Combine the sugar and eggs in a large mixing bowl. With an electric mixer, beat on high speed until the mixture is thick and pale, about 5 minutes. Stir in the chocolate mixture, vanilla, orange liqueur, and orange zest on low speed until smooth. Stir in the flour mixture until just incorporated. Stir in the almonds.

5. Pour the batter into the prepared baking dish. Bake the brownies until they are just set in the center, 20 to 22 minutes. Let them cool completely on a wire rack.

6. Grasping the overhanging foil on either side of the pan, lift out the brownies and place them on a cutting board. Cut them into 16 squares.

Orange Brownies will keep at room temperature in an airtight container for up to 3 days.

double chocolate brownies

Makes 16 brownies Bittersweet chocolate in the batter makes these brownies extra fudgy. For Triple Chocolate Brownies, add ½ cup semisweet or milk chocolate chips.

½ cup (1 stick) unsalted butter
2 ounces (2 squares) unsweetened chocolate
4 ounces bittersweet chocolate
⅔ cup unbleached all-purpose flour
½ teaspoon baking powder
¼ teaspoon salt
1 cup sugar
3 large eggs
1 teaspoon pure vanilla extract

1. Preheat the oven to 350 degrees. Line an 8-inch square baking pan with heavy-duty aluminum foil, making sure that the foil is tucked into all the corners and that there is at least 1 inch overhanging the top of the pan on all sides.

2. Put 1 inch of water in the bottom of a double boiler or a medium saucepan and bring to a bare simmer. Combine the butter and both chocolates in the top of the double boiler or in a stainless-steel bowl and place it on top of the simmering water, making sure that the water doesn't touch the bottom of the bowl. Heat, whisking occasionally, until the chocolate and butter are completely melted. Set aside to cool slightly.

3. Combine the flour, baking powder, and salt in a small mixing bowl.

4. Whisk together the sugar and eggs in a large mixing bowl. With a wooden spoon, stir in the chocolate mixture and vanilla. Stir in the flour mixture until just incorporated.

5. Pour the batter into the prepared baking pan. Bake the brownies until they are just set in the center, 25 to 30 minutes. Let them cool completely on a wire rack.

6. Grasping the overhanging foil on either side of the pan, lift out the brownies and place them on a cutting board. Cut them into 16 squares.

Double Chocolate Brownies will keep at room temperature in an airtight container for up to 3 days.

The Best Chocolate for Brownies

Does the type of chocolate you use in brownies dictate how good they are? Yes and no. I have found no difference between brownies baked with a premium brand and those baked with Baker's Chocolate, an inexpensive supermarket brand. But when I make Instant Homemade Microwave Brownies (page 142) with unsweetened cocoa powder, I find that richer, darker premium cocoa makes better brownies than does pallid supermarket cocoa. So I'm cheap when buying unsweetened chocolate, but extravagant when it comes to cocoa powder.

add-on brownies

If you like nuts, dried fruit, and/or chocolate chips in your brownies, you'll need a sturdy batter that produces thicker, more substantial brownies. Get creative here or consult my list of favorite add-on combinations.

½ cup (1 stick) unsalted butter
2 ounces (2 squares) unsweetened
  chocolate
¾ cup unbleached all-purpose flour
½ teaspoon baking powder
¼ teaspoon salt
1 cup sugar
2 large eggs
1 teaspoon pure vanilla extract
1 cup any combination chopped nuts,
  chocolate or peanut butter chips,
  and/or chopped dried fruit

1. Preheat the oven to 350 degrees. Line an 8-inch square baking pan with heavy-duty aluminum foil, making sure that the foil is tucked into all the corners and that there is at least 1 inch overhanging the top of the pan on all sides.

2. Put 1 inch of water in the bottom of a double boiler or medium saucepan and bring to a bare simmer. Combine the butter and chocolate in the top of the double boiler or in a stainless-steel bowl and set on top of the simmering water, making sure that the water doesn't touch the bottom of the bowl. Heat, whisking occasionally, until the chocolate and butter are completely melted. Set aside to cool slightly.

3. Combine the flour, baking powder, and salt in a small mixing bowl.

4. Whisk together the sugar and eggs in a large mixing bowl. With a wooden spoon, stir in the chocolate mixture and vanilla. Stir in the flour mixture until just incorporated. Stir in the add-ons.

5. Pour the batter into the prepared baking dish. Bake the brownies until they are just set in the center, 30 to 35 minutes. Let them cool completely on a wire rack.

6. Grasping the overhanging foil on either side of the pan, lift out the brownies and place them on a cutting board. Cut them into 16 squares.

Add-On Brownies will keep at room temperature in an airtight container for up to 3 days.

Brownie Add-Ons

I'm a minimalist when it comes to brownies. Like most kids, I usually like them straight with a glass of milk. But I admit to a weakness for brownies with dried cherries, milk chocolate chips, and walnuts. When you want your chocolate spiked with something crunchy or chewy, here are some add-on combinations that make sense:

* ½ to ¾ cup any combination chopped walnuts, pecans, and almonds
* ½ cup each semisweet, milk, and white chocolate chips
* ½ cup chopped walnuts and ½ cup dried cherries
* ½ cup white chocolate chips and ½ cups dried cranberries
* ½ cup chopped roasted peanuts and ½ cup raisins
* ½ cup chopped roasted peanuts and ½ cup peanut butter chips
* ½ cup chopped hazelnuts and ½ cup milk chocolate chips
* ½ cup sweetened flaked coconut and ½ cup chopped pecans
* ½ cup chopped walnuts, ½ cup semisweet chocolate chips, and ½ cup mini marshmallows

instant homemade microwave brownies

Makes 16 brownies

This recipe is perfect for those nights, after dinner, when you just wish you could wave a magic wand and have warm brownies to eat. Another plus—this recipe, although very rich-tasting, is relatively low in fat. Like a lot of food cooked in the microwave, these brownies will harden as they cool, so eat them while they're hot. Microwave brownies are very good right out of the oven, so finishing a panful shouldn't be a problem.

Nonstick cooking spray
1½ cups sugar
¾ cup unsweetened Dutch-process cocoa powder
¾ cup unbleached all-purpose flour
½ cup (1 stick) unsalted butter, melted and slightly cooled
3 large eggs
1 teaspoon pure vanilla extract
¾ cup chopped walnuts

1. Coat the inside of an 8-inch square glass baking dish with cooking spray.

2. Whisk together the sugar, cocoa powder, and flour in a medium mixing bowl.

3. Whisk together the cooled melted butter, eggs, and vanilla in a large mixing bowl. With a wooden spoon, stir in the flour mixture until well combined.

4. Scrape the batter into the prepared dish. Microwave on high until the brownies are just set in the center, 4 to 7 minutes, depending on the power and size of your oven. Let the brownies cool on a wire rack for 5 minutes.

5. Cut the brownies into 16 squares. Serve them immediately.

Kids Can Help

Because Instant Homemade Microwave Brownies are so simple and don't require getting anywhere near a hot oven, this is a great recipe for kids, seven and older, who like to cook. They can measure and mix all the ingredients (you might want to melt the butter for the younger ones) and scrape the batter into the baking dish. The dish will be hot when the brownies are ready, so removing it from the microwave should be mom's job.

chocolate-mint brownies
with white chocolate chips

Makes 16 brownies

This is about as baroque as I like to get with brownies. White chocolate, which can sometimes be cloying, is a wonderfully creamy and sweet counterpoint to the intense dark chocolate and bracing mint.

½ cup (1 stick) unsalted butter
2 ounces (2 squares) unsweetened chocolate
¾ cup unbleached all-purpose flour
½ teaspoon baking powder
¼ teaspoon salt
1 cup sugar
2 large eggs
1 teaspoon pure vanilla extract
½ teaspoon pure peppermint extract
1 cup white chocolate chips

1. Preheat the oven to 350 degrees. Line an 8-inch square baking pan with heavy-duty aluminum foil, making sure that the foil is tucked into all the corners and that there is at least 1 inch overhanging the top of the pan on all sides.

2. Put 1 inch of water in the bottom of a double boiler or a medium saucepan and bring to a bare simmer. Combine the butter and unsweetened chocolate in the top of the double boiler or in a stainless-steel bowl and place it on top of the simmering water, making sure that the water doesn't touch the bottom of the bowl. Heat, whisking occasionally, until the chocolate and butter are completely melted. Set aside to cool slightly.

3. Combine the flour, baking powder, and salt in a small mixing bowl.

4. Whisk together the sugar and eggs in a large mixing bowl. With a wooden spoon, stir in the chocolate mixture and extracts. Stir in the flour mixture until just incorporated. Stir in the white chocolate chips.

5. Pour the batter into the prepared baking pan. Bake the brownies until they are just set in the center, 30 to 35 minutes. Let them cool completely on a wire rack.

6. Grasping the overhanging foil on either side of the pan, lift out the brownies and place them on a cutting board. Cut them into 16 squares.

Chocolate-Mint Brownies with White Chocolate Chips will keep at room temperature in an airtight container for up to 3 days.

raspberry brownies

I love the combination of tart berries and rich, dark chocolate. This is one of the simplest ways to put the two together.

½ cup (1 stick) unsalted butter
2½ ounces bittersweet chocolate
½ cup unbleached all-purpose flour
½ teaspoon baking powder
¼ teaspoon salt
1¼ cups sugar
2 large eggs
½ teaspoon pure vanilla extract
1 pint fresh raspberries, or 1 pint
    frozen whole raspberries, thawed and
    patted dry with paper towels

1. Preheat the oven to 350 degrees. Line an 8-inch square baking pan with heavy-duty aluminum foil, making sure that the foil is tucked into all the corners and that there is at least 1 inch overhanging the top of the pan on all sides.

2. Put 1 inch of water in the bottom of a double boiler or a medium saucepan and bring to a bare simmer. Combine the butter and chocolate in the top of the double boiler or in a stainless-steel bowl and set it on top of the simmering water, making sure that the water doesn't touch the bottom of the bowl. Heat, whisking occasionally, until the chocolate and butter are completely melted. Set aside to cool slightly.

3. Combine the flour, baking powder, and salt in a small mixing bowl.

4. Whisk together the sugar and eggs in a large mixing bowl. With a wooden spoon, stir in the chocolate mixture and vanilla. Stir in the flour mixture until just incorporated. Gently stir in the raspberries.

5. Pour the batter into the prepared baking pan. Bake the brownies until they are just set in the center, about 35 minutes. Let them cool for at least 20 minutes so that they are warm but not hot, or cool them completely on a wire rack.

6. Grasping the overhanging foil on either side of the pan, lift out the brownies and place them on a cutting board. Cut them into 16 squares.

Raspberry Brownies will keep at room temperature in an airtight container for up to 3 days.

A Good Excuse to Make Raspberry Brownies

How long has it been since you've had a brownie sundae? These are good with vanilla ice cream and Simple Warm Chocolate Sauce (page 41) on top.

cream cheese brownies

Makes 16 brownies

This is a classic subcategory of brownie that's tangy as well as chocolatey and sweet.

For the brownie batter

½ cup (1 stick) unsalted butter
4 ounces (4 squares) unsweetened chocolate
⅔ cup unbleached all-purpose flour
½ teaspoon baking powder
¼ teaspoon salt
1¼ cups sugar
2 large eggs
2 teaspoons pure vanilla extract

For the cream cheese filling

One 8-ounce package cream cheese, softened
¼ cup sugar
1 large egg

1. Preheat the oven to 325 degrees. Adjust the oven rack to the bottom third of the oven. Line an 8-inch square baking pan with heavy-duty aluminum foil, making sure that the foil is tucked into all the corners and that there is at least 1 inch overhanging the top of the pan on all sides.

2. Make the brownies: Put 1 inch of water in the bottom of a double boiler or medium saucepan and bring to a bare simmer. Combine the butter and chocolate in the top of the double boiler or in a stainless-steel bowl and set it on top of the simmering water, making sure that the water doesn't touch the bottom of the bowl. Heat, whisking occasionally, until the chocolate and butter are completely melted. Set aside to cool slightly.

3. Combine the flour, baking powder, and salt in a small mixing bowl.

4. Whisk together the sugar and eggs in a large mixing bowl. With a wooden spoon, stir in the chocolate mixture and vanilla. Stir in the flour mixture until just incorporated.

5. Make the filling: Combine the cream cheese and sugar in a medium mixing bowl. With an electric mixer on medium-high speed beat the mixture until very smooth. Add the egg and beat again until smooth.

6. Pour all but about ½ cup of the batter into the prepared baking pan. Smooth the top with a rubber spatula. Drop the cream cheese mixture by heaping tablespoonfuls over the brownie batter and smooth with the spatula to create an even layer. Drop the remaining brownie batter in dollops on top and swirl the batter with a knife to create marbling. Do not overmix. Bake the brownies in the bottom third of the oven until they are just set in the center, 45 to 50 minutes. Let them cool completely on a wire rack.

7. Refrigerate them until they are completely chilled, at least 3 hours. Grasping the overhanging foil on either side of the pan, lift out the brownies and place them on a cutting board. Cut them into 16 squares.

Cream Cheese Brownies will keep in the refrigerator in an airtight container for up to 5 days.

caramel swirl brownies

Makes 16 brownies

I tried a number of brownie recipes using packaged caramel candies, but I was never satisfied, because the commercial candy baked up into hard little bits. Since caramel sauce is simple to make, I decided to swirl my own homemade caramel into brownie batter and see what happened. The result, while comfortingly retro, is far superior to the back-of-the-bag version.

½ cup (1 stick) unsalted butter
2 ounces (2 squares) unsweetened chocolate
¾ cup unbleached all-purpose flour
½ teaspoon baking powder
¼ teaspoon salt
1 cup sugar
2 large eggs
1 teaspoon pure vanilla extract
½ cup semisweet chocolate chips
½ cup chopped walnuts or pecans
1 recipe Homemade Caramel Sauce (page 233) or ½ cup store-bought caramel sauce

1. Preheat the oven to 350 degrees. Line an 8-inch square baking pan with heavy-duty aluminum foil, making sure that the foil is tucked into all the corners and that there is at least 1 inch overhanging the top of the pan on all sides.

2. Put 1 inch of water in the bottom of a double boiler or medium saucepan and bring to a bare simmer. Combine the butter and chocolate in the top of the double boiler or in a stainless-steel bowl and set it on top of the simmering water, making sure that the water doesn't touch the bottom of the bowl. Heat, whisking occasionally, until the chocolate and butter are completely melted. Set aside to cool slightly.

3. Combine the flour, baking powder, and salt in a small mixing bowl.

4. Whisk together the sugar and eggs in a large mixing bowl. With a wooden spoon, stir in the chocolate mixture and vanilla. Stir in the flour mixture until just incorporated. Stir in the chocolate chips.

5. Stir the nuts into the caramel sauce.

6. Pour the batter into the prepared baking pan. Smooth the top with a rubber spatula. Drop the caramel mixture by heaping tablespoonfuls over the brownie batter. Swirl with a knife to create marbling. Do not overmix. Bake the brownies until they are just set in the center, 30 to 35 minutes. Let them cool completely on a wire rack. Refrigerate them until they are completely chilled.

7. Grasping the overhanging foil on either side of the pan, lift out the brownies and place them on a cutting board. Cut them into 16 squares.

Caramel Swirl Brownies will keep at room temperature in an airtight container for up to 3 days.

pantry blondies

Makes 16 blondies

When I was a kid first learning how to bake, I discovered the blondie recipe in *The Joy of Cooking*. Even when my mother had run out of chocolate, she always had all the ingredients to make these delicious bars. I still turn to this recipe, slightly adapted, when I'm desperate for something sweet but don't have much to work with.

1 cup unbleached all-purpose flour
1 teaspoon baking powder
¼ teaspoon salt
½ cup (1 stick) unsalted butter
1 cup firmly packed light brown sugar
1 large egg
1 teaspoon pure vanilla extract
¾ cup chopped walnuts

1. Preheat the oven to 350 degrees. Line an 8-inch square baking pan with heavy-duty aluminum foil, making sure that the foil is tucked into all the corners and that there is at least 1 inch overhanging the top of the pan on all sides.

2. Combine the flour, baking powder, and salt in a small mixing bowl.

3. Melt the butter in a medium saucepan over low heat. Remove it from the heat. With a wooden spoon, stir in the brown sugar until it is dissolved. Quickly whisk in the egg and vanilla. Stir in the flour mixture until just incorporated. Stir in the walnuts.

4. Pour the batter into the prepared baking pan. Bake the blondies until they are just set in the center, 25 to 30 minutes. Let them cool completely on a wire rack.

5. Grasping the overhanging foil on either side of the pan, lift out the blondies and place them on a cutting board. Cut them into 16 squares.

Pantry Blondies will keep at room temperature in an airtight container for up to 3 days.

coconut-ginger blondies

Makes 16 blondies If you stock your pantry well, with crystallized ginger and flaked sweetened coconut, you will also be able to make this more exotic blondie variation at a moment's notice. A handful of crunchy cashews is optional.

1 cup unbleached all-purpose flour
1 teaspoon baking powder
1 teaspoon ground ginger
¼ teaspoon salt
½ cup (1 stick) unsalted butter
1 cup firmly packed light brown sugar
1 large egg
2 tablespoons dark rum (optional)
1 teaspoon pure vanilla extract
¾ cup sweetened flaked coconut
¼ cup finely chopped crystallized ginger
½ cup chopped unsalted cashews
  (optional)

1. Preheat the oven to 350 degrees. Line an 8-inch square baking pan with heavy-duty aluminum foil, making sure that the foil is tucked into all the corners and that there is at least 1 inch overhanging the top of the pan on all sides.

2. Combine the flour, baking powder, ground ginger, and salt in a small mixing bowl.

3. Melt the butter in a medium saucepan over low heat. Remove it from the heat. With a wooden spoon, stir in the brown sugar until it is dissolved. Quickly whisk in the egg, rum (if you are using it), and vanilla. Stir in the flour mixture until just incorporated. Stir in the coconut and crystallized ginger, and cashews, if you are using them.

4. Pour the batter into the prepared baking pan. Bake the blondies until they are just set in the center, 25 to 30 minutes. Let them cool completely on a wire rack.

5. Grasping the overhanging foil on either side of the pan, lift out the blondies and place them on a cutting board. Cut them into 16 squares.

Coconut-Ginger Blondies will keep at room temperature in an airtight container for up to 3 days.

date-nut blondies

Dates, nuts, and spices transform the Pantry Blondie recipe into something entirely different. To save time, you may buy chopped dates and walnut pieces.

¾ cup unbleached all-purpose flour
¼ cup old-fashioned rolled oats
  (not instant)
1 teaspoon baking powder
¼ teaspoon salt
¼ teaspoon ground cinnamon
⅛ teaspoon ground nutmeg
½ cup (1 stick) unsalted butter
1 cup firmly packed light brown sugar
1 large egg
1 teaspoon pure vanilla extract
¾ cup chopped walnuts, pecans, or
  almonds
½ cup chopped dates

1. Preheat the oven to 350 degrees. Line an 8-inch square baking pan with heavy-duty aluminum foil, making sure that the foil is tucked into all the corners and that there is at least 1 inch overhanging the top of the pan on all sides.

2. Combine the flour, oats, baking powder, salt, cinnamon, and nutmeg in a medium mixing bowl.

3. Melt the butter in a medium saucepan over medium heat. Remove it from the heat. With a wooden spoon, stir in the brown sugar until it is dissolved. Quickly whisk in the egg and vanilla. Stir in the flour mixture until just incorporated. Stir in the nuts and dates.

4. Pour the batter into the prepared baking pan. Bake the blondies until they are just set in the center, 25 to 30 minutes. Let them cool completely on a wire rack.

5. Grasping the overhanging foil on either side of the pan, lift out the blondies and place them on a cutting board. Cut them into 16 squares.

Date-Nut Blondies will keep at room temperature in an airtight container for up to 3 days.

peanut butter blondies

The combination of chocolate and peanut butter probably predates the printing press and will still be around after cookbooks have been replaced by on-line recipe files. But most recipes that I've tried just don't excite me. If the peanut butter flavor is not assertive enough, the chocolate frosting overwhelms the bland blondies. The solution is a good dose of chopped salted peanuts, which gives the blondies texture as well as strong peanut flavor to contrast with the smooth, dark chocolate glaze. This is one of my favorite bar recipes.

1 cup plus 2 tablespoons unbleached all-purpose flour
¼ teaspoon baking powder
¼ teaspoon baking soda
¼ teaspoon salt
6 tablespoons (¾ stick) unsalted butter
1 cup firmly packed light brown sugar
½ cup natural smooth peanut butter
2 large eggs
1 teaspoon pure vanilla extract
½ cup chopped salted peanuts
½ recipe Chocolate Glaze (recipe follows)

1. Preheat the oven to 350 degrees. Line an 8-inch square baking pan with heavy-duty aluminum foil, making sure that the foil is tucked into all the corners and that there is at least 1 inch overhanging the top of the pan on all sides.

2. Combine the flour, baking powder, baking soda, and salt in a small mixing bowl.

3. Melt the butter in a medium saucepan over medium heat. With a wooden spoon, stir in the brown sugar until dissolved. Remove the pan from the heat and stir in the eggs and vanilla. Stir in the flour mixture until just incorporated. Stir in the peanuts.

4. Pour the batter into the prepared baking pan. Bake the blondies until they are just set in the center, 25 to 30 minutes. Let them cool completely on a wire rack.

5. Spread the glaze over the blondies with an offset spatula. Allow the glaze to set, about 2 hours.

6. Grasping the overhanging foil on either side of the pan, lift out the blondies and place them on a cutting board. Cut them into 16 squares.

Peanut Butter Blondies will keep at room temperature in an airtight container for up to 3 days.

A Good Excuse to Make Peanut Butter Blondies

If you are at all competitive about how well your contribution sells at a bake sale, try this recipe. Although other brownies and blondies may taste great, Peanut Butter Blondies, with their shiny dark chocolate icing, have a visual appeal that makes them fly off the table before the rest.

chocolate glaze

Makes 1 cup, enough to thickly glaze 24 large cookies or a batch of Peanut Butter Blondies (opposite)

This glaze is only for the patient, since it takes a couple of hours to harden.

8 ounces bittersweet chocolate, finely chopped
2 tablespoons vegetable oil
1 tablespoon corn syrup

1. Put 1 inch of water in the bottom of a double boiler or medium saucepan and bring to a bare simmer. Combine the chocolate, oil, and corn syrup in the top of the double boiler or in a stainless-steel bowl and set it on top of the simmering water, making sure that the water doesn't touch the bottom of the bowl. Heat, whisking occasionally, until the chocolate and oil are completely melted.

2. Dip the cookies in the glaze, or pour the glaze over cookies, and allow the glaze to harden, about 2 hours. If the glaze gets too thick, reheat it over simmering water. Store glazed cookies at room temperature in an airtight container.

Cutting Bars Neatly

The most difficult thing about making brownies, blondies, and bars is removing them neatly from the pan and cutting them into squares without mangling them or having them fall apart. I've found two tricks that help. I line my baking pan with a sheet of heavy-duty aluminum foil large enough to overhang the sides by one inch. Not only does this make cleanup easy, but it lets you remove the whole panful of brownies without having to dig into the corners with a spatula and risk losing some of the brownies in the process.

As for cutting the bars into squares, one simple trick that I highly recommend is placing the pan of cooled bars into the refrigerator for five or ten minutes to give them a little chill. A quick stop in the refrigerator won't affect their fresh-baked flavor; instead it will temporarily make the bars harder and easier to cut cleanly.

maple walnut blondies

Pure maple syrup sweetens this batter and maple extract, available in most supermarkets, gives it an extra flavor boost.

1 cup unbleached all-purpose flour
1 teaspoon baking powder
¼ teaspoon salt
½ cup (1 stick) unsalted butter
½ cup firmly packed light brown sugar
½ cup pure maple syrup
1 large egg
1 teaspoon pure vanilla extract
½ teaspoon pure maple extract
¾ cup chopped walnuts

1. Preheat the oven to 350 degrees. Line an 8-inch square baking pan with heavy-duty aluminum foil, making sure that the foil is tucked into all the corners and that there is at least 1 inch overhanging the top of the pan on all sides.

2. Combine the flour, baking powder, and salt in a small mixing bowl.

3. Melt the butter in a medium saucepan over low heat. Remove it from the heat. With a wooden spoon, stir in the brown sugar and maple syrup until they are dissolved. Quickly whisk in the egg, vanilla, and maple extract. Stir in the flour mixture until just incorporated. Stir in the walnuts.

4. Pour the batter into the prepared baking pan. Bake the blondies until they are just set in the center, 25 to 30 minutes. Let them cool completely on a wire rack.

5. Grasping the overhanging foil on either side of the pan, lift out the blondies and place them on a cutting board. Cut them into 16 squares.

Maple-Walnut Blondies will keep at room temperature in an airtight container for up to 3 days.

whole wheat blondies

These are chewy and wholesome, reminiscent of graham crackers. When I want something decadent, I make them the base for a gooey sundae of coffee ice cream, Marshmallow Fluff, and hot fudge sauce.

1 cup whole wheat flour
1 teaspoon baking powder
1/8 teaspoon salt
1/2 cup (1 stick) unsalted butter
1 cup firmly packed light brown sugar
1 large egg
1 teaspoon pure vanilla extract
3/4 cup chopped walnuts

1. Preheat the oven to 350 degrees. Line an 8-inch square baking pan with heavy-duty aluminum foil, making sure that the foil is tucked into all the corners and that there is at least 1 inch overhanging the top of the pan on all sides.

2. Combine the flour, baking powder, and salt in a small mixing bowl.

3. Melt the butter in a medium saucepan over low heat. Remove it from the heat.

With a wooden spoon, stir in the brown sugar until it is dissolved. Quickly whisk in the egg and vanilla. Stir in the flour mixture until it is just incorporated. Stir in the walnuts.

4. Pour the batter into the prepared baking pan. Bake the blondies until they are just set in the center, 25 to 30 minutes. Let them cool completely on a wire rack.

5. Grasping the overhanging foil on either side of the pan, lift out the blondies and place them on a cutting board. Cut them into 16 squares.

Whole Wheat Blondies will keep at room temperature in an airtight container for up to 3 days.

granola bars

Makes 16 bars

Granola bars are great when you want something chewy, wholesome, and not too sweet. They don't fall apart easily and they stay fresh, wrapped in plastic, for almost a week. Use whatever combination of nuts, seeds, and dried fruits you and your kids like, sticking to the proportions below. You'll find whole wheat flour, flax seeds, and dried fruit at the health foods store.

¾ cup old-fashioned rolled oats (not instant)
¼ cup chopped almonds, pecans, or walnuts
2 tablespoons flax seeds
2 tablespoons unsalted sunflower seeds or pumpkin seeds
½ cup whole wheat flour
½ teaspoon baking powder
¼ teaspoon salt
½ teaspoon ground cinnamon
½ cup canola or vegetable oil
½ cup firmly packed dark brown sugar
1 large egg
1 teaspoon pure vanilla extract
½ cup raisins, dried cherries, cranberries, or any other chopped dried fruit

1. Preheat the oven to 350 degrees. Line an 8-inch square baking pan with heavy-duty aluminum foil, making sure that the foil is tucked into all the corners and that there is at least 1 inch overhanging the top of the pan on all sides.

2. Spread the oats, nuts, flax seeds, and sunflower or pumpkin seeds on a baking sheet and bake them until they are lightly toasted, stirring once or twice with a spoon, about 10 minutes. Remove the pan from the oven and let the mixture cool completely.

3. Combine the flour, baking powder, salt, and cinnamon in a small mixing bowl.

4. Combine the oil and brown sugar in a large mixing bowl and mix them until smooth. Stir in the egg and vanilla. Stir in the flour mixture until it is just combined. Stir in the oat mixture until well combined. Stir in the raisins or dried fruit.

5. Pour the batter into the prepared baking pan. Bake the bars until they are set, 25 to 30 minutes. Let them cool completely on a wire rack.

6. Grasping the overhanging foil on either side of the pan, lift out the bars and place them on a cutting board. Cut them into 16 squares.

Granola Bars will keep at room temperature in an airtight container for up to 5 days.

four-layer bars

Makes 16 bars This is a venerable back-of-the-can recipe, adapted to my taste. The slightly tart apricots balance the other very sweet ingredients. Of course, you may adapt my recipe to your taste, substituting dried cherries or cranberries for the apricots. You can also substitute other chopped nuts for the almonds, using whatever you like best or happen to have on hand.

5 tablespoons unsalted butter, melted
1 cup graham cracker crumbs (from about 8 whole graham crackers)
1 cup finely chopped almonds
½ cup chopped dried apricots
½ cup semisweet or milk chocolate chips
1½ cups sweetened flaked coconut
One 7-ounce can sweetened condensed milk

1. Preheat the oven to 325 degrees. Line an 8-inch square baking pan with heavy-duty aluminum foil, making sure that the foil is tucked into all the corners and that there is at least 1 inch overhanging the top of the pan on all sides.

2. Combine the melted butter and graham cracker crumbs in a medium mixing bowl and stir until all the crumbs are moistened. Sprinkle the mixture across the bottom of the prepared baking pan and press with your fingertips into an even layer.

3. Sprinkle the chopped almonds and apricots evenly over the crumbs. Sprinkle the chocolate chips over the almonds and apricots. Sprinkle the coconut over the chocolate chips. With a large spoon, press down on the coconut firmly to pack together the layers. Drizzle the condensed milk evenly over the coconut. Bake the bars until the coconut begins to color, 25 to 27 minutes. Let the pan cool completely on a wire rack. Refrigerate the bars for 10 minutes.

4. Grasping the overhanging foil on either side of the pan, lift out the bars and place them on a cutting board. Cut them into 16 squares.

Four-Layer Bars will keep, wrapped in plastic and at room temperature, for 4 or 5 days.

s'mores bars

Makes 12 bars This is a variation on Four-Layer Bars, with marshmallows rather than sweetened condensed milk holding the ingredients together. A lot of kids prefer these to Four-Layer Bars (page 155), maybe because they completely lack nutritional value whereas Four-Layer Bars at least have dried fruit.

5 tablespoons unsalted butter, melted
1 cup graham cracker crumbs (from about 8 whole graham crackers)
1 cup finely chopped walnuts
2 cups miniature marshmallows
1 cup milk chocolate chips

1. Preheat the oven to 325 degrees. Line an 8-inch square baking pan with heavy-duty aluminum foil, making sure that the foil is tucked into all the corners and that there is at least 1 inch overhanging the top of the pan on all sides.

2. Combine the melted butter and graham cracker crumbs in a medium mixing bowl and stir until all the crumbs are moistened. Sprinkle the mixture across the bottom of the prepared baking pan and press it with your fingertips into an even layer.

3. Sprinkle the chopped walnuts evenly over the crumbs. Bake for 10 minutes.

Remove the pan from the oven and sprinkle the marshmallows and chocolate chips evenly over the nuts. Return the pan to the oven and bake until the marshmallows are golden, another 13 to 15 minutes. Let the pan cool completely on a wire rack. Refrigerate it for 10 minutes.

4. Grasping the overhanging foil on either side of the pan, lift out the bars and place them on a cutting board. Cut them into 16 squares.

S'mores Bars will keep, wrapped in plastic and at room temperature, for 4 or 5 days.

A Good Excuse to Make S'mores Bars

No recipe in this chapter has fewer ingredients. Make these and see how little work you can get away with and still bake something great.

apricot linzer bars

Makes 16 bars   I love the combination of nut cake and jam. Instead of rolling out a lattice top, I save time and effort by just dropping teaspoonfuls of dough over the filling. As the bars bake, the topping spreads to cover the apricots. After all, you're going to be cutting them into bars (and ruining the lattice) anyway.

For the filling
- ½ cup dried apricots
- ½ cup apricot preserves
- 1 tablespoon strained fresh lemon juice

For the crust and crumb
- 1 cup blanched whole almonds
- 1½ cups unbleached all-purpose flour
- 1 teaspoon baking powder
- ¼ teaspoon ground cloves
- ¼ teaspoon salt
- ¾ cup granulated sugar
- ¾ cup (1½ sticks) unsalted butter, melted
- 1 large egg
- 1 teaspoon pure vanilla extract
- ¼ cup sliced almonds

For the topping
- Confectioners' sugar

1. Preheat the oven to 350 degrees. Line an 8-inch square baking pan with heavy-duty aluminum foil, making sure that the foil is tucked into all the corners and that there is at least 1 inch overhanging the top of the pan on all sides.

2. Make the filling: Place the apricots in a small saucepan and cover them with water. Bring the liquid to a boil, remove the pan from the heat, and let the fruit stand for 5 minutes. Drain, coarsely chop the apricots, and combine them with the preserves and lemon juice in a small mixing bowl. Set them aside.

3. Make the crust and crumb: Place the whole almonds in a food processor and grind them fine. Be careful not to overprocess, or the almonds will release their oil. Transfer the almonds to a medium mixing bowl and combine them with the flour, baking powder, ground cloves, and salt.

4. Combine the granulated sugar and melted butter in a large mixing bowl with a wooden spoon until smooth. Stir in the egg and vanilla. Stir in the flour-and-almond mixture until the ingredients are well combined.

5. Place half the crust and crumb batter in the baking pan and smooth it with a metal spatula into an even layer. Spread the filling across the crust with the spatula. Drop the remaining crust and crumb batter by heaping teaspoonfuls across the top of the filling. Sprinkle the top evenly with the sliced almonds. Bake the bars until the top is golden brown, 40 to 45 minutes. Let the pan cool completely on a wire rack.

6. Grasping the overhanging foil on either side of the pan, lift out the crumb bars and place them on a cutting board. Cut 16 squares. Dust the squares with confectioners' sugar just before serving.

Apricot Linzer Bars will keep at room temperature in an airtight container for up to 3 days.

marshmallow treats

Makes 16 small or 4 extra-large bars

These bars aren't baked, so I probably shouldn't include them in this book, but what kind of mom would I be if I never made Marshmallow Treats for my kids? This is an adaptation of the back-of-the-box recipe. I like to make my treats with butter instead of margarine, and I like them extra-thick. I cut them into 12 squares, but I've been seeing extra-large marshmallow treats in places like Starbucks. If you want the supersize, double the recipe, use a 9 x 11-inch baking pan, and cut the bars into 8 squares.

3 tablespoons unsalted butter
One 10-ounce package regular
    marshmallows
½ teaspoon pure vanilla extract
¼ teaspoon salt
4 cups puffed rice cereal
Nonstick cooking spray

1. Line an 8-inch square baking pan with heavy-duty aluminum foil, making sure that the foil is tucked into all the corners and that there is at least 1 inch overhanging the top of the pan on all sides.

2. Melt the butter in a large saucepan over low heat. Add the marshmallows, vanilla, and salt and stir with a wooden spoon

until melted. Remove the pan from the heat and stir in the rice cereal until it is evenly coated.

3. Turn the mixture into the prepared baking pan. Spray a rubber spatula with cooking spray and spread the mixture evenly across the pan. The pan will be full, with the Marshmallow Treats coming almost to the top. Let the pan cool completely.

4. Grasping the overhanging foil on either side of the pan, lift out the bars and place them on a cutting board. Cut them into 16 squares.

Marshmallow Treats will keep, wrapped in plastic and at room temperature, for 2 to 3 days.

www.ricekrispies.com

Perusing the recipes that Kellogg's has posted on its official Rice Krispies site, you get the feeling that the more things change, the more they stay the same. With your high-speed Internet connection, you can find all the ingenious ideas you used to be able to send away for after saving a couple of box tops—like how to coat fish fillets or cover a cauliflower-cheese casserole with crushed Rice Krispies.

I myself don't feel the need to incorporate Rice Krispies into every dish that I cook. But there was one sweet on-line idea that really appealed to me: marshmallow treat ice cream cups. If you love marshmallow topping on your ice cream sundae, you might want to try this idea.

Coat the inside of a 12-cup muffin tin with nonstick cooking spray. Make the Marshmallow Treat mixture as directed on the facing page. Divide the mixture among the cups and press it into and up the sides of the muffin cups with the back of a spoon sprayed with nonstick cooking spray. Let the cups cool completely.

After the cups have completely cooled, they just slide out of the muffin tins. (If you are not going to use them immediately, store them at room temperature in an airtight container for up to 1 day.)

I scooped some coffee ice cream into my cups, poured a little Simple Warm Chocolate Sauce (page 41) over each portion, and topped it with a maraschino cherry.

caramel nut squares

Makes 16 squares

Caramel Nut Squares, Lemon Squares (opposite), and Raspberry Cheesecake Bars (page 162) all require a prebaked shortbread crust. Don't let this extra step deter you from trying these recipes. They are all wonderful and surprisingly easy to make. I've pared down the recipes so they require as little work as possible. The shortbread dough doesn't have to be rolled, just patted flat in the baking dish.

For the crust

1 cup unbleached all-purpose flour
1/3 cup confectioners' sugar
2 tablespoons cornstarch
1/4 teaspoon salt

For the caramel filling

7 tablespoons unsalted butter, chilled
   and cut into 12 pieces
2 tablespoons unsalted butter
1/2 cup plus 2 tablespoons firmly packed
   light brown sugar
1/4 cup light corn syrup
1/4 cup heavy cream
2 cups coarsely chopped pecans
1 teaspoon pure vanilla extract

1. Preheat the oven to 350 degrees. Line a 9 x 13-inch baking pan with heavy-duty aluminum foil, making sure that the foil is tucked into all the corners and that there is at least 1 inch overhanging the top of the pan on all sides.

2. Make the crust: Combine the flour, confectioners' sugar, cornstarch, and salt in a medium mixing bowl. With an electric mixer, mix on low speed to combine. Add the butter and mix on low speed until the ingredients just begin to come together in clumps. Sprinkle this mixture across the bottom of the prepared pan and press with your fingertips into an even layer. Place the pan in the freezer for 15 minutes and then bake the crust until the edges are just golden, 18 to 20 minutes.

3. Make the filling: When the crust comes out of the oven, reduce the oven temperature to 325 degrees. Combine the butter, brown sugar, and corn syrup in a medium saucepan and bring to a boil, stirring frequently with a wooden spoon. Boil for 1 minute, stir in the heavy cream and pecans, and boil for another 3 minutes, stirring frequently. Stir in the vanilla.

4. Pour the hot filling on top of the warm crust. Use the back of the spoon to distribute the nuts evenly across the pan. Return the pan to the oven and bake until the filling is bubbling and slightly browned, 18 to 20 minutes. Transfer the pan to a wire rack and let it cool completely.

5. Lift the foil from the pan onto a cutting board and use a sharp chef's knife to cut 16 squares.

Caramel Nut Squares will keep in an airtight container for 2 to 3 days.

A Good Excuse to Make Caramel Nut Squares

These make a nice gift at holiday time, packed in pretty tissue paper and cellophane.

lemon squares

Makes 16 squares

The topping for these squares is easy in the extreme—just whisk together the ingredients and pour them over the partially baked crust. Through the alchemy of baking and chilling, the result is a perfect lemon custard that would make any pastry chef proud. Wait and dust the squares with powdered sugar just before serving, because the sugar will dissolve into the crust if the squares are allowed to stand for a long period of time.

For the crust
1 cup unbleached all-purpose flour
1/3 cup confectioners' sugar
2 tablespoons cornstarch
1/4 teaspoon salt
7 tablespoons unsalted butter, chilled and cut into 12 pieces

For the lemon filling
1 cup granulated sugar
3 large eggs
3 tablespoons unbleached all-purpose flour
Pinch of salt
1 teaspoon grated lemon zest
1/2 cup strained fresh lemon juice

For the topping
Confectioners' sugar

1. Preheat the oven to 350 degrees. Line an 8-inch square baking pan with heavy-duty aluminum foil, making sure that the foil is tucked into all the corners and that there is at least 1 inch overhanging the top of the pan on all sides.

2. Make the crust: Combine the flour, confectioners' sugar, cornstarch, and salt in a medium mixing bowl. With an electric mixer, mix on low speed to combine. Add the chilled butter and mix on low speed until the ingredients just begin to come together in clumps. Sprinkle this mixture evenly across the bottom of the prepared baking pan and press with your fingertips into an even layer. Place the pan in the freezer for 15 minutes and then bake the crust until it is light golden, about 20 minutes.

3. Make the filling: While the crust is baking, whisk together the granulated sugar, eggs, flour, and salt until smooth. Whisk in the lemon zest and juice. When the crust comes out of the oven, reduce the oven temperature to 300 degrees. Pour the filling on top of the warm crust. Return the pan to the oven and bake until the filling is just set in the center, about 20 minutes. Transfer the pan to a wire rack and let it cool completely.

4. Lift the foil from the pan onto a cutting board and use a sharp chef's knife to cut 16 squares.

Lemon Squares will keep in an airtight container in the refrigerator for up to 3 days. Sift some confectioners' sugar over the bars just before serving.

raspberry cheesecake bars

Makes 16 bars

If your family is a cheesecake family, then you must try this recipe. It's just like cheesecake, but easier to make and serve. No water bath is required, you don't need a springform pan, and you end up with pretty squares. Blueberries or blackberries may be substituted for the raspberries if you like.

For the crust

- 1 cup unbleached all-purpose flour
- 1/3 cup confectioners' sugar
- 2 tablespoons cornstarch
- 1/4 teaspoon salt
- 7 tablespoons unsalted butter, chilled and cut into 12 pieces

For the raspberry filling

- 1 pound cream cheese, softened
- 1/2 cup granulated sugar
- 2 large eggs
- 1 teaspoon pure vanilla extract
- 1 cup fresh raspberries or 1 cup frozen whole raspberries, thawed and patted dry with paper towels

1. Preheat the oven to 350 degrees. Adjust the oven rack to the bottom third of the oven. Line an 8-inch square baking pan with heavy-duty aluminum foil, making sure that the foil is tucked into all the corners and that there is at least 1 inch overhanging the top of the pan on all sides.

2. Make the crust: Combine the flour, confectioners' sugar, cornstarch, and salt in a medium mixing bowl. With an electric mixer, mix on low speed to combine. Add the butter and mix on low speed until the ingredients just begin to come together in clumps. Sprinkle this mixture across the bottom of the baking pan and press it with your fingertips into an even layer. Place the pan in the freezer for 15 minutes and then bake the crust until it is light golden, 20 to 22 minutes. Remove the pan from the oven, reduce the oven temperature to 325 degrees, and let the crust cool until just warm to the touch.

3. Make the filling: Combine the cream cheese and granulated sugar in a large mixing bowl. With an electric mixer on medium-high speed, beat the mixture until very smooth. Add the eggs and vanilla and beat again until smooth.

4. Pour the filling on top of the warm crust. Smooth the top with a rubber spatula. Scatter the berries over the top of the filling. Bake until the filling is just set in the center, 50 to 55 minutes. Let the pan cool completely on a wire rack. Refrigerate until the bars are completely chilled, at least 3 hours.

5. Grasping the overhanging foil on either side of the pan, lift the foil from the pan onto a cutting board. Cut 16 squares.

Raspberry Cheesecake Bars will keep in the refrigerator in an airtight container for up to 2 days.

blueberry-cornmeal crumb squares

Makes 16 bars

This is such a wonderful recipe—a layer of fresh blueberries between a cornmeal-and-almond crust and crunchy crumbs. It's also pretty simple. The dough is divided in half, one part used for the crust and the other part for the topping. Other fresh fruit may be substituted—raspberries, halved strawberries, diced peaches, plums, or apples. Just don't forget the cornstarch; it's what jells the filling and keeps the bars from getting soggy. These are best eaten the day they are made, although they will keep overnight. Longer than that and they lose their crunch.

For the filling

1 pint fresh blueberries, picked over for stems, or 1 pint frozen blueberries, thawed and patted dry with paper towels
¼ cup sugar
½ teaspoon grated lemon zest
2 teaspoons cornstarch

For the crust and crumb

¾ cup whole almonds
½ cup yellow cornmeal
2 cups unbleached all-purpose flour
1 cup sugar
¼ teaspoon salt
1 cup (2 sticks) unsalted butter, melted

1. Preheat the oven to 350 degrees. Line an 8-inch square baking pan with heavy-duty aluminum foil, making sure that the foil is tucked into all the corners and that there is at least 1 inch overhanging the top of the pan on all sides.

2. Make the filling: Combine the blueberries, sugar, lemon zest, and cornstarch in a medium mixing bowl. Let the mixture stand, stirring once or twice, until the sugar is dissolved.

3. Make the crust and crumb: Grind the almonds coarsely in a food processor. Be careful not to overprocess, or the almonds will release their oil. Add the cornmeal, flour, sugar, and salt and pulse once or twice to combine. Add the melted butter and pulse once or twice until all the ingredients are moistened.

4. Sprinkle half of the mixture across the bottom of the prepared baking pan and press it with your fingertips into an even layer. Place the other half of the mixture in the freezer for 5 minutes. Spread the filling evenly across the crust. Scatter the remaining crumb mixture over the blueberries, squeezing it into pea-size crumbs as you do so. Bake until the berries are bubbling and the top is golden, 45 to 50 minutes. Let the pan cool completely on a wire rack.

5. Grasping the overhanging foil on either side of the pan, lift out the crumb bars and place them on a cutting board. Cut 16 squares.

Blueberry-Cornmeal Crumb Squares are best the day they are made, but they will keep for 2 days at room temperature in an airtight container.

MOM'S APPLE PIE:
no-fail pies, tarts, quiches, and cobblers

CLOCKWISE FROM TOP: Rustic Apple Tart with Rich Cream Cheese Crust, Little Lemon Curd Tarts, Thanksgiving Day Pumpkin Pie

We all know that motherhood is not a pie-baking

contest. But wouldn't it be nice to add pie baking to your resume anyway? Or at least know, come November, where to find a simple, reliable recipe for apple pie? The twenty or so recipes that follow will get you through Thanksgiving and beyond. There are classic recipes for apple, pumpkin, blueberry, and walnut pies that would make June Cleaver proud. But if you don't own a rolling pin, don't despair. Take a look at the recipes for cobblers, crisps, betties, and crumb-crust tarts and pies at the end of the chapter, none of which require that you roll out dough. Once you master these supersimple desserts, you may even decide to invest in a rolling pin and take your pie making to the next level.

Back to those prize-winning pies: I use two basic types of pie dough, both made with butter. For me, flavor is everything, and butter tastes better than vegetable shortening or lard. Buttery Pie Dough is made from just flour, butter, salt, and water. It's rich and flaky, a perfect foil for extra-sweet pies such as Apple, Maple-Walnut, and Blueberry Crumb. Sweet Pie Dough has some added sugar and eggs and bakes up sweet and rather crisp like a cookie, just the thing for spicy pumpkin filling. It's sturdy enough to roll into Apple and Raisin Turnovers that won't leak any juice while you're holding them.

I've paired my crusts and fillings according to my own taste. Once you've worked with both doughs, you can make your own matches. Buttery Pie Dough and Sweet Pie Dough can be used interchangeably in most of the recipes, and if you decide that you prefer your Blueberry Crumb Pie with Sweet Pie Dough or you would rather risk a little leaking for Apple and Raisin Turnovers using Buttery Pie Dough, that's fine.

To guarantee tenderness, Buttery Pie Dough should be handled as little as possible. Make sure your butter is well chilled and your water is icy cold. Turn off the mixer as soon as the dough comes together. Don't worry if you can still see pea-size pieces of butter in the dough. It's these butter pockets that will make the dough flaky. Always chill the dough before rolling it out. Try to roll out the dough quickly. The fewer passes with the rolling pin, the better. By the same token, don't beat up the dough with the rolling pin. Use firm but gentle pressure for the most tender crust.

Sweet Pie Dough can take more handling. It actually benefits from a little kneading before you roll it out—to soften up the dough and help prevent it from cracking as you roll it out. Both types of dough should be well chilled before they are rolled out. If your dough is warm, it will get sticky. And if your dough is sticking, you are more likely to add flour during rolling, which will toughen the crust.

For hassle-free rolling, lightly dust your work surface and rolling pin with flour and slide an offset spatula under the dough frequently to make sure that it's not sticking to your work surface. Turn the dough by about 90 degrees every couple of rolls so that you wind up with a round piece of dough rather than a long, skinny one. If you don't have a rolling pin and you want to buy one, I recommend a thick wooden cylinder without handles. Rolling pins with handles give you less control over the dough, and rolling pins that are tapered are tricky to work with. For cutting strips for a lattice top, a fluted pastry wheel is nice but not necessary. A sharp paring knife or pizza cutter will do the same job, without producing the fancy edges.

When you fit your dough into the pie plate, press it firmly into the sides of the plate but don't stretch it. Dough that has been stretched will shrink back into the pan during baking. Also, to combat shrinking, make sure your crust is well chilled (I like to put my pie plate with its crust in the freezer for at least 15 minutes) before baking. Glass pie plates are great, because with glass you can actually see how your bottom crust is browning so you'll never remove the pie from the oven before it's done.

Is this too much information for you? If you have to have pastry crust, but don't want the hassle of rolling dough, check out the Rustic Apple and Peach Tarts with Rich Cream Cheese Crust. The dough is mixed in a food processor in seconds. Instead of using a rolling pin, you simply pat the dough into rustic rounds. If you've made Play-Doh pizza, you're familiar with the technique.

Then there are cobblers, crisps, and betties, which provide the same satisfying combination of juicy fruit and crisp pastry without any rolling. Simple Peach Cobbler has a topping that's like cookie dough. Spoon the dough over some sliced peaches and it will spread during baking for a crisp-on-the-outside, buttery-on-the-inside cover. Simple Berry Crisp gets its crunch from a sliced almond and crumb topping that's scattered over your choice of strawberries, blueberries, or raspberries. Simple Apple Brown Betty is the simplest of all. Buttered breadcrumbs provide the crispy contrast to the juicy fruit. Any of these recipes can be prepared for the oven in about 15 minutes, and they are great choices for everyday dessert or casual entertaining. The only downside to serving cobblers, crisps, and betties is that they look rather messy when portioned out. I serve them in bowls rather than on dessert plates to keep each portion somewhat contained.

Last but not least are pies and tarts with cookie crumb crusts. Just grind up some graham crackers or chocolate wafer cookies in the food processor, or buy boxes of crumbs in the baking aisle of the supermarket. Moisten the crumbs with butter, press the crust into a pie or tart pan, and, voilà! Pie crust! With crusts this simple, you want to keep the fillings simple too. Spread some Milk Chocolate Ganache on a tart shell made of chocolate cookie crumbs and you have a perfect chocolate dessert. Cookie crumb crusts make sensational bases for ice cream pies. Coffee-Toffee Ice Cream Pie combines cookie crumbs, caramel, peanuts, and coffee ice cream. Just before serving, you pour hot fudge sauce over individual slices. If you don't like coffee, I've suggested a bunch of other crumb crust and ice cream combinations. It was a happy day when I perfected my Lime-Coconut Pie recipe. I finally had a dessert that was just as refreshing as Lemon Meringue Pie, but without the hassle of baking a pastry crust or the stress of making a meringue topping. I always started to weep before I was ready to serve dessert.

I expected my family to wolf down all of the cookies I made while putting together this book. But I was really surprised at everyone's excitement when I was making pies. The sight of six Little Lemon Curd Tarts inspired my five-year-old to challenge me and my husband to a pie-eating contest. We had a hard time slowing down in order to let her win! Pie is often reserved for special occasions. There's a good reason for this. A Lattice-Top Apple Pie is really special and takes some time and effort. But you don't have to wait for a major holiday to delight your family with this type of dessert. Make some Spiced Apple and Raisin Turnovers any old fall weekend and watch them disappear.

buttery pie dough

Makes 2 disks,
enough dough for
two 9-inch pie shells,
two 10-inch tart shells,
or 1 double-crust pie

If you are making a single-crust pie or tart, you have two options: Cut the recipe in half, or make the whole recipe and freeze half of the dough for another single-crust pie.

2½ cups unbleached all-purpose flour
½ teaspoon salt
1 cup (2 sticks) chilled unsalted butter,
  cut into 16 pieces
¼ cup plus 2 tablespoons ice water

1. Combine the flour and salt in the bowl of an electric mixer fitted with a paddle attachment. Add the butter and mix on low speed until the mixture resembles coarse meal.

2. Add ¼ cup of the water and continue to mix on low speed until the dough just begins to come together. If the mixture is too dry to come together, add more of the water, 1 teaspoon at a time, until the dough begins to form clumps.

To mix the dough by hand: Combine the flour and salt in a large mixing bowl. Cut the butter into 1-tablespoon chunks and add it to the bowl. Cut the butter into the flour mixture by squeezing the butter and flour together with your fingers, until the butter is evenly distributed and the mixture resembles coarse meal. Do this quickly so the butter doesn't melt in your hands. Sprinkle ¼ cup of water over the mixture and stir with a fork until the dough begins to hold together. If the mixture is too crumbly and dry to come together, sprinkle another teaspoon or two of water over the bowl and continue to mix with a fork until it holds together.

3. Turn the dough out onto a lightly floured work surface and divide it in half. Press each half into a 6-inch disk and wrap it in plastic. Refrigerate the dough for at least 1 hour and for up to 2 days.

Buttery Pie Dough may be frozen, wrapped in plastic and then aluminum foil, for up to 1 month. Defrost it in the refrigerator overnight.

To Prevent Your Pie Crust from Shrinking

If you are simply filling a pie or tart shell without prebaking the crust, there is little need to worry about the pastry shrinking or bubbling up in spots. The heavy filling will keep the crust flat and in place.

Placed in the oven on its own, however, without the weight of any filling to keep it in place, a pie shell tends to shrink. A shrunken pie shell is not as pleasing to look at as is a beautifully shaped shell. More important, a shrunken crust won't do as good a job of holding the filling.

You can take steps to make sure that your crust holds its shape in the oven:

* **Avoid stretching the dough** as you press it into the pan. Dough that is stretched will shrink back to its original position when baked.
* **Pricking the bottom of the crust** with a fork prevents small pockets of air trapped in the dough from expanding into unsightly bubbles as the crust bakes.
* **Weighing the dough down** with dried beans for the first part of the baking time will help hold the dough in place, the same way that filling a pie shell with apples prevents the dough from shrinking. Cut out a 10-inch circle of parchment paper or aluminum foil and place it in the pie shell. Pour 2 cups of dried beans into the shell. Bake the pie shell as directed in the recipe.

sweet pie dough

Makes 2 disks,
enough dough for
two 9-inch pie shells,
two 10-inch tart shells,
or 1 double-crust pie

Unlike Buttery Pie Dough, Sweet Pie Dough actually benefits from some handling. Knead it a few times on a lightly floured surface and it will roll out beautifully with no cracks or crumbles around the edges.

2½ cups unbleached all-purpose flour
¼ cup plus 2 tablespoons sugar
½ teaspoon salt
½ cup (1 stick) chilled unsalted butter, cut into ¼-inch dice
2 large eggs, lightly beaten

1. Combine the flour, sugar, and salt in the bowl of an electric mixer fitted with a paddle attachment. Add the butter and mix on low speed until the mixture resembles coarse meal.

2. Add the eggs and continue to stir on low speed until the dough just begins to come together.

To mix the dough by hand: Combine the flour, sugar, and salt in a large mixing bowl. Cut the butter into 1-tablespoon chunks and add it to the bowl. Cut the butter into the flour mixture by squeezing the butter and flour together with your fingers until the butter is evenly distributed and the mixture resembles coarse meal. Do this quickly so the butter doesn't melt in your hands. Pour the eggs over the mixture and stir with a fork until the dough begins to hold together.

3. Turn the dough out onto a lightly floured work surface and divide it in half. Knead each half into a smooth, round ball. Press each ball into a 6-inch disk and wrap it in plastic. Refrigerate the dough for at least 1 hour and for up to 2 days.

Sweet Pie Dough may be frozen, wrapped in plastic and then aluminum foil, for up to 1 month. Defrost it in the refrigerator overnight.

lattice-top apple pie

**Makes one
9-inch pie;
8 to 10 servings**

When I first started baking apple pie for Thanksgiving, I simply placed sugared apple slices in a pie shell, covered them with a lattice top, and baked. The pie looked great as it went into the oven, but no matter how many apples I piled into my shell, they shrunk so much that when I removed the pie from the oven, there was a space of a few inches between my crisp top and the fruit below. The pie tasted fine, but it was difficult to cut without destroying the decorative lattice I had worked so hard to weave. When I cooked the apples before placing them in the shell, cooking off some of their moisture, the pie was much better. The apples were preshrunk, so the lattice top still sat directly on top of the filling when the pie came out of the oven. What's more, there was no extra liquid to make the bottom crust soggy.

Weaving a lattice isn't as complicated as the directions make it sound. It's like making a pot holder at camp—over, under, over, under. If you don't remember, ask your kids to remind you how it's done.

For the filling

**3½ pounds firm, tart apples, such as
  Granny Smith**
¼ cup (½ stick) unsalted butter
⅔ cup sugar
1 teaspoon ground cinnamon

2 disks Buttery Pie Dough (page 169)
1 large egg, lightly beaten

1. Make the filling: Peel, core, and cut the apples into ½-inch-thick slices. Melt the butter over medium heat in a sauté or frying pan large enough to hold the apple slices. Add the apples and cook them until they begin to release some of their juices, about 2 minutes. Stir in the sugar and cinnamon and cook, stirring occasionally, until the apples are softened but still pretty firm, another 5 to 7 minutes. Remove the pan from the heat and allow the apples to cool completely.

2. Preheat the oven to 400 degrees. Position the oven rack in the bottom third of the oven.

3. Make the lattice top: Turn one chilled dough disk out onto a lightly floured work surface and sprinkle it with a little bit of flour. With a lightly floured rolling pin, roll the dough into an 11-inch round, rotating the dough as you roll and sliding a flat metal spatula underneath occasionally to make sure that the dough does not stick to the work surface. Using a ruler and a fluted pastry wheel or sharp paring knife, cut the dough into eight 1-inch-wide strips. Line up half of the strips vertically, 1 inch apart, on a baking sheet lined with parchment paper. Fold every other strip in half toward you. Place a strip so that it lies horizontally 1 inch above the folded edge. Unfold the folded strips. Now fold back the vertical strips that hadn't been folded last time so that they

Apples for Baking

Apples used in pies and tarts should hold their shape during baking. You don't want to buy apples that turn to applesauce. Granny Smith and Golden Delicious are two widely available varieties that are reliably firm. I prefer Granny Smiths for their tart taste, but if you like a sweeter pie, you might try Golden Delicious. There are also plenty of regional varieties that make splendid pies. At your local orchard or farmstand in the fall, look for Braeburn, Cortland, Gravenstein, Macoun, Northern Spy, and Winesap apples, all of which bake up beautifully.

fold over the horizontal strip. Place another strip horizontally above the first one, 1 inch from the folded edge. Unfold the folded strips. Turn the baking sheet 180 degrees and repeat, weaving in the two remaining strips horizontally. (The lattice may be wrapped in plastic and frozen for up to 1 month. Let it stand on the counter for 5 to 10 minutes to soften before laying it on top of the filled pie.)

4. For the bottom crust, turn the other dough disk out onto the lightly floured work surface and sprinkle with a little bit of flour. With a lightly floured rolling pin, roll the dough into an 11-inch round, rotating the dough as you roll it and sliding a flat metal spatula underneath occasionally to make sure that the dough does not stick to the work surface. Lift the dough by folding it in half over the rolling pin and gently place it on top of a 9-inch pie pan. Press the dough firmly against the

sides of the pan, being careful not to stretch the dough, or your pie shell will shrink as it bakes. Trim the excess dough with scissors or a sharp paring knife so that it overhangs the pie pan by one inch. Fold the extra inch toward the center of the pie along the rim. Crimp the doubled dough, pinching it at 1-inch intervals between your thumb and index finger, to form a decorative edge. Place the pie shell and the lattice in the freezer for 15 minutes to chill. (The rolled pie shell can be wrapped in plastic and frozen for up to 1 month. Bake it directly from the freezer.)

5. Remove the pie shell and lattice from the freezer and scrape the cooled apple filling into the shell. Slide the frozen lattice from the parchment onto the pie, adjusting the strips so that they are straight and even. Trim the strips so that they overhang the rim of the pie by 1 inch. Pinch the ends of the strips so that they form part of the rim. Brush the lattice and rim with the beaten egg. Place the pie on a baking sheet (in case some of the filling bubbles over) and bake the pie in the bottom third of the oven until the crust is golden brown and the filling is bubbling, 45 to 50 minutes. Let the pie cool completely on a wire rack.

Lattice-Top Apple Pie is best eaten on the day it is baked. Wrap leftovers in plastic and store at room temperature for up to 2 days.

Kids Can Help

Weaving a lattice with your child is a fun and gratifying project.

blueberry crumb pie

A crumb topping is a simple alternative to a top crust of pastry. An equal amount of any other berry or stone fruit may be substituted here, but blueberries are the simplest to prepare. Peaches, nectarines, plums, and apricots should be peeled, pitted, and cut into ½-inch-thick slices. Strawberries should be hulled and halved (if they are small, you may leave them whole).

1 disk Buttery Pie Dough (page 169)

For the filling

3½ tablespoons cornstarch
2 tablespoons water
5 cups fresh blueberries, rinsed, patted dried, and picked over for stems
⅔ cup granulated sugar
¼ teaspoon ground nutmeg

For the crumb topping

½ cup (1 stick) unsalted butter, melted
½ cup firmly packed light brown sugar
1½ cups unbleached all-purpose flour
1 large egg yolk, lightly beaten

1. Preheat the oven to 400 degrees. Position the oven rack in the bottom third of the oven.

2. Turn the chilled dough out onto a lightly floured work surface and sprinkle it with a little bit of flour. With a lightly floured rolling pin, roll the dough into an 11-inch round, rotating the dough as you roll it and sliding a flat metal spatula underneath occasionally to make sure that the dough does not stick to the work surface. Lift the dough by folding it in half over the rolling pin, and gently place it on top of a 9-inch pie pan.

3. Press the dough firmly against the sides of the pan, being careful not to stretch the dough, or your pie shell will shrink as it bakes. Trim the excess dough with scissors or a sharp paring knife so that it over-hangs the pie pan by 1 inch. Fold the extra inch toward the center of the pie along the rim. Crimp the doubled dough, pinching it at 1-inch intervals between your thumb and index finger, to form a decorative edge. Place the pie shell in the freezer while you mix the filling and make the crumb topping. (The rolled pie shell can be wrapped in plastic and frozen for up to 1 month. Bake the pie shell directly from the freezer.)

4. Make the filling: Combine the cornstarch and water in a small bowl and stir until smooth. Combine the blueberries, granulated sugar, and nutmeg in a large mixing bowl. Stir in the dissolved cornstarch and let the mixture stand, stirring it occasionally, until the sugar dissolves, about 15 minutes.

Kids Can Help

Who else do you think is going to pick all of those blueberries?

5. Make the crumb topping: Combine the melted butter, brown sugar, and flour in a medium mixing bowl. Pinch the mixture between your fingers to form large (about ½-inch) crumbs.

6. Remove the pie shell from the freezer and scrape the blueberry filling into the shell. Scatter the crumbs over the berries. Brush the rim of the pie crust with the egg yolk. Place the pie on a baking sheet (in case some of the filling bubbles over) and bake the pie in the bottom third of the oven until the crust is golden brown and the filling is bubbling, 45 to 50 minutes. Let the pan cool completely on a wire rack.

Blueberry Crumb Pie is best eaten on the day it is baked. Wrap leftovers in plastic and store at room temperature for up to 2 days.

Pie Crust Edges

A fluted edge is standard, but there are other simple ways of making a decorative rim:

* As an alternative to forming a fluted pie crust edge with your fingers, simply press the tines of a fork into the edge all around the pie.
* Roll the extra dough into three long ¼-inch-thick ropes and braid them. Affix the braid to the edge using a lightly beaten egg as glue, and brush the braid itself with egg.
* Roll the extra dough to a ⅛-inch thickness and cut out shapes with small cookie cutters. Affix the shapes to the edge using a lightly beaten egg as glue, and brush the edge and shapes with egg.

maple walnut pie

Makes one 9-inch pie;
6 to 8 servings

I like this better than traditional pecan pie, which is often too sweet. Maple Walnut Pie gets great flavor as well as sweetness from the maple syrup. Pecans may be used instead of walnuts if you like.

1 disk Buttery Pie Dough (page 169)

For the filling

3 large eggs plus 1 egg yolk
4½ tablespoons unsalted butter, melted and cooled
½ cup sugar
¼ cup plus 2 tablespoons light corn syrup
¼ cup plus 2 tablespoons pure maple syrup
2 cups walnut pieces

1. Preheat the oven to 350 degrees. Position the oven rack in the middle of the oven.

2. Turn the chilled dough out onto a lightly floured work surface and sprinkle it with a little bit of flour. With a lightly floured rolling pin, roll the dough into an 11-inch round, rotating the dough as you roll it and sliding a flat metal spatula underneath occasionally to make sure that the dough does not stick to the work surface. Lift the dough by folding it in half over the rolling pin, and gently place it on top of a 9-inch pie pan.

3. Press the dough firmly against the sides of the pan, being careful not to stretch the dough, or your pie shell will shrink as it bakes. Trim the excess dough with scissors or a sharp paring knife so that it over-hangs the pie pan by 1 inch. Fold the extra inch toward the center of the pie along the rim. Crimp the doubled dough, pinch-ing it at 1-inch intervals between your thumb and index finger, to form a decora-tive edge. Prick the bottom all over with a fork. Place the pie shell in the freezer for 15 minutes to firm up. (The pie shell can be wrapped in plastic and frozen for up to 1 month. Bake the pie shell directly from the freezer.)

4. Cut out a 10-inch circle of parchment paper or aluminum foil and place it in the pie shell. Pour 2 cups of dried beans into the shell. Bake the crust until it has begun to turn a light gold color, about 20 minutes. Remove the pie shell from the oven, lift the parchment and beans from the shell, and return the pie shell to the oven. Cook it until light golden, another 10 to 12 minutes.

5. While the shell is baking, make the filling: In a medium mixing bowl, whisk together the 3 whole eggs, cooled melted butter, sugar, corn syrup, and maple syrup. Stir in the walnuts.

6. Remove the pie shell from the oven, turn the oven temperature down to 325 degrees, and scrape the filling into the shell. Brush the rim of the pie shell with the egg yolk. Bake the pie until the filling is just set, 40 to 45 minutes. Let the pan cool completely on a wire rack.

Maple Walnut Pie is best eaten on the day it is baked. Wrap leftovers in plastic and store at room temperature for up to 2 days.

chocolate chip–pecan tart

**Makes one 10-inch tart;
8 to 10 servings**

Semisweet chocolate chips are the starting point of all home baking, according to my children. Here is the chocolate chip recipe for this chapter: a big chocolate chip cookie baked in a tart shell.

1 disk Buttery Pie Dough (page 169)

For the filling

1 cup firmly packed light brown sugar
**¼ cup plus 2 tablespoons unbleached
    all-purpose flour**
½ cup (1 stick) unsalted butter, melted
2 large eggs
1 teaspoon pure vanilla extract
1 cup coarsely chopped pecans
1 cup semisweet chocolate chips

1. Preheat the oven to 325 degrees.

2. Turn the chilled dough out onto a lightly floured work surface and sprinkle it with a little bit of flour. With a lightly floured rolling pin, roll the dough into a 12-inch round, rotating the dough as you roll it and sliding a flat metal spatula underneath occasionally to make sure that the dough does not stick to the work surface. Lift the dough by folding it in half over the rolling pin, and gently place it on top of a 10-inch tart pan with a removable bottom. Press the dough firmly against the sides of the pan, being careful not to stretch the dough, or your tart shell will shrink as it bakes. Trim off all but ½ inch of the dough along the edge of the tart pan. Fold the extra dough into the pan and press it firmly against the sides. Prick the bottom of the tart shell with a fork and place the pan in the freezer while you mix the filling. (The rolled tart shell can be wrapped in plastic and frozen for up to 1 month. Bake it directly from the freezer.)

3. Make the filling: Combine the sugar and flour in a large mixing bowl. Add the melted butter, eggs, and vanilla and stir with a wooden spoon or electric mixer until smooth. Stir in the pecans and chocolate chips.

4. Take the tart shell out of the freezer. Pour the filling into the shell and bake the tart until golden and the filling is just set, 45 to 50 minutes. Let the tart cool completely on a wire rack before serving.

Chocolate Chip–Pecan Tart will keep, wrapped in plastic and stored at room temperature, for up to 3 days.

 **A Good Excuse to Make
Chocolate Chip–Pecan Tart**

You might want to bring this along on a picnic, since it travels well and won't fall apart if jostled a little in the trunk of your car.

little lemon curd tarts

Makes six 4-inch tarts

It's difficult to portion out one big lemon tart neatly. The filling tends to ooze. That's why I like to make individual lemon tarts and let everyone eat his or her own. Try a simple garnish of sugared lemon slices or blueberries. It takes just a few seconds to cover the fruit in sugar, and it looks so pretty. There's plenty of dough here to make six individual tarts. I like to divide the dough into six pieces and roll each tart shell from a fresh piece of dough, rather than rolling and rerolling scraps. This method ensures that each tart crust is as tender as possible.

1 disk Sweet Pie Dough (page 171)
1 recipe Lemon Curd (page 231)
6 thinly sliced lemon slices or 18
    blueberries (optional)

1. Preheat the oven to 325 degrees.

2. Divide the chilled dough into 6 equal pieces. Wrap 5 pieces in plastic and place them in the refrigerator. Turn the other piece of dough out onto a lightly floured work surface and sprinkle it with a little bit of flour. Knead the dough several times to soften and smooth it out. With a lightly floured rolling pin, roll the dough into a $\frac{1}{8}$-inch thickness, rotating the dough as you roll it and sliding a flat metal spatula underneath occasionally to make sure that the dough does not stick to the work surface. Lift the dough by folding it in half over the rolling pin, and gently place it on top of a 6-inch tart pan with a removable bottom. Press the dough firmly against the sides of the pan, being careful not to stretch the dough, or your tart shells will shrink as they bake. Trim off all but $\frac{1}{2}$ inch of the dough along the edge of the tart pan. Fold the extra dough into the

pan and press it firmly against the sides. Prick the bottom of the tart shell with a fork. Repeat with the remaining 5 dough pieces. Place the tart shells in the freezer for 15 minutes to firm up. (The rolled tart shells can be wrapped in plastic and frozen for up to 1 month. Bake them directly from the freezer.)

3. Remove the tart shells from the freezer, place them on a large baking sheet, and bake them until golden brown, 25 to 30 minutes. Remove the tart shells from the oven and let them cool completely on a wire rack.

4. To assemble the tarts, remove the sides of each tart pan. Spoon about $\frac{1}{4}$ cup of the lemon curd into each tart shell and smooth the filling with a small spatula.

5. To garnish, make lemon twists by cutting each lemon slice halfway through and twisting the cut ends. Dip the slices in sugar and place one twist on top of each tart. Or dip the berries in sugar and place three sugared berries on top of each tart. Serve immediately.

quiche lorraine

Makes one
10-inch quiche;
6 to 8 servings

What can I say? My mom used to make a version of this savory pie, and sometimes I get nostalgic for it even though it's out of fashion and the cardiologist wouldn't recommend it as an alternative to bran flakes. But it won't kill you if you eat it every once in a while, and it's a real treat that your own kids are sure to remember.

1 disk Buttery Pie Dough (page 169)

For the filling
4 ounces thick-cut bacon, cut into
   1-inch pieces
3 large eggs
1 cup half-and-half
$\frac{1}{2}$ cup freshly grated Parmesan cheese
$\frac{1}{4}$ teaspoon salt
Ground black pepper
Pinch of ground nutmeg

1. Preheat the oven to 350 degrees. Position the oven rack in the middle of the oven.

2. Turn the chilled dough out onto a lightly floured work surface and sprinkle it with a little bit of flour. With a lightly floured rolling pin, roll the dough into an 11-inch round, rotating the dough as you roll and sliding a flat metal spatula underneath occasionally to make sure that the dough does not stick to the work surface. Lift the dough by folding it in half over the rolling pin, and gently place it on top of a 10-inch tart pan with a removable bottom. Press the dough firmly against the sides of the pan, being careful not to stretch the dough, or your pie shell will shrink as it bakes. Trim the excess dough with scissors or a sharp paring knife so that it overhangs the tart pan by 1 inch.

Fold the extra inch toward the center of the pan along the rim. Crimp the doubled dough, pinching it at 1-inch intervals between your thumb and index finger, to form a decorative edge. Prick the bottom of the crust all over with a fork. Place the tart shell in the freezer for 15 minutes to firm up. (The tart shell can be wrapped in plastic and frozen for up to 1 month. Bake it directly from the freezer.)

3. Cut out a 10-inch circle of parchment paper or aluminum foil and place it in the tart shell. Pour 2 cups of dried beans into the shell. Bake the tart crust until it has begun to turn a pale gold color, about 20 minutes. Remove the shell from the oven, lift the parchment and beans from the shell, and return the tart pan to the oven. Cook the shell until it is golden, another 10 to 12 minutes.

4. While the tart shell is baking, make the filling: Over medium heat, sauté the bacon in a medium sauté pan until the fat is just rendered but the slices are not yet crisp. Remove the bacon with a slotted spoon and drain it on paper towels. In a large mixing bowl, whisk together the eggs, half-and-half, Parmesan, salt, pepper, and nutmeg.

5. Remove the tart shell from the oven and turn the oven temperature up to 375 degrees. Scatter the bacon pieces across the bottom of the tart shell. Pour the egg mixture into the shell. Bake the quiche until the filling is just set and slightly puffed, about 30 minutes. Let it cool for at least 30 minutes on a wire rack and serve it warm, or let it cool completely and serve it at room temperature.

Quiche Lorraine is best eaten on the day it is baked. Wrap leftovers in plastic and store in the refrigerator for up to 2 days.

thanksgiving day pumpkin pie

**Makes one
9-inch pie;
8 to 10 servings**

I like to keep Thanksgiving Day dessert simple, since I'm either traveling somewhere or putting together a big dinner for a lot of friends and relatives at home. Pumpkin pie definitely has the advantage over apple pie, since it requires only a single crust and the filling is just whisked together. Partially baking the pie shell before pouring in the filling ensures a crisp crust. Be careful not to bake the pie for too long. The center should still be jiggly when you remove the pie from the oven. The filling will continue to cook from the residual heat as the pie cools.

1 disk Sweet Pie Dough (page 171)

For the filling

**4 large eggs, at room temperature, plus
1 large egg yolk, gently beaten, for
glazing**
One 15-ounce can pumpkin purée
**1¼ cups half-and-half, at room
temperature**
1 cup firmly packed dark brown sugar
2 teaspoons ground cinnamon
1 teaspoon ground ginger
½ teaspoon ground nutmeg
½ teaspoon salt

1. Preheat the oven to 350 degrees. Position the oven rack in the middle of the oven.

2. Turn the chilled dough out onto a lightly floured work surface and sprinkle it with a little bit of flour. With a lightly floured rolling pin, roll the dough into an 11-inch round, rotating the dough as you roll and sliding a flat metal spatula underneath occasionally to make sure that the dough does not stick to the work surface. Lift the dough by folding it in half over the rolling pin, and gently place it on top of a 9-inch pie pan. Press the dough firmly against the sides of the pan, being careful not to stretch the dough, or your pie shell will shrink as it bakes. Trim the excess dough with scissors or a sharp paring knife so that it overhangs the pie pan by 1 inch. Fold the extra inch toward the center of the pie along the rim. Crimp the doubled dough, pinching it at 1-inch intervals between your thumb and index finger, to form a decorative edge. Prick the bottom all over with a fork. Place the pie shell in the freezer for 15 minutes to firm up. (The pie shell can be wrapped in plastic and frozen for up to 1 month. Bake it directly from the freezer.)

3. Cut out a 10-inch circle of parchment paper or aluminum foil and place in the pie shell. Pour 2 cups of dried beans into the shell. Bake the crust until it has begun to turn a pale gold color, about 20 minutes. Remove the pie shell from the oven and lift the parchment and beans from the shell. Increase the oven temperature to 375 degrees. Place the oven rack in the lower third of the oven. Return the pie shell to the oven and bake it for 10 to 12 minutes.

4. While the shell is baking, make the filling: Combine the whole eggs, pumpkin, half-and-half, brown sugar, cinnamon, ginger, nutmeg, and salt in a large mixing bowl and stir together with a wooden spoon or electric mixer until smooth.

5. Scrape the filling into the hot shell. Brush the rim of the pie shell with the egg yolk. Bake the pie in the bottom third of the oven. Check after 20 minutes; if the rim of the crust is very brown, tent the pie with a sheet of lightly greased aluminum foil. Continue to bake until the pie the center jiggles slightly but the rest of the pie is set, another 15 to 20 minutes. Let the pie cool completely on a wire rack.

Thanksgiving Day Pumpkin Pie is best eaten on the day it is baked. Wrap leftovers in plastic and store at room temperature for up to 2 days.

jam tart with cutout top crust

Makes 6 to 8 servings

Although you may weave a lattice to top the tart, I like to cover the top with shapes I've cut with cookie cutters. I've used hearts in several sizes, stars, and letters of the alphabet, and they all look cute.

1 disk Sweet Pie Dough (page 171)
1 cup best-quality fruit preserves
Confectioners' sugar

1. Turn the chilled dough out onto a lightly floured work surface and sprinkle it with a little bit of flour. Knead the dough several times to soften and smooth it out. With a lightly floured rolling pin, roll the dough into a ⅛-inch thickness, rotating the dough as you roll and sliding a flat metal spatula underneath occasionally to make sure that the dough does not stick to the work surface. Lift the dough by folding it in half over the rolling pin, and gently place it on top of a 6-inch tart pan with a removable bottom. Trim off all but ½ inch of the dough from the edge of the pan. Fold the extra dough into the pan and press it firmly against the sides. Prick the bottom of the tart shell with a fork and place the pan in the refrigerator.

2. For the cookie cutouts, reroll the trimmed dough to a ⅛-inch thickness, rotating the dough as you roll and sliding a flat metal spatula underneath occasionally to make sure that the dough does not stick to the work surface. Cut the rolled dough into shapes of your choice and

transfer these shapes to a baking sheet lined with parchment paper. Place the baking sheet in the refrigerator for 15 minutes.

3. Preheat the oven to 350 degrees. Position the oven rack in the bottom third of the oven.

4. Place the jam in a food processor and process until very smooth. Scrape the jam into the chilled tart shell and smooth it with a spatula. Position the cookie shapes over the jam, covering most of the tart but allowing some of the jam to peek through. Bake the tart in the bottom third of the oven until the crust is golden brown and the filling is bubbling, 30 to 35 minutes. Let the tart cool completely on a wire rack. Dust with confectioners' sugar just before serving.

Jam Tart is best served on the day it is made.

A Good Excuse to Make Jam Tart

This dessert is cute on Valentine's Day. Use strawberry or raspberry jam, and heart-shaped cookie cutters for the top crust.

spiced apple and raisin turnovers

Makes about 24 turnovers

Turnovers are fun, which is reason enough to make them. But if you need another reason, they are also economical and convenient. Filled, unbaked turnovers can be frozen and baked a couple at a time whenever you need a warm apple dessert.

For the filling

2 tablespoons unsalted butter
2 pounds (about 4 large) firm, tart apples, such as Granny Smiths, peeled, cored, and cut into ½-inch dice
⅓ cup plus 2 tablespoons sugar
¼ teaspoon salt
¼ teaspoon ground ginger
Pinch of ground cloves
⅓ cup raisins
½ teaspoon ground cinnamon

2 disks Sweet Pie Dough (page 171)
1 large egg, lightly beaten

1. Make the filling: Melt the butter over medium heat in a large saucepan. Add the apples and cook them until they begin to release some of their juices, 4 to 5 minutes. Stir in ⅓ cup of the sugar, the salt, ginger, and cloves and cook, stirring occasionally, until the apples are very soft and most of the liquid has evaporated, 7 to 10 minutes. Remove the pan from the heat, stir in the raisins, and allow the apples to cool completely. (The cooled filling may be made in advance and refrigerated for up to 1 day.)

2. Preheat the oven to 400 degrees.

3. Combine the remaining 2 tablespoons sugar and the cinnamon in a small bowl. On a lightly floured work surface with a lightly floured rolling pin, roll out 1 chilled dough disk to ⅛-inch thickness and cut out as many 4-inch rounds as you can, using a biscuit cutter or the bottom of a tart pan as your guide. Transfer the circles to baking sheets lined with parchment paper. Reroll the scraps and repeat with the remaining dough. Repeat with the remaining dough disk.

4. Spoon a heaping tablespoonful of the cooled apple and raisin filling onto the center of each round. Fold the round over and seal it by pressing the edges together with the tines of a fork. (Filled turnovers may be frozen on a baking sheet, transferred to a zipper-lock plastic freezer bag, and frozen for up to 1 month. Let the turnovers stand at room temperature for 10 minutes before proceeding with the recipe.) Brush the turnovers with the beaten egg and sprinkle them with the cinnamon sugar.

5. Bake until the turnovers are golden, about 20 minutes. Let them cool for 10 minutes and serve them warm, or let them cool completely and then reheat them in a 350-degree oven for 10 minutes.

Spiced Apple and Raisin Turnovers are best served on the day they are made.

Kids Can Help

I put my older child to work sealing the turnovers with a fork. I love the way they look, even if the edges aren't always perfect.

rustic apple tart with rich cream cheese crust

Makes 4 to 6 servings

I've come to rely on this recipe not only because it is supersimple but because everyone loves it. The cream cheese dough is not rolled but simply pressed into a rough round. The apples don't have to be precooked. The combination of tart apples and rich, tangy dough is irresistible.

For the filling

2 large tart apples, such
    as Granny Smiths
2 tablespoons strained fresh lemon
    juice
¼ cup plus 2 tablespoons sugar
¼ teaspoon ground cinnamon

1 recipe Rich Cream Cheese Tart Dough
    (opposite), rolled into one 10-inch or
    4 small crusts, and chilled for at least
    1 hour
1 large egg yolk, lightly beaten
Vanilla Whipped Cream (page 230) or
    vanilla ice cream (optional)

1. Preheat the oven to 400 degrees.

2. Make the filling: Peel the apples and cut them in half. Remove the cores with a paring knife. Cutting from blossom end to stem end, slice each half into ¼-inch-thick slices.

3. Combine the apple slices with the lemon juice, ¼ cup of the sugar, and the cinnamon in a large mixing bowl. Stir to combine. Let the apples stand until the sugar is dissolved, about 15 minutes, stirring once or twice.

4. Place a shaped large dough round on a baking sheet. Arrange the apple slices in 2 concentric circles on the large dough round or in one circle on the small rounds, overlapping the apple slices slightly. Brush the rim of the crust with the egg yolk. Sprinkle the apples with the remaining 2 tablespoons sugar. Bake until golden, 30 to 35 minutes.

Serve warm or at room temperature with Vanilla Whipped Cream or ice cream on the side.

Rustic Apple Tart is best served on the day it is made.

A Good Excuse to Make Rustic Apple Tart with Rich Cream Cheese Crust

If I'm having eight or fewer people for Thanksgiving, I might double this recipe and make eight individual tarts. The dough can be made and shaped weeks ahead of time, and the rest of the prep is minimal, leaving lots of time to prepare the rest of the meal.

rustic peach tart with rich cream cheese crust

Makes 6 to 8 servings

This is the summertime version of the previous recipe. A dash of cardamom lends an exotic note to the rustic tart, but cinnamon or ground ginger may be substituted.

For the filling

3 medium ripe peaches
2 tablespoons strained fresh lemon juice
¼ cup plus 2 tablespoons sugar
¼ teaspoon ground cardamom

1 recipe Rich Cream Cheese Tart Dough (recipe follows), rolled into 1 large or 4 small crusts, and chilled for at least 1 hour
1 large egg yolk, lightly beaten
Vanilla Whipped Cream (page 230) or vanilla ice cream (optional)

1. Preheat the oven to 400 degrees.

2. Make the filling: Peel the peaches and cut them in half. Remove the pits. Cutting from blossom end to stem end, slice each half into ¼-inch-thick slices.

3. Combine the peach slices with the lemon juice, ¼ cup of the sugar, and the cardamom in a large mixing bowl. Stir to combine. Let the peaches stand until the sugar is dissolved, about 15 minutes, stirring once or twice.

4. Place a shaped large dough round on a baking sheet. Arrange the slices in 2 concentric circles on the large dough round or in 1 circle on the small rounds, overlapping them slightly. Brush the lip of the dough with the beaten egg yolk. Sprinkle the peaches with the remaining 2 tablespoons sugar. Bake the tart or tarts until golden, 30 to 35 minutes.

Serve the tart(s) warm or at room temperature with Vanilla Whipped Cream or ice cream on the side.

Rustic Peach Tart is best served on the day it is made.

rich cream cheese tart dough

Makes 1 large free-form tart crust or 4 small tart crusts

The richest and most delicious pastry dough I know. An added bonus—it's also the easiest.

½ cup (4 ounces) chilled cream cheese, cut into 6 pieces
½ cup (1 stick) chilled unsalted butter, cut into 8 pieces
1 cup unbleached all-purpose flour, plus extra for shaping
½ cup sugar
⅛ teaspoon salt

1. Line a baking sheet with parchment paper.

2. Place the cream cheese, butter, 1 cup flour, salt, and sugar in a food processor. Process until the dough just comes together. It will be sticky.

3. Sprinkle the parchment paper with flour. Turn the dough out onto the sheet and, with floured hands, press the dough into a rough 10-inch circle or four 5-inch circles. Roll about ½ inch of the edge of the circle inward to create a lip to catch the juices. Refrigerate the crust for 1 hour or wrap the baking sheet in plastic and refrigerate it for up to 24 hours until you are ready to use it.

Shaped Rich Cream Cheese Tart Dough, wrapped in plastic, may be frozen for up to 2 months and used directly from the freezer.

Pairing Fruit for Cobblers, Crisps, and Betties

Cobblers, crisps, and betties can be made year round with seasonal fruit. Just substitute about 4 cups of any prepared fruit for the peaches, berries, and apples in the recipe of your choice. Desserts made with just one type of fruit are simplest, but pairing two kinds of fruit can be really wonderful. Everyone knows that strawberries and rhubarb are a good match. But think about the following combinations when shopping for your next cobbler, crisp, or betty:

* **Apricots and cherries:** Use 3 cups halved and pitted apricots and 1 cup pitted cherries.
* **Peaches and blackberries:** Use 3 cups pitted and sliced peaches and 1 cup blackberries.
* **Mangoes and raspberries:** Use 3 cups peeled, pitted, and sliced mangoes and 1 cup raspberries.
* **Pears and cranberries:** Use 3¼ cups peeled, cored, and sliced pears and ¾ cup fresh or frozen cranberries.
* **Apples and raisins:** Use 4 cups peeled, cored, and sliced apples and ½ cup raisins.

simple apple brown betty

Makes 6 to 8 servings

It doesn't get any simpler than this—sliced apples baked under a topping made of buttery breadcrumbs. Apple Brown Betty isn't as rich as cobbler or pie, so if you are looking for luxury, serve this with vanilla ice cream on the side.

2 pounds tart apples, such as Granny
  Smiths
2/3 cup firmly packed dark brown sugar
1 tablespoon cornstarch
1/4 cup (1/2 stick) unsalted butter
4 slices firm white sandwich bread
  (about 4 ounces)
1/4 teaspoon ground cinnamon

1. Preheat the oven to 375 degrees.

2. Peel, halve, and core the apples and cut each half into 3 or 4 wedges. Combine the apples, 1/3 cup of the brown sugar, and the cornstarch in a medium mixing bowl and let the fruit stand, stirring once or twice, until the sugar is moistened, about 15 minutes.

3. Make the topping: Melt 3 tablespoons of the butter in a butter warmer or small saucepan. Tear the bread into large pieces, place them in a food processor, and process into coarse crumbs. Transfer the crumbs to a small bowl and toss them with the melted butter, the remaining 1/3 cup brown sugar, and the cinnamon.

4. Transfer the apples to an 8-inch square baking pan. Scatter the crumb mixture over the fruit. Dot the crumbs with the remaining 1 tablespoon butter.

5. Bake the betty until the fruit is bubbling and the topping is golden, 40 to 45 minutes. Serve warm with ice cream.

Simple Apple Brown Betty is best served on the day it is made.

simple peach cobbler

Makes 6 to 8 servings This simple fruit dessert consists of butter cookie dough spooned on top of sweetened sliced peaches. Truth be told, I prefer this cobbler to any kind of pie, and I make it all year-round, with apples in the fall and strawberries in June. Any fruit or combination of fruits can be substituted for the peaches, depending on your mood and the availability of the fruit. See Pairing Fruit for Cobblers, Crisps, and Betties (page 186) for some suggestions.

2 pounds ripe peaches
¾ cup sugar
1 tablespoon cornstarch
½ cup (1 stick) unsalted butter, softened
1 large egg yolk
½ teaspoon pure vanilla extract
1 teaspoon grated lemon zest
½ cup unbleached all-purpose flour
¼ teaspoon baking powder
Pinch of salt

1. Preheat the oven to 375 degrees.

2. Peel, halve, and pit the peaches. Slice each half into 3 or 4 wedges. Combine the peaches, ¼ cup of the sugar, and the cornstarch in a large mixing bowl. Let the fruit stand, stirring occasionally, until the sugar dissolves, 5 to 7 minutes.

3. Make the dough: Cream together the butter and remaining ½ cup sugar in a medium mixing bowl with a wooden spoon or an electric mixer until smooth. Beat in the egg yolk, vanilla, and lemon zest until the batter is smooth, scraping down the sides of the bowl once or twice as necessary. Add the flour, baking powder, and salt and stir until just combined.

4. Transfer the peaches to an 8-inch square baking pan. Drop the dough in rounded tablespoonfuls over the fruit. Bake until the fruit is bubbling and the crust is golden, 50 to 55 minutes. Let the cobbler cool slightly and serve it warm.

Simple Peach Cobbler is best served on the day it is made.

How to Peel Peaches

Firm, underripe peaches can be peeled easily with a vegetable peeler or sharp paring knife. But ripe fruit that is even a little bit yielding begins to fall apart under the pressure of a peeler or knife. To remove the skins from ripe peaches, bring several inches of water to a boil in a large saucepan. Immerse the peaches in the water for 30 seconds to 1 minute, remove them with a slotted spoon, and allow them to cool slightly. You should be able to slide the skins away from the flesh with your fingers.

simple berry crisp

For people who like a little crunch in their fruit desserts, a berry crisp with sliced almonds is just the ticket. Use a variety of berries, or choose your favorite.

2 pints any combination of fresh picked-over or hulled blueberries, strawberries, and/or raspberries

⅓ cup plus 2 tablespoons firmly packed light brown sugar

½ teaspoon pure almond extract

1 tablespoon cornstarch

¼ cup sliced almonds

½ cup unbleached all-purpose flour

⅛ teaspoon ground cinnamon

Pinch of salt

¼ cup (½ stick) unsalted butter, chilled and cut into small pieces

1. Preheat the oven to 425 degrees.

2. Combine the berries, ⅓ cup of the brown sugar, the almond extract, and cornstarch in a medium mixing bowl. Stir to combine, mashing some, but not all, of the berries with the back of the spoon to release some of their juices. Stir once or twice while preparing the topping.

3. Make the topping: Combine the almonds, flour, cinnamon, salt, and the remaining 2 tablespoons brown sugar in a medium mixing bowl and stir to combine. Add the butter and mix on low speed with an electric mixer just until clumps begin to form, 1 to 2 minutes. Do not overmix.

4. Spread the berry mixture across the bottom of an 8-inch square baking pan. Scatter the topping over the berries. Bake the berry crisp until the berries are bubbling and the topping is golden, about 30 minutes. Serve it warm.

Simple Berry Crisp is best served on the day it is made.

milk chocolate ganache tart

This is one of the simplest recipes in this chapter, and the best one for chocolate lovers. Serve it with a big bowl of strawberries on the side.

For the chocolate cookie crust

1⅓ cups (about 30 cookies) Nabisco
   Famous Chocolate Wafer crumbs
Pinch of salt
5 tablespoons unsalted butter, melted

1 recipe Milk Chocolate Ganache
   (page 227)
Unsweetened cocoa powder for dusting

1. Preheat the oven to 350 degrees.

2. Make the crust: Place the cookies and salt in a food processor and grind into fine crumbs. Add the melted butter and process until the crumbs are moistened.

3. Turn the crumbs into a 10-inch tart pan with a removable bottom. Press the mixture evenly across the bottom of the pan and all the way up the sides, packing it tightly with your fingertips so it is even and compacted. (The crust can be prepared up to 1 week in advance, wrapped in plastic, and frozen.) Bake the crust until it is crisp, 6 to 8 minutes. Let it cool completely on a wire rack.

4. Place the ganache in a large mixing bowl, and, using an electric mixer fitted with a whisk attachment, whip the ganache until it holds soft peaks, 2 to 3 minutes. Spread the ganache evenly across the bottom of the tart shell. Refrigerate the tart for up to 6 hours before serving.

Just before serving, sift some cocoa powder over the ganache. Milk Chocolate Ganache Tart is best served on the day it is made.

lime-coconut pie

Makes one 9-inch pie;
8 servings

Key lime and lemon meringue pies are refreshing, but let's face it, they are a pain. I developed this icebox pie so that I'd have a simple citrus summer dessert and never have to make a meringue pie topping again.

For the graham cracker crust

1⅓ cups graham cracker crumbs (from about 20 whole graham crackers)
5 tablespoons unsalted butter, melted
2 tablespoons sugar

For the filling

One 15-ounce can cream of coconut (such as Coco Lopez)
⅔ cup lowfat plain yogurt
½ cup strained fresh lime juice (from 3 to 4 limes)
2 teaspoons grated lime zest
3 tablespoons cold water
2 teaspoons unflavored gelatin

1. Preheat the oven to 350 degrees.

2. Make the crust: Combine the graham cracker crumbs, melted butter, and sugar in a medium bowl and stir until all the crumbs are moistened. Press the graham cracker mixture evenly across the bottom and all the way up the sides of a 9-inch pie plate. Place the crust in the freezer for 15 minutes. (The crust can be prepared up to 1 week in advance, wrapped in plastic, and frozen.) Bake the crust until the crust is golden, about 15 minutes. Let it cool completely on a wire rack.

3. Make the filling: Whisk together the cream of coconut, yogurt, lime juice, and lime zest in a large mixing bowl.

4. Place the water in a small metal bowl and sprinkle the gelatin over the water. Let the mixture stand until the gelatin softens, about 10 minutes. Set the bowl over a small saucepan of barely simmering water; whisk the liquid until the gelatin dissolves, about 1 minute. Whisk the gelatin into the coconut mixture.

5. Pour the filling into the crust, cover with plastic wrap, and chill to set, for at least 4 hours or for up to 1 day.

Improvising Ice-Cream Pies

Ice cream pies are a great option when you want a do-ahead summer dessert. After you make a graham cracker crust (just follow the directions in the recipe for Lime-Coconut Pie, page 191) or a chocolate cookie crust (see Coffee-Toffee Ice-Cream Pie, opposite), you can create any number of pies using any flavor of ice cream and complementary sauces and garnishes. Here are a few of my favorite combinations, just to give you an idea of the possibilities. I've listed the ingredients working from the bottom of the pie to the top.

* **S'mores Ice-Cream Pie:** Graham cracker crust, cooled Hot Fudge Sauce (page 232), chocolate ice cream, warmed Hot Fudge Sauce, and Marshmallow Fluff

* **Banana Split Ice-Cream Pie:** Graham cracker crust, Homemade Caramel Sauce (page 233), sliced bananas, vanilla ice cream, warmed Hot Fudge Sauce (page 232), Vanilla Whipped Cream (page 230), and a maraschino cherry to garnish each slice

* **Strawberry-Blueberry Ice-Cream Pie:** Graham cracker crust, Homemade Caramel Sauce (page 233), strawberry ice cream, Warm Blueberry Sauce (page 31), Vanilla Whipped Cream (page 230), and a fresh strawberry to garnish each slice

* **Peppermint Patty Ice-Cream Pie:** Chocolate cookie crust, chopped chocolate-mint candies, chocolate chip mint ice cream, and warmed Hot Fudge Sauce (page 232)

* **Peanut Butter Fudge Ice-Cream Pie:** Chocolate cookie crust, cooled Hot Fudge Sauce (page 232), chocolate–peanut butter cup ice cream, Peanut Butter–Caramel Sauce (page 234), and a miniature peanut butter cup to garnish each slice

coffee-toffee ice-cream pie

Makes one 10-inch pie; 8 servings

Ice cream pies are a favorite summer dessert of mine. With companies like Häagen-Dazs and Ben and Jerry's constantly introducing new superpremium flavors to the market, the possibilities are endless. Coffee, caramel, and hot fudge are a classic combination. See "Improvising Ice Cream Pies" (opposite) for more ideas.

For the chocolate cookie crust

1⅓ cups (about 30 cookies) Nabisco Famous Chocolate Wafers crumbs
⅛ teaspoon salt
5 tablespoons unsalted butter, melted

1 recipe Homemade Caramel Sauce (page 233), warmed
⅓ cup chopped salted peanuts
1 pint coffee ice cream, softened
Hot Fudge Sauce (page 232)

1. Preheat the oven to 350 degrees.

2. Make the crust: Place the cookies and salt in a food processor and grind into fine crumbs. Add the melted butter and process until the crumbs are moistened. Turn the crumbs into a 10-inch tart pan with a removable bottom. Press the mixture evenly across the bottom of the pan and all the way up the sides, packing it tightly with your fingertips so it is even and compacted. (The crust can be prepared up to 1 week in advance, wrapped in plastic, and frozen.) Bake the crust until crisp, 6 to 8 minutes. Let it cool completely on a wire rack.

3. Spread the warm Homemade Caramel Sauce across the bottom of the pie shell. Sprinkle evenly with the peanuts. Let cool.

4. Spread the softened ice cream evenly over the caramel. Cover the pan with plastic wrap and freeze the tart for at least 1 hour or for up to 1 week.

5. To serve, let the pie stand at room temperature for about 10 minutes to soften slightly.

Cut slices with a sharp knife. Spoon some Hot Fudge Sauce over each slice and serve immediately.

BIRTHDAYS AND BEYOND: cakes for all occasions

LEFT TO RIGHT: Classic Yellow Layer Cake with Vanilla Birthday Cake Frosting, Devil's Food Cupcakes with Chocolate Butter Icing

For my first child's first birthday, I made a

chocolate Bavarian cake glazed with bittersweet chocolate ganache and decorated with candied rose petals. I was working as a pastry chef at a fine restaurant, and I couldn't conceive of anything simpler. When my second child's first birthday rolled around, I was in a different frame of mind. At home with two kids, I barely had time to put away the laundry. So I made a Yellow Layer Cake with fluffy white Birthday Cake Frosting and decorated it with pink and yellow Necco wafers. Nobody was disappointed. Both cakes were really pretty, tasted great, and were made by Mom.

In this chapter, I'll take you through the cake recipes I have come to rely on since I made the transition from pastry chef to mom. I've pretty much abandoned fancy cakes that require sugar syrups, mousse fillings, glazes, and marzipan decorations. But I certainly haven't given up on cake. In fact, I probably make more cakes now than ever before. The fuller my life gets, the more there is to celebrate. And there's no substitute for cake when I want to mark an occasion, whether it's our anniversary, our daughter's first dance recital, or the last day of winter vacation. I just make sure now that my cakes are easy to make and delicious even when unadorned. A lackluster sponge cake can be made enjoyable with fillings, frostings, and decorative frills, but a mediocre piece of pound cake sitting on a plate has nowhere to hide.

For everyday eating, I rely on a few pound cake and snacking cake recipes that are foolproof and utterly delicious. A good pound cake is rich and buttery without being heavy and greasy. It keeps wonderfully at room temperature for several days and refrigerated for up to one week. A pound cake is the perfect cake to bake and have around to satisfy those urges for something sweet. Toasted pound cake, served with fruit and whipped cream or ice cream, is a really great dessert classic that never goes out of style.

Snacking cakes, baked in a square pan and cut into squares for eating out of hand, are less rich than pound cakes. Bake some Gingerbread Squares at lunch time and serve them as after-school treats. Carrot Cake, dressed up with Cream Cheese and Honey Frosting, is a good bake sale choice because it can be cut into nice, neat squares. These cakes couldn't be simpler to make; if I were going to make cake every day, I'd choose one of these recipes for convenience and honest flavor.

A step up from pound cakes and snacking cakes are Bundt cakes, which are just as simple to make but seem special because of the decorative pan they're baked in. These cakes do double duty. Plain, Apple-Raisin Bundt

Cake and Coconut Bundt Cake are great with coffee, tea, or milk in the afternoon. Add some warm Caramel Sauce, and the apple-raisin cake makes a beautiful fall dessert. With Warm Blueberry Sauce, the coconut cake will thrill dinner guests in the summer.

I usually make cheesecakes and flourless chocolate cakes on request. Do you know someone who just loves cheesecake? Here are the recipes you can rely on to treat that person to his or her favorite, whether it is New York Cheesecake, Chocolate Cheesecake, or a spicy Pumpkin Cheesecake with a gingersnap cookie crumb crust. If you've never baked a flourless cake, you might begin with Chocolate Truffle Cake. No one will believe that this decadent flourless chocolate cake contains only four ingredients and takes just a few minutes to prepare.

Last but not least are layer cakes and cupcakes. I make cupcakes all the time. Every school party—Halloween, Valentine's Day, St. Patrick's Day—I'm in the classroom passing out cupcakes with orange, pink, or green sprinkles to match the occasion. I think I enjoy making them as much as the kids like eating them. Yellow cake and devil's food cake recipes will probably keep you covered if you only make cupcakes occasionally. I've thrown in a few extras—Granola Cupcakes and Strawberry Cupcakes—for variety.

Following tradition, I usually make layer cakes on birthdays. Just a few favorite cakes—vanilla, chocolate, lemon, and coconut—combined with a couple of frostings give me plenty of combinations for the year. For my husband, I'll frost Lemon Layer Cake with Vanilla Whipped Cream, since that's his favorite. Both of my girls prefer Classic Yellow Layer Cake with Birthday Cake Frosting, the choice of small children everywhere. Yes, I have even baked birthday cakes for myself. If I make my own Devil's Food Layer Cake and cover it with Chocolate Butter Icing, I know I'll get to lick the bowl. I've written down a few pointers for frosting and decorating the layers (see "Frosting and Decorating Layer Cakes," page 222), but I don't make a production out of it anymore. Some fresh flowers placed around the base of the cake will do if you are serving cake to grown-ups. Sprinkles pressed into the sides or arranged in a decorative pattern across the top of the cake will please kids. And those candles that you can't blow out are always a hit.

Instructions and tips are included in each recipe, but there are a few general things you'll want to keep in mind when baking any of the cakes in this chapter. Although it may seem inconvenient, take the time to bring your ingredients to room temperature before you begin to mix your batter.

Butter, milk, and eggs that are cold from the refrigerator will yield a curdled batter that won't rise as well as a nice, smooth one. If you forget to take your butter out of the refrigerator, cut it into small pieces and let it sit on a plate in the kitchen for 10 minutes to soften. Warm cold milk for a few seconds in the microwave. Break cold eggs into a bowl and place the bowl on top of a larger bowl of warm water for 5 minutes. (Angel Food Cake is the exception here. As per the recipe, the egg whites should be cold.)

There are some recipes that I think are best made with all-purpose flour. Snacking cakes that you cut into large squares and eat by hand need the sturdy texture that all-purpose flour provides. Upside-down cakes also need to be a little tougher, to serve as a base for their thick fruit and syrup toppings. But for most cake recipes, I urge you to try cake flour (although all-purpose flour will work in all the recipes that follow). Cake flour has less protein than all-purpose flour and gives cakes a finer crumb and softer texture. It really does make a difference. When shopping, read the boxes carefully. Don't buy "self-rising" cake flour by accident; it has added baking powder.

simply perfect pound cake

"You can't fake pound cake," a good friend nodded approvingly when she tasted my version. This is the real thing—rich and buttery, but not heavy at all. Serve it with berries and ice cream, dollops of Lemon Curd (page 231), or on its own.

Nonstick cooking spray
4 large eggs, at room temperature, lightly beaten
2 teaspoons pure vanilla extract
1½ cups cake flour (not self-rising)
¾ teaspoon baking powder
¼ teaspoon salt
1 cup (2 sticks) unsalted butter, softened
1¼ cups sugar

1. Preheat the oven to 325 degrees. Coat the inside of a 9 x 5-inch loaf pan with cooking spray and dust it with flour, knocking out any extra flour.

2. Combine the eggs and vanilla in a glass measuring cup and lightly beat. Combine the cake flour, baking powder, and salt in a medium mixing bowl.

3. Combine the butter and sugar in a large mixing bowl and cream with an electric mixer on medium-high speed until fluffy, about 3 minutes, scraping down the sides of the bowl once or twice as necessary.

4. With the mixer on medium-low speed, pour the egg mixture into the bowl in a slow stream, stopping the mixer once or twice to scrape down the sides.

5. Turn the mixer to low speed and add the flour mixture, ½ cup at a time, scraping down the sides of the bowl after each addition. After the last addition, mix for 30 seconds on medium speed.

6. Scrape the batter into the prepared pan and smooth the top with a rubber spatula. Bake the cake until it is golden and a toothpick inserted in the center comes out clean, about 1 hour and 15 minutes. Let the cake cool in the pan for about 5 minutes, invert it onto a wire rack, and then turn it right side up on a rack to cool completely.

Simply Perfect Pound Cake will keep at room temperature, wrapped in plastic, for up to 3 days or refrigerated for up to 1 week.

marble pound cake

As a kid, I thought that my grandmother's marble cake was magical. My own children were similarly amazed by the swirly patterns in each slice of this pound cake. When you can't decide between chocolate and vanilla, here's your recipe.

Nonstick cooking spray
3 ounces semisweet or bittersweet chocolate, finely chopped
4 large eggs, at room temperature, lightly beaten
2 teaspoons pure vanilla extract
1½ cups cake flour (not self-rising)
¾ teaspoon baking powder
¼ teaspoon salt
1 cup (2 sticks) unsalted butter, softened
1¼ cups sugar

1. Preheat the oven to 325 degrees. Coat the inside of a 9 x 5-inch loaf pan with cooking spray and dust it with flour, knocking out any extra flour.

2. Put 1 inch of water in the bottom of a double boiler or a small saucepan and bring to a bare simmer. Place the chocolate in the top of the double boiler or in a stainless-steel bowl big enough to rest on top of the saucepan, and set the bowl on top of the simmering water, making sure that the water doesn't touch the bottom of the bowl. Heat, whisking occasionally, until the chocolate is completely melted. Set aside to cool.

3. Combine the eggs and vanilla in a glass measuring cup and lightly beat. Combine the cake flour, baking powder, and salt in a medium mixing bowl.

4. Combine the butter and sugar in a large mixing bowl and cream with an electric mixer on medium-high speed until fluffy, about 3 minutes, scraping down the sides of the bowl once or twice as necessary.

5. With the mixer on medium-low speed, pour the egg mixture into the bowl in a slow stream, stopping the mixer once or twice to scrape down the bowl.

6. Turn the mixer to low speed and add the flour mixture, ½ cup at a time, scraping down the sides of the bowl after each addition. After the last addition, mix for 30 seconds on medium speed.

7. Scrape half the batter into a medium mixing bowl and set aside. Add the melted chocolate and stir until combined.

8. Scrape half the yellow batter into the prepared loaf pan and smooth the top with a rubber spatula. Scrape half the chocolate batter into the prepared pan and smooth the top. Repeat the layers with the remaining batters. Run a butter knife blade through the batter to create marbling. Do not overmix.

9. Bake the pound cake until it is golden and a toothpick inserted in the center comes out clean, about 1 hour and 15 minutes. Let the cake cool in the pan for about 5 minutes, invert it onto a wire rack, and then turn it right side up on a rack to cool completely.

Marble Pound Cake will keep at room temperature, wrapped in plastic, for up to 3 days or refrigerated for up to 1 week.

lemon poppy seed pound cake

Makes 8 to 10 servings Abundant poppy seeds give this pound cake flavor, color, and crunch. To dress it up, serve it with Quick Crème Fraîche (page 229).

Nonstick cooking spray
4 large eggs, at room temperature, lightly beaten
1 teaspoon pure vanilla extract
1½ cups cake flour (not self-rising)
¾ teaspoon baking powder
¼ teaspoon salt
¼ cup poppy seeds
1 tablespoon grated lemon zest
1 cup (2 sticks) unsalted butter, softened
1½ cups sugar
¼ cup strained fresh lemon juice

1. Preheat the oven to 325 degrees. Coat the inside of a 9 x 5-by-3-inch loaf pan with cooking spray and dust it with flour, knocking out any extra flour.

2. Combine the eggs and vanilla in a glass measuring cup and lightly beat. Combine the cake flour, baking powder, salt, poppy seeds, and lemon zest in a medium mixing bowl.

3. Combine the butter and 1¼ cups of the sugar in a large mixing bowl and cream with an electric mixer on medium-high speed until fluffy, about 3 minutes, scraping down the sides of the bowl once or twice as necessary.

4. With the mixer on medium-low speed, pour the egg mixture into the bowl in a slow stream, stopping the mixer once or twice to scrape down the bowl.

5. Turn the mixer to low speed and add the flour mixture, ½ cup at a time, scraping down the sides of the bowl after each addition. After the last addition, mix for 30 seconds on medium speed.

6. Scrape the batter into the prepared pan and smooth the top with a rubber spatula. Bake the cake until it is golden and a toothpick inserted in the center comes out clean, about 1 hour and 15 minutes. Let the cake cool in the pan for about 5 minutes, invert it onto a wire rack, and then turn it right side up on a rack.

7. While the cake is cooling, make the syrup. Combine the remaining ¼ cup sugar and the lemon juice in a small saucepan and cook over low heat until the sugar dissolves. Poke the warm pound cake all over with a toothpick. Brush the glaze on the warm cake until all of the glaze is absorbed. Let the cake cool completely.

Lemon Poppy Seed Pound Cake will keep at room temperature, wrapped in plastic, for up to 3 days or refrigerated for up to 1 week.

cornmeal-orange pound cake

Makes 8 to 10 servings

Cornmeal and brown sugar give this pound cake a distinctive texture, slightly crunchy and a little more dense than plain pound cake. This cake is very good unadorned for breakfast or in the afternoon. Spread some cream cheese frosting over the top and serve the cake with sliced strawberries for a lovely dessert.

Nonstick cooking spray
4 large eggs, at room temperature, lightly beaten
1 teaspoon pure vanilla extract
1 cup cake flour (not self-rising)
½ cup yellow cornmeal
1¼ teaspoons baking powder
¼ teaspoon salt
1 tablespoon grated orange zest
1 cup (2 sticks) unsalted butter, softened
1 cup firmly packed light brown sugar
Cream Cheese and Butter Frosting (page 228) or Cream Cheese and Honey Frosting (page 228), optional

1. Preheat the oven to 325 degrees. Coat the inside of a 9 x 5-inch loaf pan with cooking spray and dust it with flour, knocking out any extra flour.

2. Combine the eggs and vanilla in a glass measuring cup and lightly beat. Combine the cake flour, cornmeal, baking powder, salt, and orange zest in a medium mixing bowl.

3. Combine the butter and brown sugar in a large mixing bowl and cream with an electric mixer on medium-high speed until fluffy, about 3 minutes, scraping down the sides of the bowl once or twice as necessary.

4. With the mixer on medium-low speed, pour the egg mixture into the bowl in a slow stream, stopping the mixer once or twice to scrape down the bowl.

5. Turn the mixer to low speed and add the flour mixture, ½ cup at a time, scraping down the sides of the bowl after each addition.

6. Scrape the batter into the prepared pan and smooth the top with a rubber spatula. Bake the cake until it is golden and a toothpick inserted in the center comes out clean, about 1 hour and 15 minutes. Let the cake cool in the pan for about 5 minutes, invert it onto a wire rack, and then turn it right side up on a rack. Let it cool completely. Frost the cake with Cream Cheese Frosting if desired.

Cornmeal-Orange Pound Cake will keep at room temperature, unfrosted and wrapped in plastic, for up to 3 days or, frosted and refrigerated, for up to 1 week.

gingerbread squares

This is a very simple recipe for snacking cake when you want something quick with a lot of sugar and spice.

Nonstick cooking spray
¾ cup boiling water
½ cup dark molasses
1 teaspoon baking soda
1¼ cups unbleached all-purpose flour
1 teaspoon baking powder
¼ teaspoon salt
1½ teaspoons ground ginger
½ teaspoon ground cinnamon
¼ cup (½ stick) unsalted butter, softened
½ cup firmly packed light brown sugar
1 large egg yolk

1. Preheat the oven to 350 degrees. Coat the inside of an 8-inch square baking pan with cooking spray.

2. Pour the boiling water into a glass measuring cup and stir in the molasses and baking soda. Set aside to cool.

3. Combine the flour, baking powder, salt, ginger, and cinnamon in a medium mixing bowl.

4. Combine the butter and sugar in a large mixing bowl and cream with an electric mixer on medium-high speed until fluffy, about 3 minutes, scraping down the sides of the bowl once or twice as necessary.

5. Add the egg yolk and beat until smooth, scraping down the sides of the bowl once or twice as necessary. Beat in half the molasses mixture on medium speed and then half the flour mixture. Scrape down the bowl and repeat with the remaining molasses mixture and the remaining flour mixture.

6. Scrape the batter into the prepared pan and smooth the top with a rubber spatula. Bake until a toothpick inserted in the center comes out clean, about 30 minutes. Let the gingerbread cool in the pan for about 15 minutes, invert it onto a wire rack, and then turn it right side up on a rack to cool completely. Cut into 9 squares and serve.

Gingerbread Squares will keep, covered in plastic wrap at room temperature, for up to 3 days.

carrot cake squares

Makes 9 squares The secret ingredient in my carrot cake may surprise you—it's butter. Most recipes call for oil, ostensibly for health reasons, but butter just tastes better. And let's be honest—are you really so concerned about cholesterol if you're planning on covering the cake with cream cheese frosting?

Nonstick cooking spray
2 large eggs, at room temperature
¼ cup milk, at room temperature
1⅓ cups unbleached all-purpose flour
1 teaspoon baking powder
1 teaspoon ground cinnamon
¼ teaspoon salt
½ cup (1 stick) unsalted butter, softened
1 cup firmly packed light brown sugar
2 cups peeled and grated carrots (about 4 medium carrots)
½ cup chopped walnuts
Cream Cheese and Butter Frosting (page 228) or Cream Cheese and Honey Frosting (page 228)

1. Preheat the oven to 350 degrees. Coat the inside of an 8-inch square baking pan with cooking spray and dust with flour, knocking out any extra flour. Combine the eggs and milk in a glass measuring cup and lightly beat.

2. Combine the flour, baking powder, cinnamon, and salt in a medium mixing bowl.

3. Combine the butter and sugar in a large mixing bowl and cream with an electric mixer on medium-high speed until fluffy, about 3 minutes, scraping down the sides of the bowl once or twice as necessary.

4. With the mixer on medium-low speed, pour one-third of the egg mixture into the bowl in a slow stream. Add one-third of the flour mixture. Add another third of the egg mixture and another third of the flour mixture. Add the remaining egg mixture and then the remaining flour mixture. Scrape down the sides of the bowl and beat on medium speed for 1 minute. Stir in the carrots and walnuts.

5. Scrape the batter into the prepared pan and smooth the top with a rubber spatula. Bake the cake until it is golden and a toothpick inserted in the center comes out clean, 35 to 40 minutes. Let the cake cool in the pan for about 15 minutes, invert it onto a wire rack, and then turn it right side up on a rack to cool completely.

6. Frost with Cream Cheese and Butter Frosting or Cream Cheese and Honey Frosting and cut into 9 squares.

Carrot Cake Squares will keep, covered with plastic wrap and refrigerated, for up to 2 days.

chocolate-buttermilk squares

Makes 9 squares This one-bowl recipe is simple enough to make as an after-school snack. Use premium Dutch-process cocoa for the richest taste. I like Pernigotti or Van Leer (see Mail-Order and Online Resources, page 273).

Nonstick cooking spray
1¾ cups unbleached all-purpose flour
¾ cup unsweetened Dutch-process cocoa powder
1 cup sugar
1 teaspoon baking soda
¼ teaspoon salt
1 cup buttermilk
½ cup (1 stick) unsalted butter, melted
2 teaspoons pure vanilla extract

1. Preheat the oven to 350 degrees. Coat the inside of an 8-inch square baking pan with cooking spray.

2. Combine the flour, cocoa powder, sugar, baking soda, and salt in a large mixing bowl. With a wooden spoon or electric mixer, stir in the buttermilk, melted butter, and vanilla until just combined.

3. Scrape the batter into the prepared pan and smooth the top with a rubber spatula. Bake until a toothpick inserted in the center comes out clean, about 35 minutes. Let the cake cool in the pan for about 10 minutes, invert it onto a wire rack, and then turn it right side up on a rack to cool completely. Cut into 9 squares.

Chocolate-Buttermilk Squares will keep, wrapped in plastic at room temperature, for up to 2 days.

sour cream coffee bundt cake

Makes 8 to 10 servings Sour Cream Coffee Bundt Cake should be in every mom's repertoire. This particular recipe was given to my mom by a neighbor many years ago, and she still makes it today when she wants to bring someone a cake.

Nonstick cooking spray
½ cup firmly packed light brown sugar
½ cup finely chopped pecans
1½ teaspoons ground cinnamon
3 large eggs, at room temperature
1½ cups full-fat sour cream, at room temperature
2 teaspoons pure vanilla extract
3 cups unbleached all-purpose flour
1½ teaspoons baking powder
1½ teaspoons baking soda
½ teaspoon salt
1 cup (2 sticks) unsalted butter, softened
1½ cups granulated sugar

1. Preheat the oven to 350 degrees. Coat the inside of a 12-cup Bundt pan with cooking spray and dust it with flour, knocking out any extra flour.

2. Combine the brown sugar, pecans, and cinnamon in a small bowl. Combine the eggs, sour cream, and vanilla in a large glass measuring cup and lightly beat. Combine the flour, baking powder, baking soda, and salt in a medium mixing bowl.

3. Combine the butter and granulated sugar in a large mixing bowl and cream with an electric mixer on medium-high speed until fluffy, about 3 minutes, scraping down the sides of the bowl once or twice as necessary.

4. With the mixer on medium-low speed, pour one-third of the egg mixture into the bowl in a slow stream. Add one-third of the flour mixture. Add another third of the egg mixture and another third of the flour mixture. Add the remaining egg mixture and then the remaining flour mixture. Scrape down the sides of the bowl and beat on medium for 1 minute.

5. Scrape one-third of the batter into the prepared pan and sprinkle with one-third of the pecan mixture. Repeat two more times. Bake the cake until it is golden and a toothpick inserted in the center comes out clean, 55 to 60 minutes. Let the cake cool in the pan for about 15 minutes, invert it onto a wire rack, and then turn it right side up on a rack to cool completely.

Sour Cream Coffee Bundt Cake will keep at room temperature for up to 2 days, covered with a cake dome.

A Good Excuse to Make Sour Cream Coffee Bundt Cake

Why not invite the moms of some of your kids' friends over for coffee some morning, so you can all get to know each other a little better? If you all work, make it a weekend, when the dads can babysit.

mississippi mud bundt cake

Makes 8 to 10 servings I developed this recipe for *Bon Appétit* magazine; they were looking for simple desserts to follow barbecue dinners. This homey Southern-style cake delivers a good dose of sweetness—just what I want after a spicy dinner of chicken and ribs.

2 cups unbleached all-purpose flour
2 teaspoons baking soda
1 teaspoon salt
1 cup (2 sticks) unsalted butter, cut into pieces
6 ounces (6 squares) unsweetened chocolate, finely chopped
½ cup brewed espresso or very strong coffee
1½ cups sugar
½ cup bourbon
4 large eggs, at room temperature
2 teaspoons pure vanilla extract
Espresso-Bourbon Glaze (page 232)

1. Preheat the oven to 350 degrees. Butter a 12-cup Bundt pan.

2. Combine the flour, baking soda, and salt in a medium mixing bowl.

3. Combine the butter, chocolate, and espresso in a medium saucepan. Stir over low heat until the chocolate and butter have melted. Remove the pan from the heat. Add the sugar and bourbon and whisk until the sugar has dissolved and the mixture is smooth.

4. Place the eggs and vanilla in a large mixing bowl and mix with a wooden spoon or electric mixer on low speed. Gradually beat in the chocolate mixture. Add the flour mixture and stir until just combined. Scrape the batter into the prepared pan and smooth the top with a rubber spatula.

5. Bake until a toothpick inserted in the center of the cake comes out clean, about 45 minutes. Let the cake cool in the pan for about 5 minutes, invert it onto a wire rack, and then turn it right side up on a rack to cool completely.

6. Place the cake atop a wire rack set over a baking sheet. Slowly drizzle the glaze over the cake, allowing it to run down the sides of the cake, covering as much of the cake as possible. Spoon any glaze drippings from the baking sheet over the cake. Let the glaze set for 30 minutes.

Mississippi Mud Bundt Cake will keep for 2 days at room temperature, covered with a cake dome.

coconut bundt cake

Makes 8 to 10 servings I love unsweetened dried coconut, which is available in natural food stores, because it's fluffy and light, not heavy and sticky-sweet like the sweetened flaked coconut sold in supermarkets. Stirred into yellow cake batter, coconut gives this Bundt cake a slightly chewy texture and a great coconut flavor. If you are a coconut-and-chocolate person, serve this cake with Simple Warm Chocolate Sauce. If you are a coconut-and-fruit person, serve it with Warm Blueberry Sauce.

Nonstick cooking spray
3 large eggs, at room temperature
1 cup whole milk
2 teaspoons pure vanilla extract
2 cups cake flour (not self-rising)
1½ teaspoons baking powder
½ teaspoon salt
1 cup (2 sticks) unsalted butter, softened
1⅓ cups sugar
1½ cups unsweetened shredded coconut
Simple Warm Chocolate Sauce (page 41) or Warm Blueberry Sauce (page 31), optional

1. Preheat the oven to 350 degrees. Coat the inside of a 12-cup Bundt pan with cooking spray and dust it with flour, knocking out any extra flour.

2. Combine the eggs, milk, and vanilla in a glass measuring cup and lightly beat. Combine the cake flour, baking powder, and salt in a medium mixing bowl.

3. Combine the butter and sugar in a large mixing bowl and cream with an electric mixer on medium-high speed until fluffy, about 3 minutes, scraping down the sides of the bowl once or twice as necessary.

4. With the mixer on medium-low speed, pour one-third of the egg mixture into the bowl in a slow stream. Add one-third of the flour mixture. Add another third of the egg mixture and another third of the flour mixture. Add the remaining egg mixture and then the remaining flour mixture. Scrape down the sides of the bowl and beat on medium speed for 1 minute. Stir in the coconut.

5. Scrape the batter into the prepared pan and smooth the top with a rubber spatula. Bake the cake until it is golden and a toothpick inserted in the center comes out clean, 35 to 40 minutes. Let the cake cool in the pan for about 15 minutes, invert it onto a wire rack, and then turn it right side up on a rack to cool completely.

6. Spoon some Simple Warm Chocolate Sauce or Warm Blueberry Sauce on each slice just before serving, if desired.

Coconut Bundt Cake will keep at room temperature for up to 2 days, covered with a cake dome.

apple-raisin bundt cake

This homey cake, dotted with apple chunks and raisins, is perfect as an after-school snack with a tall glass of milk. Serve it with some warm caramel sauce and it becomes a formidable dessert.

Nonstick cooking spray
2 large eggs, at room temperature
1 teaspoon pure vanilla extract
2 cups cake flour (not self-rising)
¾ teaspoon baking soda
¼ teaspoon salt
1½ teaspoons ground cinnamon
¼ teaspoon ground nutmeg
½ cup (1 stick) unsalted butter, softened
1⅓ cups sugar
2 medium apples such as Granny Smiths (about ¾ pound), peeled, cored, and cut into ¼-inch dice
½ cup raisins
1 recipe Homemade Caramel Sauce (page 233; optional), warmed

1. Preheat the oven to 350 degrees. Coat the inside of a 12-cup Bundt pan with cooking spray and dust it with flour, knocking out any extra flour.

2. Combine the eggs and vanilla in a glass measuring cup and lightly beat. Combine the flour, baking soda, salt, cinnamon, and nutmeg in a medium mixing bowl.

3. Combine the butter and sugar in a large mixing bowl and cream with an electric mixer on medium-high speed until fluffy, about 3 minutes, scraping down the sides of the bowl once or twice as necessary.

4. With the mixer on medium-low speed, pour the egg mixture into the bowl in a slow stream, stopping the mixer once or twice to scrape down the sides of the bowl.

5. Turn the mixer to low speed and add the flour mixture, ½ cup at a time, scraping down the sides of the bowl after each addition. Stir in the apples and raisins.

6. Scrape the batter into the prepared pan and smooth the top with a rubber spatula. Bake the cake until it is golden and a toothpick inserted in the center comes out clean, about 1 hour. Let the cake cool in the pan for about 5 minutes, invert it onto a wire rack, and then turn it right side up on a rack to cool completely.

7. If you wish, pour a few tablespoons of warm Homemade Caramel Sauce onto a dessert plate and cover it with a slice of cake.

Apple-Raisin Bundt Cake will keep at room temperature for up to 5 days, covered with a cake dome.

angel food cake

Makes one
9-inch tube cake;
8 to 10 servings

Although grown-ups like this cake because it is fat-free, kids like it because it is sweet, sweet, sweet. For the tallest, lightest cake possible, make sure that your egg whites are cold when you whip them. Whip them on medium speed (not high, or you might overwhip them) just until they hold soft peaks—not until they are stiff; stiff egg whites tend to collapse when combined with the flour. Whisking the flour mixture and then straining it into the egg whites lessens the chance of deflating the whites.

1 cup cake flour (not self-rising)
1½ cups sugar
¼ teaspoon salt
12 large cold egg whites
1 teaspoon cream of tartar
2 teaspoons pure vanilla extract

1. Preheat the oven to 325 degrees. Have ready a 9-inch ungreased angel food tube pan with a removable bottom.

2. Combine the cake flour, ¾ cup of the sugar, and the salt in a medium mixing bowl and whisk thoroughly to break up any lumps. Set aside.

3. Place the egg whites in a large mixing bowl and whip them with an electric mixer fitted with a whisk attachment on medium speed until frothy. Add the cream of tartar and continue to beat on medium until the egg whites begin to turn white. With the mixer still on medium speed, pour in the remaining ¾ cup sugar in a slow, steady stream and whip until the whites are shiny white and until when the whisk is lifted from the mixture the egg whites just hold soft, floppy peaks. Stir in the vanilla until just mixed in.

4. Place a small fine-mesh strainer over the bowl of egg whites and strain about ¼

cup of the flour mixture into the egg white mixture. Gently fold in the flour mixture with a rubber spatula. Repeat with the remaining flour mixture in ¼-cup increments until all of it has been folded in. Pour the batter into the tube pan and smooth the top with a rubber spatula. Bake the cake until it is golden brown and the top springs back when you touch it, about 50 minutes.

5. Remove the pan from the oven. If your pan has feet, invert the pan onto a heat-proof surface and allow it to cool. If your pan doesn't have feet, invert 4 drinking glasses on the counter and rest the inverted pan on top of the glasses to allow

A Good Excuse to Make Angel Food Cake

Make this cake if someone you'll be feeding is watching his or her cholesterol and fat intake. See "Five Good Things to Do with Angel Food Cake" (opposite) for some fat- and calorie-laden add-ons if you are worried that the rest of your family and guests might not have their sweet and fat tooths satisfied.

air to circulate around the cake while it cools. Let the cake cool in the pan for at least 1 hour or for up to 6 hours.

6. To remove the cake from the pan, run a sharp paring knife around the edges, being careful to leave the golden crust intact. Remove the sides of the pan. Invert the cake onto a serving platter. Run the paring knife under the removable bottom of the pan and lift it off the cake. Serve the cake plain or frost as desired.

Angel Food Cake will keep at room temperature, under a cake dome, for 2 to 3 days.

Five Good Things to Do with Angel Food Cake

Angel Food Cake, so white and plain, cries out for colorful and flavorful adornments and accompaniments. Here are some of my favorites:

1. Glaze it with Milk Chocolate Ganache (page 227) or set slices on top of some Hot Fudge Sauce (page 232) and top with small scoops of ice cream.
2. Add 2 teaspoons grated orange zest or 1 teaspoon grated lemon zest to the batter with the vanilla. Serve the cake with sliced strawberries and Vanilla Whipped Cream (page 230).
3. Whisk 1 tablespoon instant espresso powder into the flour mixture. Drizzle the finished cake with Espresso-Bourbon Glaze (page 232) and serve with small scoops of chocolate and coffee ice cream.
4. Fold in 1 cup miniature chocolate chips after all of the flour has been added. Serve the cake with warm Peanut Butter–Caramel Sauce (page 234).
5. Serve the cake with fresh raspberries and/or a simple raspberry sauce: Purée 1 pint fresh or frozen raspberries in a blender or food processor. Strain the sauce through a fine-mesh strainer into a bowl and stir in 1 tablespoon fresh lemon juice and 2 tablespoons confectioners' sugar or more to taste.

 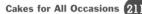

plum upside-down cake

**Makes one
9-inch cake;
6 to 8 servings**

For a long time, I avoided upside-down cake, because those rings of canned pineapple just didn't appeal to me. When I realized that other fruits could be substituted, I reconsidered.

Although this recipe is not difficult, it has more steps than most of the cakes in this book. The fruit must be cooked in syrup, arranged in the pan, and allowed to cool. The batter must be made with separated eggs. And then there is the issue of unmolding the cake: Don't panic if some of your fruit sticks when you remove the cake from the pan. Simply place the fruit back on the cake. This may sound like a lot of work, but on the bright side you'll have a delicious cake that comes out of the pan already decorated with shiny, caramelized fruit.

For the fruit

6 tablespoons (¾ stick) unsalted butter
6 medium plums, pitted, halved, and cut
    into ½-inch-thick slices
½ cup sugar
½ teaspoon ground cinnamon

For the cake

Nonstick coating spray
1⅓ cups unbleached all-purpose flour
1½ teaspoons baking powder
¼ cup yellow cornmeal
½ teaspoon salt
4 large eggs, at room temperature,
    separated
½ cup (1 stick) unsalted butter,
    softened
1 cup sugar
1 teaspoon pure vanilla extract
⅔ cup whole milk, at room temperature

1. Make the fruit: Melt the butter in a large skillet over medium heat. Add the plums, sugar, and cinnamon and cook, stirring frequently, until the sugar is dissolved and the fruit is coated with glossy syrup, 4 to 5 minutes. Remove the skillet from the heat. Using a slotted spoon or spatula, remove the fruit to a plate to cool slightly. Leave the syrup in the skillet.

2. Coat the inside of a 9-inch round cake pan with cooking spray. Arrange the cooled fruit in 3 concentric circles in the pan. Bring the syrup to a boil in the skillet and cook it over medium heat for 3 minutes. Pour it over the fruit. Set the fruit aside to cool completely.

3. Make the cake batter: Preheat the oven to 350 degrees. Combine the flour, baking powder, cornmeal, and salt in a medium mixing bowl. Set aside.

4. Place the egg whites in a large mixing bowl and, with an electric mixer fitted with a whisk attachment, beat the whites on high speed until they just hold stiff peaks. Do not overwhip. The whites should look smooth, not grainy.

 **A Good Excuse to Make
Plum Upside-Down Cake**

Bored with the same old fruit pie or cobbler recipe you rely on during the summer? Make this wonderful cake instead.

Upside-Down Cake Variations

If you'd prefer, you can substitute 5 large peaches or nectarines, pitted, halved, and cut into ½-inch-thick slices. Five medium Granny Smith apples or 6 ripe Bosch pears, peeled, cored, and cut into ½-inch-thick slices, will work, too. If you must have pineapple, the simplest thing to do is to buy a 20-ounce can of sliced, unsweetened pineapple, drain the fruit on paper towels, and cook it in the butter and sugar until the sugar is just dissolved, 1 to 2 minutes.

5. Combine the butter and sugar in another large mixing bowl and cream together on medium-high speed with the mixer until fluffy, 2 to 3 minutes. With the mixer on medium speed, add the yolks one at a time, scraping down the sides of the bowl after each addition. Stir in the vanilla.

6. With the mixer on medium speed, alternately add the flour mixture and the milk, a third at a time, scraping down the sides of the bowl, and mixing until the batter is just smooth. Gently fold in the egg whites until all the white streaks are gone. Scrape the batter into the prepared pan and smooth the top with a rubber spatula. Bake the cake until it is golden and a toothpick inserted in the center comes out without any batter on it (though there may be some sticky fruit juices on the toothpick), 50 to 55 minutes. Let the cake cool completely in the pan.

7. To unmold, place the pan on the stovetop over very low heat for about 1 minute. Run a sharp paring knife around the edge of the cake to loosen it. Place a serving plate over the cake pan and invert it. If any fruit sticks to the bottom of the pan, carefully place it back on top of the cake.

Plum Upside-Down Cake will keep at room temperature for up to 1 day, covered with a cake dome.

classic yellow layer cake or cupcakes

**Makes two
9-inch cake layers
or 16 cupcakes**

A great-tasting and simple recipe that makes perfect layer cake or cupcakes.
Fill and frost layers with Vanilla Birthday Cake Frosting (page 225) or Chocolate
Birthday Cake Frosting (page 226) for a classic kid-friendly cake. Or fill with Lemon
Curd (page 231) and frost with Vanilla Whipped Cream (page 230) for a less
sugary cake.

**Nonstick cooking spray
4 large eggs, at room temperature
½ cup whole milk, at room temperature
1 tablespoon pure vanilla extract
2¼ cups cake flour (not self-rising)
1½ cups sugar
2 teaspoons baking powder
½ teaspoon salt
1 cup (2 sticks) unsalted butter,
     softened and cut into 16 pieces**

1. Preheat the oven to 350 degrees. Coat
the insides of two 9-inch round cake pans
with cooking spray. Line the bottoms and
sides with parchment paper and coat that
with spray as well. Dust the bottoms and
sides of the pans with flour, knocking out
any extra flour. For cupcakes, coat the
muffin tins with cooking spray and dust
with flour, or line the muffin tins with
paper liners.

2. Combine the eggs, milk, and vanilla in
a medium mixing bowl and beat lightly
with a fork. Set aside.

3. Combine the cake flour, sugar, baking
powder, and salt in a large mixing bowl.
Add the butter and, with an electric mixer
fitted with the paddle attachment, mix on
low speed until the butter pieces are no
larger than small peas.

4. Pour in about two-thirds of the egg
mixture and mix on low speed until all
the ingredients are moistened. Scrape
down the sides of the bowl with a rubber
spatula and mix on medium-high speed
for 1 minute. Stir in the remaining egg
mixture on low speed until combined.
Scrape down the sides of the bowl again
and mix on medium-high speed again for
another 30 seconds.

5. Scrape the batter into the prepared pans
and smooth the top with a rubber spatula.
Bake until the cake is light golden and a
toothpick inserted in the center comes out
clean, about 20 minutes for cupcakes,
25 to 30 minutes for layer cake. Let the
cake cool in the pan for about 5 minutes,
invert it onto a wire rack, and then turn it
right side up on a rack to cool completely.

Classic Yellow Layer Cake or Cupcakes will
keep, wrapped in plastic, at room temperature for up to 1 day or refrigerated for
up to 3 days. Frost as desired.

lemon layer cake or cupcakes

Makes two 9-inch cake layers or 16 cupcakes

This is the perfect cake for lemon lovers. I like to fill Lemon Layer Cake with Lemon Curd (page 231) and frost it with Vanilla Whipped Cream (page 230). For decoration, dip very thin slices of lemon in sugar and arrange them on top of the cake immediately before serving. Frost cupcakes with Vanilla Whipped Cream or Quick "Crème Fraîche" (page 229).

Nonstick cooking spray
4 large eggs, at room temperature
$\frac{1}{2}$ cup whole milk, at room temperature
$\frac{1}{4}$ cup strained fresh lemon juice
1 teaspoon pure vanilla extract
2 teaspoons grated lemon zest
$2\frac{1}{2}$ cups cake flour (not self-rising)
$1\frac{1}{2}$ cups sugar
2 teaspoons baking powder
$\frac{1}{2}$ teaspoon baking soda
$\frac{1}{2}$ teaspoon salt
1 cup (2 sticks) unsalted butter, softened and cut into 16 pieces

1. Preheat the oven to 350 degrees. Coat the inside of two 9-inch cake pans with cooking spray. Line the bottom and sides with parchment paper and coat that with spray as well. Dust the bottom and sides of the pans with flour, knocking out any excess flour. For cupcakes, coat the inside of muffin tins with cooking spray and dust with flour, or line the muffin tins with paper liners.

2. Combine the eggs, milk, lemon juice, vanilla, and lemon zest in a medium mixing bowl and beat together lightly with a fork. Set aside.

3. Combine the cake flour, sugar, baking powder, baking soda, and salt in a large mixing bowl. Add the butter and mix on low speed with an electric mixer fitted with the paddle attachment until the butter pieces are no larger than small peas.

4. Stir in about two-thirds of the egg mixture and mix on low speed until all the ingredients are moistened. Scrape down the sides of the bowl with a rubber spatula and mix on medium-high speed for 1 minute. Stir in the remaining egg mixture on low speed until combined. Scrape down the sides of the bowl again and mix on medium-high speed again for another 30 seconds.

5. Scrape the batter evenly into the prepared pans and smooth the top with a rubber spatula. Bake until the cake is light golden and just set, and a toothpick inserted in the center comes out clean, about 20 minutes for cupcakes, 25 to 30 minutes for cake layers. Let the cake cool in the pan for about 5 minutes, invert it onto a wire rack, and then turn it right side up on a rack to cool completely.

Lemon Layer Cake or Cupcakes will keep, wrapped in plastic, at room temperature for up to 1 day or refrigerated for up to 3 days. Frost as desired.

devil's food layer cake or cupcakes

Makes two 9-inch cake layers or 16 cupcakes

Here's where to turn when you need a chocolate layer cake or cupcakes. Shiny Chocolate Butter Icing (page 227) complements the dark chocolate cake. Fill this cake with Coconut Custard Filling (page 229) if you like chocolate and coconut together.

Nonstick cooking spray
1/2 cup unsweetened cocoa powder such as Hershey's (do not use Dutch-process cocoa for this recipe), plus extra for dusting the pans
6 tablespoons boiling water
2/3 cup full-fat sour cream, at room temperature
2 large eggs, at room temperature
2 teaspoons pure vanilla extract
2 cups cake flour (not self-rising)
1 cup granulated sugar
1/2 cup firmly packed light brown sugar
3/4 teaspoon baking soda
1/2 teaspoon salt
1 cup (2 sticks) unsalted butter, softened and cut into 16 pieces

1. Preheat the oven to 350 degrees. Coat the insides of two 9-inch round cake pans with cooking spray. Line the bottom and sides with parchment paper and coat that with spray as well. Dust the bottoms and sides of the pans with cocoa powder, knocking out any extra. For cupcakes, coat muffin tins with cooking spray and dust with cocoa, or line the muffin tins with paper liners.

2. Whisk together the cocoa powder and boiling water in a small bowl until smooth. Set aside to cool. Combine the sour cream, eggs, and vanilla in a medium mixing bowl and beat lightly with a fork. Set aside.

3. Combine the flour, granulated sugar, brown sugar, baking soda, and salt in a large mixing bowl. Add the butter and, with an electric mixer fitted with the paddle attachment, mix on low speed until the butter pieces are no larger than small peas.

4. Stir in about two-thirds of the egg mixture and mix on low speed until all the ingredients are moistened. Scrape down the sides of the mixer bowl with a rubber spatula and mix on medium-high speed for 1 minute. Stir in the remaining egg mixture on low speed until combined. Scrape down the sides of the bowl again and mix on medium-high speed again for another 30 seconds. Add the cocoa mixture and beat on medium-high speed until combined, scraping down the sides of the bowl once or twice as necessary.

 A Good Excuse to Make Devil's Food Cupcakes

When you don't want to make brownies or cookies for a bake sale, these always-popular cupcakes are a luscious alternative.

5. Scrape the batter into the prepared pans and smooth the tops with a rubber spatula. Bake until a toothpick inserted in the center comes out clean, about 20 minutes for cupcakes, 30 to 35 minutes for layer cake. Let the cake cool in the pan for about 5 minutes, invert it onto a wire rack, and then turn it right side up on a rack to cool completely.

Devil's Food Layer Cake or Cupcakes will keep, wrapped in plastic, at room temperature for up to 1 day or refrigerated for up to 3 days. Frost as desired.

Muffins into Cupcakes

What's the difference between a cupcake and a muffin? Not much. Muffins are made from a thicker batter than are classic cupcakes, so they can handle all kinds of goodies that you might want to stir in. You may transform many of the muffins in Mom's Café: Muffins, Quick Breads, Biscuits, and Scones into cupcakes simply by frosting them. Here are some suggestions:

* Best Blueberry Muffins (page 49) with Quick "Crème Fraîche" (page 229)
* Lemon-Ginger Muffins (page 53) with Quick "Crème Fraîche" (page 229)
* Pumpkin Spice Muffins (page 54) with Cream Cheese and Butter Frosting (page 228)
* Chocolate Chip Muffins (page 55; skip the Cinnamon-Sugar topping) with Chocolate Butter Icing (page 227)
* Raspberry-Cornmeal Muffins (page 58) with Vanilla Whipped Cream (page 230)

coconut cream layer cake or cupcakes

Makes two 9-inch cake layers

Coconut milk can be found in the Asian or Latin foods aisle of the supermarket. Coconut extract should be in the baking aisle, near the vanilla. Fill with Coconut Custard Filling (page 229) and frost with Vanilla Whipped Cream (page 230). To decorate the cake, toast ½ cup sweetened flaked coconut on a baking sheet in a preheated 350-degree oven until golden, let cool completely, and press the toasted coconut onto the sides of the frosted cake.

Nonstick cooking spray
3 large eggs, at room temperature
1 cup unsweetened coconut milk (not cream of coconut), at room temperature
2 teaspoons pure coconut extract
1 teaspoon pure vanilla extract
2 cups cake flour (not self-rising)
1½ cups sugar
2½ teaspoons baking powder
½ teaspoon salt
1 cup (2 sticks) unsalted butter, softened and cut into 16 pieces

1. Preheat the oven to 350 degrees. Coat the inside of two 9-inch cake pans with cooking spray. Line the bottom and sides with parchment paper and coat that with spray as well. Dust the bottom and sides of the pans with flour, knocking out any extra flour. For cupcakes, coat the inside of the muffin tins with cooking spray and dust with flour, or line the muffin tins with paper liners.

2. Combine the eggs, coconut milk, and extracts in a medium mixing bowl and beat together lightly with a fork. Set aside.

3. Combine the flour, sugar, baking powder, and salt in a large mixing bowl. Add the butter and mix on low speed with an electric mixer fitted with the paddle attachment until the butter pieces are no larger than small peas.

4. Stir in about two-thirds of the egg mixture on low speed until all the ingredients are moistened. Scrape down the sides of the bowl with a rubber spatula and mix on medium-high speed for 1 minute. Stir in the remaining egg mixture on low speed until combined. Scrape down the sides of the bowl again and mix on medium-high speed again for another 30 seconds.

5. Scrape the batter evenly into the prepared pans and smooth the top with a rubber spatula. Bake until the cake is light golden and a toothpick inserted in the center comes out clean, about 20 minutes for cupcakes, 25 to 30 minutes for layer cake. Let the cake cool in the pan for about 5 minutes, invert it onto a wire rack, and then turn it right side up on a rack to cool completely.

Coconut Cream Layer Cake or Cupcakes will keep, wrapped in plastic, at room temperature for up to 1 day or refrigerated for up to 3 days. Frost as desired.

strawberry cupcakes with vanilla whipped cream and strawberry roses

Makes 12 cupcakes

A dozen small strawberries carved into "roses" make a simple but special garnish for these birthday cupcakes with the classic flavors of berries and cream.

Nonstick cooking spray (optional)
1½ cups unbleached all-purpose flour
1 teaspoon baking powder
¼ teaspoon salt
¾ cup sugar, plus more for dipping the strawberries
13 tablespoons unsalted butter, softened
3 large eggs
1 teaspoon pure vanilla extract
¼ cup best-quality strawberry jam
12 small strawberries, washed and stems trimmed
1 recipe Vanilla Whipped Cream (page 230)

1. Preheat the oven to 350 degrees. Line a 12-cup muffin tin with paper liners or coat the tins with cooking spray.

2. Combine the flour, baking powder, and salt in a medium mixing bowl. Combine the sugar and butter in a large mixing bowl and beat with an electric mixer on medium-high speed until fluffy, 3 to 5 minutes, scraping down the sides of the bowl once or twice as necessary. Add the eggs one at a time and beat until well mixed, scraping down the sides of the bowl after each addition. Add the vanilla and beat until smooth. Pour in the dry ingredients. Beat on medium-high speed, scraping down the sides of the bowl once or twice, for 2 to 3 minutes.

3. Fill each muffin cup about one-third full. Drop 1 teaspoon of jam onto the center of each cupcake. Top each cupcake with the remaining batter so that muffin cups are two-thirds full. Bake the cupcakes until they are pale golden, 17 to 19 minutes. Let them cool in the pan for about 5 minutes, invert them onto a wire rack, and then turn them right side up on a rack to cool completely.

4. To carve the strawberry roses, with a sharp paring knife, make two small cuts on either side on the upper third (the stem end) of each berry and shave two "petals" away from the center. Bend the cut sections slightly away from the center of the berry, leaving the bottoms of the petals attached. Make four similar cuts underneath and a little bit to the side of the upper cuts.

5. Just before serving, top each cupcake with a generous dollop of Vanilla Whipped Cream. Dip each strawberry "rose" in sugar and place it on top of the whipped cream on each cupcake.

Wrap unfrosted cupcakes individually in plastic and then aluminum foil and freeze them for up to 1 month.

A Good Excuse to Make Strawberry Cupcakes

These are perfect for a birthday in June (or whenever strawberries are in season near you).

brownie cupcake sundaes with peanut butter–caramel sauce

If you are baking cupcakes for a brownie lover, this is your recipe. These cupcakes are dense and fudgy, rather than light and tender like Devil's Food Cupcakes. Homemade Caramel Sauce (page 233) may be substituted for the Peanut Butter–Caramel Sauce if you like. These cupcakes are cute garnished with a Chocolate-Dipped Pretzel (page 235).

Nonstick cooking spray (optional)
6 tablespoons (¾ stick) unsalted butter, cut into 6 pieces
7 ounces semisweet or bittersweet chocolate, finely chopped
¾ cup unbleached all-purpose flour
¼ cup unsweetened Dutch-process cocoa powder
½ teaspoon baking powder
⅛ teaspoon salt
3 large eggs
1 cup sugar
1 teaspoon pure vanilla extract
¾ cup chopped unsalted peanuts (optional)
Vanilla ice cream
Peanut Butter–Caramel Sauce (page 234)

1. Preheat the oven to 350 degrees. Line a 12-cup muffin tin with paper liners or coat the tins with cooking spray.

2. Put 1 inch of water in the bottom of a double boiler or medium saucepan and bring to a bare simmer. Combine the butter and chocolate in the top of the double boiler or in a stainless-steel bowl and set it on top of the simmering water, making sure that the water doesn't touch the bottom of the bowl. Heat, whisking occasionally, until the chocolate and butter are completely melted. Set aside to cool slightly.

3. Combine the flour, cocoa powder, baking powder, and salt in a medium mixing bowl.

4. Whisk together the eggs and sugar in a large mixing bowl. With a wooden spoon, stir in the chocolate mixture and vanilla. Stir in the flour mixture until just combined. Stir in ½ cup of the peanuts if desired.

5. Fill each muffin cup about three-quarters full. Bake the cupcakes until the tops are dry, 18 to 20 minutes. Let them cool in the pan for about 5 minutes, invert them onto a wire rack, and then turn them right side up on a rack to cool completely.

6. Place the cupcakes in dessert bowls alongside a scoop of vanilla ice cream. Pour some warm Peanut Butter–Caramel Sauce over each portion, sprinkle each cupcake with some of the remaining ¼ cup chopped peanuts, if desired, and serve immediately.

Wrap unfrosted cupcakes individually in plastic and then aluminum foil and freeze them for up to 1 month.

granola cupcakes with orange cream cheese frosting

Makes 12 cupcakes Officially, these are healthy, since they are made with toasted rolled oats. They are perfect for a birthday party in a nutrition-conscious schoolroom. Chopped pecans or almonds may be substituted for the walnuts.

Nonstick cooking spray (optional)
10 tablespoons (1¼ sticks) unsalted butter, softened
½ cup old-fashioned rolled oats (not instant)
½ cup finely chopped walnuts
1 cup unbleached all-purpose flour
2 teaspoons baking powder
¼ teaspoon salt
1 cup sugar
2 large eggs
⅔ cup whole milk
2 teaspoons pure vanilla extract
Cream Cheese and Honey Frosting made with orange zest (page 228)

1. Preheat the oven to 350 degrees. Line a 12-cup muffin tin with paper liners or coat the muffin tins with cooking spray.

2. Melt 2 tablespoons of the butter. Spread the oats and walnuts on a baking sheet and toss with the melted butter to coat. Bake until the mixture is fragrant and lightly toasted, stirring once or twice, 10 to 12 minutes. Let the mixture cool completely.

3. Combine the flour, baking powder, and salt in a medium mixing bowl. Stir in the cooled oats and nuts. Combine the sugar and remaining 8 tablespoons (1 stick) butter in a large mixing bowl and beat with an electric mixer on medium-high speed until fluffy, 3 to 5 minutes, scraping down the sides of the bowl once or twice as necessary. Add the eggs one at a time and beat until well mixed, scraping down the sides of the bowl after each addition. Add the milk and vanilla and beat until smooth. Stir in the dry ingredients. Beat on medium-high speed, scraping down the sides of the bowl once or twice, for 2 to 3 minutes.

4. Fill each cup about two-thirds full. Bake the cupcakes until they are golden and a toothpick inserted in the center comes out clean, 18 to 20 minutes. Let them cool in the pan for about 5 minutes, invert them onto a wire rack, and then turn them right side up on a rack to cool completely.

5. Spread each cupcake with some Cream Cheese and Honey Frosting. Frosted cupcakes will keep in an airtight container at room temperature for up to 2 days.

Wrap unfrosted cupcakes individually in plastic and then aluminum foil and freeze them for up to 1 month.

Frosting and Decorating Layer Cakes

I am a big fan of the homemade look when it comes to frosted and decorated cakes. I prefer simple cakes for aesthetic reasons; cakes that look homemade are just more charming to me than are perfectly finished bakery cakes. And I prefer simple cakes for practical reasons; even though I went to cooking school, I'm just not as skilled as I should be with a pastry bag, and I'd rather make a polka-dot cake with Necco wafers for my two-year-old than attempt to pipe Elmo and disappoint everyone.

That said, there are a few things you can do so that your guests will realize that the thing you carry out to the table is actually a cake, with a flat rather than a domed top, nice straight sides, and maybe a couple of flourishes to mark whatever occasion you are celebrating:

* **Trim about ¼ inch from the sides of each layer with a sharp serrated knife.** Trim the top off each layer so that each layer is relatively flat. Trimming accomplishes two things: It gets rid of the sometimes tough or rubbery skin on the outside of the layers, and it evens out the layers and makes it easier to apply frosting evenly to the sides. Another benefit—you can snack on the scraps before you frost the cake. I've tried magic cake strips—the ones you wrap around the pans before placing them in the oven so that your layers will bake up evenly rather than rounded—and they have never worked for me. Cutting off the domed parts of the layers is the only way you will get a flat-topped cake.

* **Cut out a heavy-duty cardboard circle** the same size as your cake pan to serve as a base for your cake. You can buy these circles from a baking supply store or from a baking catalogue (see Mail-Order and Online Resources, page 273), but it's just as easy to use the bottom of a box. Cover the circle with aluminum foil.

* **Place a tablespoon or so of frosting on the cardboard** circle and place the bottom layer on the frosting, trimmed side up. The frosting applied to the circle will prevent your cake from sliding around as you frost it. Spread whatever filling you are using over the bottom layer, and place the second layer on top of the filling, cut side down. This configuration should give you the flattest top possible. About ¼ to ⅓ inch of the cardboard circle should be peeking out all around the bottom of the cake. This is how thick the frosting on the sides of your cake should be.

* **If you are filling the cake** with the same frosting you are using on the outside, it doesn't matter if some oozes out from the layers. If, however, you are filling the cake with something different, you don't want the filling to ooze out the sides and mix with the frosting. So if you are using a different filling, don't spread it to the edge of the layer. Leave at least a ½-inch border to allow the filling to spread without leaking when you place the second layer on top.

* **Lightly dust the tops** and sides of the cake with a pastry brush to remove the loose crumbs. This will help prevent any stray crumbs from sticking to the icing.

* **To frost a cake:** Place the cardboard-supported cake on the counter and spoon about 1½ cups of frosting on top. Using an offset spatula, spread the frosting

across the top of the cake and all the way to the edges. Run the spatula back and forth over the cake until the frosted top looks flat and none of the cake is peeking through. Now here's the hard part: Carefully pick up the cake and balance it in the palm of your left hand (or right, if you're left-handed). Working over the frosting bowl (so that when some frosting falls from the cake or spatula as you're working, it will fall back into the bowl), apply the frosting thickly to the sides in sections, rotating the cake with your left hand as you work. To smooth the sides, hold the edge of the spatula perpendicular to the side of the cake and run it around the cake, again rotating the cake with your left hand, scraping the excess frosting back into the bowl as necessary. Use the cardboard round as your guide. The frosting should come just to the edge of the cardboard. If you hold the spatula straight up as you rotate the cake, the frosted sides of your cake should turn out more or less straight. Place the cake on a serving platter. Run the spatula over the top to even out the top edges.

Frosting a cake with one hand while holding the cake in the palm of your other hand takes some concentration and practice, but it really works. Try to frost your cake when there's not much else going on in the kitchen.

A child tugging at your apron (I highly recommend that you wear one) or a dog pawing at your feet for a walk may result in the cake falling to the floor.

* **Invest in a great cake stand** or plate. A pretty cake stand compensates for an imperfect frosting job.

* **To decorate a cake:** Press shredded coconut, chopped nuts, or finely chopped chocolate against the sides of the cake. If you are using chocolate, work quickly, before it has a chance to melt against your hand.

* **Place fresh flowers around the base** of the cake. I don't like to decorate the cake itself with fresh flowers because not all flowers are edible, and even edible flowers (pansies, nasturtiums, roses, and violets are all edible) may have been treated with pesticides.

* **If you are making a cake for a children's party,** try decorating the cake with candy. I've already mentioned Necco wafers. They make pretty multicolored polka dots on a cake frosted with Vanilla or Chocolate Birthday Cake Frosting (pages 225 and 226). Gum drops, M&Ms, and nonpareils are also good choices. My daughters are both fiends for sprinkles, and I've used cake stencils to create patterns with

multicolored sprinkles on top of their cakes. I try to use candy that won't taste too awful with the cake. Red Hots might be cute for a Valentine's Day Cake, but I wouldn't use them because I can't imagine that their spicy flavor would complement any of my recipes. In general, I like minimally decorated cakes, and this is especially true when I'm using candy. You don't want a cake completely encrusted with candy. But do make sure that you have enough candy on your cake so that each child's piece of cake will have a piece of candy.

* **Even if you have never used a pastry bag,** you can probably pipe pearls around the top edge of the cake and around the base. Use a plain number 10 or number 12 tip. Hold the bag perpendicular with the tip about ½ inch from the surface of the cake. Squeeze until you've got a pearl about ½ inch in diameter. Stop squeezing before you lift the tip from the pearl, so you don't get a little point on top. Repeat around the base of the cake, holding the bag at a 45-degree angle and placing the tip about ½-inch from the bottom edge of the cake.

* **Depending on how many you use** and how pretty they are, birthday candles can be wonderful decorations. Pick up unusual candles when you see them.

Pastry Bag Basics

Piping with a pastry bag takes some practice, but once you get the hang of it, it's a lot of fun to write names or pipe simple borders with extra frosting tinted with food coloring to contrast with the frosting on your cake. You can buy plastic-coated canvas bags that are reusable, but I prefer disposable plastic bags for convenience (see Mail-Order and Online Resources, page 273). Here are a few hints to get you started:

* **Place a piping tip in the bag** and fill the bag just halfway to the top. If you fill it more than halfway, you'll have trouble twisting it closed, and your frosting will come out the top and get all over your hands.

* **Push the frosting toward the bottom** of the bag by holding the top of the bag closed with one hand and sliding the fingers of your other hand down the sides of the bag toward the bottom. Once the frosting is all in the bottom half of the bag, twist the bag tightly several times to seal it.

* **To pipe, hold the bag in your right hand** (or left, if you're left-handed), grasping it with your thumb and forefinger at the point where you've twisted it. Use the other three fingers to squeeze the frosting from the bag. Use your other hand to steady the bottom of the bag as you move it over the cake. Practice a few times by piping a bit of a border or a name on a plate. You can always scrape the frosting back into your frosting bowl and reuse it.

* **Large tips make quick work of decorating**, but if you want a more delicate look for your pearls, stars, and rosettes, you may use small tips with Vanilla Birthday Cake Frosting (opposite) and Chocolate Birthday Cake Frosting (page 226). With whipped cream, stick with tips that are at least ¼ inch in diameter. Forcing whipped cream through smaller tips will deflate it.

vanilla birthday cake frosting

Makes enough
to fill and frost
two 9-inch cake layers
or 24 cupcakes

This frosting is very sweet (a pound of powdered sugar will do that), and most kids love it. It's also very easy to make and very easy to work with. It pipes beautifully, if you'd like to try your hand at polka dots or pearls (see Pastry Bag Basics, opposite). If you want to add a drop or two of food coloring, you can frost your cake in pastel pink, blue, violet, green or yellow. Meringue powder is available in the baking aisle of most supermarkets and by mail (see Mail-Order and Online Resources, page 273).

1 cup (2 sticks) unsalted butter, softened
2 teaspoons pure vanilla extract
¼ teaspoon salt
One 16-ounce box confectioners' sugar
1 tablespoon meringue powder
1 tablespoon whole or lowfat milk

1. Combine the butter, vanilla, and salt in a large mixing bowl. With an electric mixer on medium-high speed, beat until the butter is fluffy, scraping down the sides of the bowl several times as necessary.

2. Add the confectioners' sugar ½ cup at a time, mixing on low speed after each addition so that the sugar doesn't fly out of the bowl. When all the sugar has been mixed into the butter, stir in the meringue powder.

3. Add the milk and beat on high speed, scraping down the sides of the bowl once or twice as necessary, until the frosting is light and fluffy, about 5 minutes.

4. Use the frosting immediately, or refrigerate it, wrapped in plastic, for up to 1 week. Bring it to room temperature and re-whip before using.

chocolate birthday cake frosting

**Makes enough
to fill and frost
two 9-inch cake layers
or 24 cupcakes**

The chocolate version of Birthday Cake Frosting is equally simple and wonderfully spreadable. When I cover a cake with this frosting, I like to spell out "Happy Birthday" with tiny nonpareil candies, and maybe use larger ones to make a border around the bottom of the cake.

1 cup (2 sticks) unsalted butter, softened

2 teaspoons pure vanilla extract

¼ teaspoon salt

One 16-ounce box confectioners' sugar

1 tablespoon meringue powder

3 to 4 tablespoons whole or lowfat milk, as needed

4 ounces unsweetened chocolate, melted and cooled

1. Combine the butter, vanilla, and salt in a large mixing bowl. With an electric mixer on medium-high speed, beat until the butter is fluffy, scraping down the sides of the bowl several times as necessary.

2. Add the confectioners' sugar ½ cup at a time, mixing on low speed after each addition so that the sugar doesn't fly out of the bowl. When all the sugar has been mixed into the butter, stir in the meringue powder.

3. Add the milk and melted chocolate and beat on high speed, scraping down the sides of the bowl once or twice as necessary, until the frosting is light and fluffy, about 5 minutes.

4. Use the frosting immediately, or refrigerate it, wrapped in plastic, for up to 1 week. Bring it to room temperature and re-whip it before using.

chocolate butter icing

Makes enough to fill and frost two 9-inch cake layers or 16 cupcakes

This is classic, shiny chocolate icing for vanilla or devil's food cake. If the icing gets too stiff to spread, microwave it for 20 to 30 seconds and whisk it until it is smooth and spreadable.

1 pound bittersweet or semisweet chocolate, finely chopped
1 cup (2 sticks) unsalted butter, cut into 16 pieces
½ cup light corn syrup
½ teaspoon salt

1. Put 2 inches of water in the bottom of a double boiler or in a medium saucepan and bring to a bare simmer. Combine the chocolate, butter, corn syrup, and salt in the top of the double boiler or in a stainless steel bowl big enough to rest on top of the saucepan, and set it on top of the simmering water, making sure that the water doesn't touch the bottom of the bowl. Heat, whisking occasionally, until the chocolate is completely melted.

2. Place the bowl on top of a larger bowl of ice water and let stand, stirring occasionally, until the frosting is spreadable, 15 to 20 minutes.

3. Use immediately, or refrigerate it, covered with plastic, for up to 1 day, microwave for 20 to 30 seconds, and then whisk until spreadable.

milk chocolate ganache

Makes about 2 cups, enough to glaze an angel food cake. Whipped, it will frost (not fill) two 9-inch cake layers or 18 cupcakes

Kids love vanilla (or granola) cupcakes frosted with this rich but kid-friendly ganache. Also try it as a simple tart filling (Milk Chocolate Ganache Tart, page 190).

10 ounces best-quality milk chocolate, such as Lindt, finely chopped
2 tablespoons unsweetened Dutch-process cocoa powder
1 cup heavy cream

1. Combine the chocolate and cocoa in a large mixing bowl. Bring the heavy cream just to a boil in a small saucepan over medium-low heat. Pour the hot cream into the bowl and let the mixture stand for 5 minutes. Whisk until smooth.

2. Pour the ganache through a strainer into a clean bowl. To use it as glaze, let the ganache cool to lukewarm and pour it over angel food cake. To whip it, first let it come to room temperature, until it is slightly thickened, about 1 hour. Then whip it with an electric mixer on medium-high speed until the ganache holds soft peaks, 2 to 3 minutes.

cream cheese and honey frosting

Makes 1¼ cups, enough to frost 1 pound cake, 12 cupcakes or muffins, or 1 pan of carrot cake squares

If you love the distinctive flavor of honey, try this frosting. It goes especially well with Cornmeal-Orange Pound Cake (page 202) and Carrot Cake Squares (page 204).

One 8-ounce package cream cheese, softened
¼ cup honey
½ teaspoon grated lemon zest or 1 teaspoon grated orange zest (optional)

1. Place the cream cheese in a medium mixing bowl. With an electric mixer, beat the cream cheese on medium-high speed until light and fluffy, 2 to 3 minutes, scraping down the sides of the bowl once or twice as necessary. Add the honey and beat again until combined.

2. Use immediately, or refrigerate it, wrapped in plastic, for up to 5 days. Re-beat to soften it before using.

cream cheese and butter frosting

Makes 1½ cups, enough to frost 12 cupcakes or muffins, or 1 pan of carrot cake squares

Classic cream cheese frosting adds richness to a variety of cakes.

One 8-ounce package cream cheese, softened
¼ cup (½ stick) unsalted butter, softened
1 cup confectioners' sugar
½ teaspoon pure vanilla extract
½ teaspoon grated lemon zest or 1 teaspoon grated orange zest (optional)

1. Combine the cream cheese and butter in a large mixing bowl. With an electric mixer, beat on medium-high speed until the mixture is light and fluffy, 3 to 4 minutes, scraping down the sides of the bowl as necessary.

2. With the mixer on low speed, add the confectioners' sugar several tablespoons at a time until all the sugar is combined, scraping down the sides of the bowl as necessary. Stir in the vanilla and zest, if you are using it. Turn the mixer to high speed and beat until very smooth, 3 to 4 minutes.

3. Use immediately, or refrigerate it, wrapped in plastic, for up to 1 week, and let the frosting come to room temperature before using.

quick "crème fraîche"

Makes about
2 cups, enough to frost
a single-layer cake or
12 cupcakes

Real crème fraîche, heavy cream made slightly tangy when combined with buttermilk and set aside, can take up to 2 days of waiting. Since I often decide on the spur of the moment to make a cake, I substitute this mixture of cream and sour cream, which can be made in an instant.

¾ cup heavy cream, chilled
5 tablespoons full-fat sour cream
2 tablespoons confectioners' sugar

1. Combine the heavy cream, sour cream, and sugar in a medium mixing bowl. With an electric mixer fitted with a whisk attachment, beat the mixture until it holds soft peaks. Do not overbeat.

2. Use immediately or refrigerate, wrapped in plastic, for up to 8 hours. Whisk it a few times by hand to aerate it before using.

coconut custard filling

Makes about
1½ cups, enough to fill
a 9-inch 2-layer cake

This recipe is adapted from one developed by my friend Roland Mesnier, who has been the pastry chef at the White House for almost twenty-five years. He is justly famous for the fantastic special occasion desserts he has served to Presidents and other heads of state, but he has also baked countless home-style birthday cakes for First Family members. Unsweetened shredded coconut is available in natural foods stores and many supermarkets.

½ cup evaporated milk
½ cup sugar
1 large egg
¼ cup (½ stick) unsalted butter
½ cup unsweetened shredded coconut
½ teaspoon pure vanilla extract

1. Combine the evaporated milk, sugar, egg, and butter in a medium saucepan and cook over medium heat, whisking constantly, until it thickens, 3 to 4 minutes.

2. Remove the pan from the heat and press the mixture through a fine strainer into a nonreactive bowl (stainless-steel, glass, or ceramic). Stir in the coconut and vanilla. Refrigerate the filling, wrapped in plastic, until chilled and very thick, at least 3 hours, before using.

vanilla whipped cream

Makes enough to frost
(not fill) two 9-inch cake
layers or 16 cupcakes

Whipped cream is one of the simplest and best cake frostings. If you ever see pasteurized organic cream, buy it. It whips up lighter and tastes fresher than the more common ultra-pasteurized type. Whatever type of cream you use, make sure your cream is well chilled before you whip it. Place the mixing bowl and whisk attachment in the freezer for 5 minutes as insurance.

1½ cups heavy cream, chilled
3 tablespoons confectioners' sugar
1 teaspoon pure vanilla extract

1. Combine the cream, sugar, and vanilla in a large mixing bowl. With an electric mixer fitted with a whisk attachment, whip on high speed until the cream just holds stiff peaks. Do not overwhip.

2. Use immediately, or refrigerate it, wrapped in plastic wrap, for up to 6 hours. Whisk it again for a couple of seconds before using.

Flavoring Whipped Cream

Vanilla is classic, but whipped cream can also be flavored with ½ teaspoon of pure almond, rum, maple, or coconut extract (these extracts are more intense than vanilla, so less is needed). Liqueurs are another option. Use up to 1½ tablespoons of coffee, hazelnut, orange, or raspberry liqueur for a more sophisticated and adult whipped cream.

lemon curd

Makes about
1¼ cups, enough to fill
1 layer cake

This versatile filling can also be used to fill tartlets or garnish slices of pound cake.

3 large eggs
6 tablespoons sugar
1 teaspoon grated lemon zest
6 tablespoons strained fresh lemon
  juice
¼ cup (½ stick) unsalted butter, cut
  into 8 pieces

1. Combine the eggs, sugar, and lemon zest in a medium heavy saucepan and whisk until smooth. Add the lemon juice and butter and cook over medium heat, whisking constantly, until the mixture is thickened, 7 to 9 minutes. Do not allow the mixture to come to a boil.

2. Pour the lemon curd through a fine strainer into a glass bowl or measuring cup. Cover the surface with plastic wrap. Refrigerate until the lemon curd is cold and thick, at least 3 hours and for up to 3 days, before using.

How to Grate Lemon Zest

Grating lemon zest is a pain, but it's the best way to add lemon flavor to baked goods. Use a box grater placed over a large cutting board. Hold the handle of the grater with one hand and hold the lemon in the other hand and scrape the lemon along the side with the smallest holes. Remove only the yellow rind, not the bitter white pith below. Tape the edge of the grater against the cutting board to remove the zest. Scrape any remaining zest from the grater with the tip of a paring knife. Gather together the zest by scraping it into a small pile on the cutting board with the blade of the knife.

espresso-bourbon glaze

Makes enough to glaze 1 bundt or angel food cake

This is a very simple glaze, good for drizzling over Bundt-style cakes.

6 tablespoons (¾ stick) unsalted butter, cut into 6 pieces
6 tablespoons firmly packed light brown sugar
2 teaspoons instant espresso powder
6 tablespoons heavy cream
1½ cups confectioners' sugar, sifted
2 tablespoons bourbon

1. Stir the butter, brown sugar, and espresso powder together in a small saucepan over medium heat until the butter melts. Stir in the heavy cream. Simmer for 1 minute. Remove from the heat.

2. Gradually add the confectioners' sugar, whisking until smooth. Mix in the bourbon. Let the glaze cool slightly before using.

hot fudge sauce

Makes about 1½ cups

Use this hot fudge sauce on brownie cupcake sundaes or angel food cake with ice cream.

¼ cup sugar
2 tablespoons unsweetened Dutch-process cocoa powder
¾ cup heavy cream
½ cup light corn syrup
2 ounces semisweet chocolate, coarsely chopped
2 tablespoons unsalted butter
1 teaspoon pure vanilla extract
⅛ teaspoon salt

1. Combine the sugar, cocoa powder, heavy cream, and corn syrup in a medium-size heavy saucepan and whisk to combine. Add the chocolate and butter and bring to a boil over medium-high heat, whisking constantly. Reduce the heat to medium-low and gently boil, without stirring, for 5 minutes.

2. Remove the pan from the heat and stir in the vanilla and salt.

3. Use immediately, or refrigerate for up to 2 weeks and reheat in a saucepan over medium-low heat, or in a microwave, before serving.

homemade caramel sauce

Homemade Caramel Sauce will keep in an airtight container at room temperature for several weeks.

½ cup sugar
2 tablespoons water
2 tablespoons unsalted butter
¼ cup heavy cream
1 teaspoon pure vanilla extract
⅛ teaspoon salt

1. Combine the sugar and water in a small saucepan. Bring to a boil and cook until the mixture turns a light amber color. Do not stir. If parts of the syrup are turning darker than others, gently tilt the pan to even out the cooking.

2. As soon as the syrup is a uniformly amber color, stir in the butter and heavy cream with a long-handled wooden spoon. The mixture will bubble up. Remove the pan from the heat and stir in the vanilla and salt.

3. Pour the sauce into a heat-proof measuring cup and let stand until the glaze is tepid and still pourable.

4. Use immediately or pour into a container, cover tightly, and keep at room temperature for up to 2 weeks. Reheat the sauce in the microwave or on the stovetop until warm and pourable.

peanut butter–caramel sauce

Makes about 1¼ cups For peanut butter fans, here's a wonderful variation on caramel sauce.

½ cup sugar
2 tablespoons water
1 cup heavy cream
⅓ cup natural smooth peanut butter
1 teaspoon pure vanilla extract

1. Combine the sugar and water in a small saucepan. Bring to a boil and cook until the mixture turns a light amber color. Do not stir. If parts of the syrup are turning darker than others, gently tilt the pan to even out the cooking.

2. As soon as the syrup is a uniformly amber color, stir in the heavy cream with a long-handled wooden spoon. The mixture will bubble up. Remove from the heat and stir in the peanut butter until smooth. Stir in the vanilla.

3. Pour the sauce into a heat-proof measuring cup and let stand until the glaze is tepid and still pourable.

4. Use immediately, or pour into a container, cover tightly, and store at room temperature for up to 2 weeks. Reheat in the microwave or on the stovetop until warm and pourable.

chocolate-dipped pretzels

Makes 48 small pretzels

You'll need only a dozen dipped pretzels to decorate a batch of devil's food cupcakes, but dipping some extra handfuls for snacking takes only a few extra minutes.

6 ounces semisweet or bittersweet chocolate
48 small pretzels or pretzel sticks

1. Place a large sheet of wax paper on a baking sheet.

2. Put 1 inch of water into the bottom of a double boiler or a medium saucepan and bring to a bare simmer. Place the chocolate in the top of the double boiler or in a stainless-steel bowl big enough to rest on top of the saucepan, and set it on top of the simmering water, making sure that the water doesn't touch the bottom of the bowl. Heat, whisking occasionally, until the chocolate is completely melted.

3. Remove the chocolate from the heat. Dip each pretzel in the chocolate to coat three-quarters of the way. Let any excess chocolate drip back into the bowl. Place each pretzel on the wax paper to cool completely. Repeat with the remaining pretzels.

Chocolate-Dipped Pretzels will keep in an airtight container at room temperature for up to 2 weeks.

 Kids Can Help

Since I always have the ingredients in my pantry, on rainy days my older daughter and I will often dip pretzels in chocolate just for fun.

ricotta cheesecake

Makes one
9-inch cake;
8 to 10 servings

This is an especially simple cheesecake because it has no crust at all. It is made with ricotta cheese, according to a traditional Italian recipe, and it's lighter and fluffier than New York Cheesecake (opposite).

Nonstick cooking spray
Two 15-ounce containers whole-milk
    ricotta cheese
6 large eggs, at room temperature,
    separated
2/3 cup granulated sugar
2 teaspoons pure vanilla extract
2 teaspoons grated lemon zest
1/2 teaspoon ground cinnamon
Pinch of ground nutmeg
Confectioners' sugar for dusting

1. Preheat the oven to 325 degrees. Coat the inside of a 9-inch springform pan with cooking spray.

2. Place the ricotta cheese in a strainer set over a bowl and let stand for 15 minutes, stirring occasionally, to drain off excess moisture.

3. Place the egg whites in a large mixing bowl and beat on high speed with an electric mixer fitted with a whisk attachment until the whites just hold stiff peaks. Do not overwhip. The whites should look smooth, not grainy.

4. Combine the egg yolks and granulated sugar in another large mixing bowl and beat on high speed until pale yellow, about 5 minutes. Stir in the ricotta, vanilla, lemon zest, cinnamon, and nutmeg until just combined. Fold the egg whites into the ricotta mixture with a rubber spatula. Place the prepared springform pan on a baking sheet and pour in the filling.

5. Bake the cheesecake until it is deep golden brown and pulling away from the sides of the pan, about 1 hour and 20 minutes. As soon as the cake is out of the oven, run a sharp paring knife around the edge of the pan to separate the cheesecake from the sides of the pan. Transfer the pan to a wire rack and let the cheesecake cool completely. Cover it with plastic wrap and refrigerate it until serving, at least 6 hours and up to 1 day.

Before serving, remove the sides of the pan and dust with confectioners' sugar.

new york cheesecake

Makes one 9-inch cake; 8 to 10 servings

Many cheesecake recipes call for baking the cake in a water bath to prevent curdling and cracking. But I find that preheating the oven to a very high temperature and then turning it down when the cake goes in results in a smooth cake without the hassle and without the danger of splashing hot water onto the cake or yourself. Do remember to run a paring knife around the edge of the cake as soon as it comes out of the oven. Separating the cake from the sides of the pan while it is hot will lessen the chance that the cake will crack as it cools and shrinks slightly.

For the graham cracker crust

Nonstick cooking spray
1⅓ cups graham cracker crumbs (about 20 whole graham crackers)
5 tablespoons unsalted butter, melted
2 tablespoons sugar
Pinch of salt

For the filling

Four 8-ounce packages cream cheese, softened
1¼ cups sugar
2 tablespoons unbleached all-purpose flour
4 large eggs, at room temperature
1 teaspoon grated lemon zest
1 teaspoon pure vanilla extract

1. Preheat the oven to 500 degrees.

2. Make the crust: Coat the inside of a 9-inch springform pan with cooking spray. Combine the graham cracker crumbs, melted butter, sugar, and salt in a medium mixing bowl and stir until all the crumbs are moistened. Press the graham cracker mixture evenly across the bottom and 1 inch up the sides of the pan, packing it tightly with your fingertips. Set the crust aside.

3. Make the filling: Combine the softened cream cheese, sugar, and flour in a large mixing bowl and beat with an electric mixer on high speed until very smooth, scraping down the sides of the bowl once or twice as necessary. Add the eggs, one at a time, and mix on low speed until combined, scraping down the sides of the bowl after each addition. Stir in the lemon zest and vanilla.

4. Place the prepared springform pan on a baking sheet and pour in the filling. Place the cheesecake in the oven and bake it for 10 minutes. Without opening the oven door, reduce the oven temperature to 200 degrees and continue to bake the cheesecake until the perimeter is set but the center is still a little jiggly, about 1 hour and 10 minutes. As soon as the cheesecake is out of the oven, run a sharp paring knife around the edge of the pan to separate the cheesecake from the sides of the pan. Set the cheesecake on a wire rack and let it cool completely. Wrap it in plastic, and refrigerate it for at least 6 hours or overnight before unmolding and serving.

New York Cheesecake will keep, wrapped in plastic and refrigerated, for up to 1 week.

chocolate cheesecake

Makes one 9-inch cake; 8 to 10 servings

This is the cheesecake for chocolate fans.

For the chocolate cookie crust

Nonstick cooking spray
1⅓ cups crushed Nabisco Famous Chocolate Wafers (30 cookies)
2 tablespoons sugar
Pinch of salt
5 tablespoons unsalted butter, melted

For the chocolate filling

7 ounces bittersweet chocolate, finely chopped
Three 8-ounce packages cream cheese, softened
¾ cup sugar
4 large eggs, at room temperature
2 teaspoons pure vanilla extract

1. Preheat the oven to 350 degrees.

2. Make the crust: Coat the inside of a 9-inch springform pan with cooking spray. Place the crushed cookies, sugar, and salt in a food processor and grind into fine crumbs. Add the melted butter and process until the crumbs are moistened. Turn the crumb mixture into the pan and press evenly across the bottom and 1 inch up the sides of the pan, packing it tightly with your fingertips. Set aside.

3. Make the filling: Put 2 inches of water in the bottom of a double boiler or in a medium saucepan and bring to a bare simmer. Place the chocolate in the top of the double boiler or in a stainless-steel bowl big enough to rest on top of the saucepan, and set it on top of the simmering water, making sure that the water doesn't touch the bottom of the bowl.

Heat, whisking occasionally, until the chocolate is completely melted. Set aside to cool.

4. Combine the softened cream cheese and sugar in a large mixing bowl and, with an electric mixer, beat on high speed until very smooth, scraping down the sides of the bowl once or twice as necessary. Add the eggs, one at a time, and mix on low speed until combined, scraping down the bowl after each addition. Stir in the melted chocolate and vanilla.

5. Place the prepared springform pan on a baking sheet and pour in the filling. Bake the cheesecake until the perimeter is set but the center is still a little jiggly, about 55 minutes. As soon as the cheesecake is out of the oven, run a sharp paring knife around the edge of the pan to separate the cheesecake from the sides of the pan. Set the cheesecake on a wire rack and let it cool completely. Wrap it in plastic, and refrigerate it for at least 6 hours or overnight before unmolding and serving.

Chocolate Cheesecake will keep, wrapped in plastic and refrigerated, for up to 1 week.

Kids Can Help

Kids with any experience in the sandbox will be good at patting the cookie crumbs into the pan.

pumpkin cheesecake

Makes one 9-inch cake;
8 to 10 servings

This cake can stand in for pumpkin pie on Thanksgiving Day, and no one will complain. I especially like the crust, made from ground store-bought gingersnaps. The spicy flavor of the cookies complements the pumpkin filling.

For the gingersnap crust

Nonstick cooking spray
1⅓ cups crushed gingersnaps
   (25 cookies)
2 tablespoons granulated sugar
Pinch of salt
5 tablespoons unsalted butter, melted

For the pumpkin filling

Three 8-ounce packages cream cheese,
   softened
1 cup firmly packed light brown sugar
¾ teaspoon ground cinnamon
½ teaspoon ground ginger
Pinch of ground nutmeg
3 tablespoons unbleached all-purpose
   flour
4 large eggs, at room temperature
2 teaspoons pure vanilla extract
One 15-ounce can pumpkin purée

1. Preheat the oven to 500 degrees.

2. Make the crust: Coat the inside of a 9-inch springform pan with cooking spray. Place the crushed cookies, granulated sugar, and salt in a food processor and grind into fine crumbs. Add the melted butter and process until the crumbs are moistened. Turn the crumb mixture into the pan and press evenly across the bottom and 1 inch up the sides of the pan, packing it tightly with your fingertips. Set aside.

3. Make the filling: Combine the softened cream cheese, brown sugar, cinnamon, ginger, nutmeg, and flour in a large mixing bowl and, with an electric mixer on high speed, beat until very smooth, scraping down the sides of the bowl once or twice as necessary. Add the eggs, one at a time, and mix on low speed until combined, scraping down the sides of the bowl after each addition. Stir in the vanilla. Stir in the pumpkin purée until just combined.

4. Place the prepared springform pan on a baking sheet and pour in the filling. Place the cheesecake in the oven and bake it for 10 minutes. Without opening the oven door, reduce the oven temperature to 200 degrees and continue to bake the cheesecake until the perimeter is set but the center is still a little jiggly, about 1 hour and 10 minutes. As soon as the cheesecake is out of the oven, run a sharp paring knife around the edge of the pan to separate the cheesecake from the sides of the pan. Set the cheesecake on a wire rack and let it cool completely. Wrap it in plastic, and refrigerate it for at least 6 hours or overnight before unmolding and serving.

Pumpkin Cheesecake will keep, wrapped in plastic and refrigerated, for up to 1 week.

chocolate truffle cake

Makes one 9-inch cake;
10 to 12 servings

When I first developed a version of this recipe for *Instant Gratification*, my five-year-old was amazed. She thought it was made entirely of chocolate frosting. She has since called it the frosting cake. If, like my daughter, you eat the frosting and leave the cake behind, devour truffles, or drink hot fudge sauce when nobody's looking, this is the dessert for you. Three tablespoons of liqueur makes the cake just a little more grown-up, but adding liqueur is entirely optional. I use Grand Marnier, Kahlua, or Frangelico, depending on what I have in the cabinet. Sorry to be a pain, but this cake does need a water bath to ensure its creamy consistency. If the cake is baked without a water bath, the edges will dry out before the center of the cake is cooked through.

Nonstick cooking spray
1 pound bittersweet chocolate, finely
    chopped
1 cup (2 sticks) unsalted butter, cut into
    16 pieces
8 large eggs, at room temperature
3 tablespoons coffee, orange, or
    hazelnut liqueur (optional)
Unsweetened cocoa powder for dusting

1. Preheat the oven to 350 degrees. While you prepare the batter, place a roasting pan in the oven and pour in ½ inch of hot water. Line the sides of a 9-inch springform pan with parchment paper and coat it with cooking spray. Place the pan on a sheet of heavy-duty aluminum foil and mold the foil to the sides of the pan, but not over the top, to prevent water from seeping in.

2. Put 2 inches of water in the bottom of a double boiler or in a medium saucepan and bring to a bare simmer. Place the chocolate and butter in the top of the double boiler or in a stainless-steel bowl big enough to rest on top of the saucepan, and set it on top of the simmering water, making sure that the water doesn't touch the bottom of the bowl. Heat, whisking occasionally, until the chocolate and butter are completely melted. Set aside to cool.

3. Break the eggs in a medium mixing bowl and whisk to break up. Slowly whisk the eggs into the chocolate mixture until well combined. Stir in the liqueur if desired. Scrape the batter into the prepared pan.

4. Carefully place the cake pan into the roasting pan of hot water and bake until the cake is set around the edges but still loose in the center, about 30 minutes. With oven mitts, carefully lift the cake pan from the water and set it on a wire rack to cool. Cover the cake with plastic wrap and refrigerate it overnight.

5. To serve, remove the springform pan sides, invert the cake onto a sheet of waxed paper, peel off the parchment, and turn the cake right side up onto a serving platter. Dust with cocoa powder.

Chocolate Truffle Cake will keep, wrapped in plastic and refrigerated, for up to 1 week.

 ### A Good Excuse to Make Chocolate Truffle Cake

This is one of the simplest recipes in the chapter, and it is perfect for holidays and entertaining. There is no longer an excuse to buy a rich and expensive dessert at a bakery.

YEAST IS YOUR FRIEND: basic bread and pizza

CLOCKWISE FROM TOP LEFT: Pan Pizza with Turkey Sausage and Peppers, Broccoli and Three-Cheese Pizza with Whole-Wheat Pizza crust, Fresh Tomato and Parmesan Pizza

When you glimpse the familiar box of baking

soda in your cabinet, you might think comforting thoughts about Sour Cream Coffee Bundt Cake. You probably don't become anxious, the way you might when confronted with an envelope of yeast. Yet yeast is almost as simple to use as baking soda. Mix yeast with warm water, stir it into some flour and a few other ingredients and a couple of hours later you have bread—or pizza dough, sticky buns, doughnuts, focaccia. Without yeast, you can't make any of them.

Yeast-related anxiety—fear that only professional bakers can produce good bread, that homemade bread will take all day, that kneading requires the strength of a professional wrestler, that the temperature of the water or kitchen or oven will kill the yeast—is irrational. If you suffer from this syndrome, as I once did, try one of the simple recipes in this chapter and you will be cured.

Here are a few things I tell myself to relax:

I'm not trying to replicate the world-class baguettes from Poilane in Paris or the sourdough loaves from La Brea Bakery in L.A. If I were, I'd be frustrated as well as anxious. I don't have a wood-burning oven or a starter whose origins can be traced back to the nineteenth century. I'm going for something a little more elemental—bread with character that can be made, start to finish, in a couple of hours and eaten straight from my own oven. The Sicilian fennel and yellow raisin bread from Amy's Breads in New York City is divine, but so is my multigrain loaf when I'm standing at my counter and spreading still-warm slices with peanut butter and jam.

Bread does not have to take all day. None of my breads begins with a time-consuming sponge. They are all straight doughs, and all the ingredients are mixed together at one time. I always use rapid-rise yeast; it can cut rising time almost in half. (You can use regular active dry yeast; rising times will just be longer.) I've stopped wasting time fantasizing about the focaccia I had in Florence before I was married. Instead, I get to work and give my kids a taste of Italy by making Sweet Focaccia with Grapes in just about two hours.

Kneading dough takes muscle, but don't fret if you haven't been to the gym since you got pregnant. I don't have the forearms of a professional wrestler, but I have a food processor with bulging biceps that does the hard work for me in 30 to 60 seconds. Forget about bannetons, baking stones, pizza peels, or bench scrapers. The only piece of special equipment I absolutely need when making bread is my Cuisinart Deluxe 11-cup machine.

I don't use that other machine—the bread machine—because it just doesn't save me that much work and I don't like the boxy shape of bread machine bread. I either bake my bread in loaf pans or shape the dough by hand.

The array of equipment sold in baking catalogues would suggest that bread making is a science. Scales, thermometers, timers, beakers—they remind me of a laboratory, not a kitchen. But successful bread making couldn't be further from lab science. It depends on intuition and observation, skills that mothers develop out of necessity. You judge the temperature for your child's bath not with a thermometer, but with your hand. Do the same with the water for your bread; it should feel like your kid's bath water, comfortably warm, not hot. You don't use a tape measure or calendar to decide when your child's hair needs a trim; you judge by eye. Look at rising bread dough the same way. Does it look like it's doubled? Then it's time to deflate it.

Recipes using yeast do demand a little more from the baker than do, say, cake recipes, which tell you exactly how much flour to use and can predict, almost to the minute, how long the cake will need to bake. Bread recipes aren't so precise. If it's humid on the day you are baking, you might have to sprinkle a little more flour into your dough to make it come together. If it's 95 degrees outside, your dough might rise in less time than suggested. Recipes give you approximate quantities and rising times, but you have to be the ultimate judge of a dough's readiness at each stage. The more bread you make, the better judge you will be.

Although the pizza recipes come at the end of the chapter, pizza dough is a great place to start if you've never worked with yeast. There's a short ingredient list: just yeast, water, flour, salt, and oil. The dough can be mixed in the food processor in seconds. It's easy to work with. After one short rise, you just divide the dough into two lumps and shape each lump into a rough round. And, of course, you don't have to stand at the oven window worrying that it's not rising enough. You want it to be flat.

Pizza is a family favorite, simple to put together, and nutritionally sound. You can make the dough when you have the chance, freeze it, and then defrost it on the counter for a couple of hours for a quick dinner any time. When you make your own pizza, you can tailor the toppings to suit your tastes. With lean meat or seafood, low-fat cheese, and plentiful vegetables, it becomes a healthy one-dish meal. I've written down recipes for some of my family's favorite pizzas. But pizza dough, like a blank canvas, will inspire you to create your own masterpiece.

I have just one rule for pizza toppings: no low-quality convenience foods on my homemade dough. It's not a Boboli, after all. Instead of using sauce from a jar, take the time to slice some fresh tomatoes or use canned tomatoes to make a simple sauce. Grate your own cheese rather than using pre-grated cheese. Real mozzarella actually tastes like a dairy product instead of rubber. Sprinkle some fresh herbs on your pizza as it comes out of the oven, if your children will tolerate this.

Unlike cookies, brownies, cakes, and pies, which should be consumed in moderation, bread and pizza can be a large and important part of a healthy diet. Making bread is a soul-nourishing activity; homemade bread nourishes our children. These are probably the best reasons for moms to overcome their fear of yeast and get into the bread-baking habit.

fluffy white sandwich bread

Makes one
9-inch loaf

This simple loaf has so much more flavor and character than store-bought white bread. It makes the best tuna or egg salad sandwiches. I toast day-old slices for BLTs made with thick-cut bacon and end-of-summer tomatoes.

1⅓ cups whole milk
1 envelope (2½ teaspoons) rapid-rise
   yeast
3½ cups unbleached
   all-purpose flour, plus more if
   necessary
2 tablespoons sugar
2 teaspoons salt
2 tablespoons unsalted butter, melted
   and cooled
Nonstick cooking spray

1. Heat the milk over low heat in a small saucepan until just warm to the touch. Pour it into a glass measuring cup and whisk in the yeast. Let the mixture stand for 5 minutes to give the yeast a chance to dissolve.

2. Combine the flour, sugar, and salt in a food processor and pulse 2 or 3 times to combine. With the motor running, pour the milk and yeast mixture and cooled melted butter into the feed tube and process until the dough forms a smooth ball, scraping down the sides of the bowl with a rubber spatula once or twice if necessary. To knead the dough, continue to process for 1 minute.

3. Coat the inside of a large mixing bowl with cooking spray. Shape the dough into a rough ball and place it in the bowl. Cover the bowl with plastic wrap and let the dough stand in a warm, draft-free spot until the dough has doubled in size, 1 to 1½ hours.

4. Coat the inside of a 9 x 5-inch loaf pan with cooking spray. Turn the dough onto a lightly floured work surface and gently press it into a rectangle measuring about 1 inch thick and 9 inches long. Tightly roll the rectangle into a 9-inch-long cylinder and place it in the prepared pan, seam side down. Press the dough into the pan so that it touches the sides and reaches into the corners. Cover the pan with plastic wrap and let the dough rise in a warm, draft-free spot until doubled in size, 1 to 1½ hours.

5. Preheat the oven to 350 degrees.

6. Remove the plastic wrap from the loaf pan and place the pan in the oven. Bake the bread until it is golden brown and firm, 40 to 50 minutes. Remove the pan from the oven and turn the bread out onto a wire rack. Let it cool to room temperature before slicing and serving.

Fluffy White Sandwich Bread may be wrapped in plastic and then aluminum foil and frozen for up to 2 weeks.

cinnamon-raisin bread

Makes one 9-inch loaf

Homemade Cinnamon-Raisin Bread is moist and fragrant, nothing like the dry-as-dust supermarket variety. Make sure to roll the dough very tightly so that you get a good swirl, and so that the dough doesn't separate from the filling during baking. Leftovers make very good toast and great French toast.

For the bread

1⅓ cups whole milk
1 envelope (2½ teaspoons)
    rapid rise yeast
3½ cups unbleached all-purpose flour,
    plus more if necessary
2 tablespoons sugar
2 teaspoons salt
2 tablespoons unsalted butter, melted
    and cooled
Nonstick cooking spray

For the filling

1½ cup raisins
2 tablespoons sugar
1½ teaspoons ground cinnamon
1 tablespoon unsalted butter, melted
    and cooled

1. Make the dough: Heat the milk over low heat in a small saucepan until just warm to the touch. Pour it into a bowl or glass measuring cup and whisk in the yeast. Let the mixture stand for 5 minutes to give the yeast a chance to dissolve.

2. Combine the flour, sugar, and salt in a food processor and pulse 2 or 3 times to combine. With the motor running, pour the milk and yeast mixture and the cooled melted butter into the feed tube and process until the dough forms a smooth ball, scraping down the sides of the bowl with a rubber spatula once or twice if necessary. To knead, continue to process for 1 minute.

3. Coat the inside of a large mixing bowl with cooking spray. Shape the dough into a rough ball and place it in the bowl. Cover the bowl with plastic wrap and let the dough stand in a warm, draft-free spot until the dough has doubled in size, 1 to 1½ hours.

4. Make the filling: Place the raisins in a small saucepan and cover them with water. Bring the liquid to a boil, remove the pan from the heat, and let it stand for 5 minutes. Drain the raisins and pat them dry on a paper towel. Set aside. Combine 2 tablespoons sugar and the cinnamon in a small bowl.

5. Coat the inside of a 9 x 5-inch loaf pan with cooking spray. Turn the dough onto a lightly floured work surface and gently press it into a rectangle measuring about 1 inch thick and 9 inches long. Brush the

Kids Can Help

Let your child punch down the dough when you are making this or any other yeasted dough recipe that doesn't contain raw eggs. My older daughter loves to bury her hand in the risen dough and watch it deflate. It's something that involves so many of her senses—she loves the way the dough feels, the sound it makes as it sinks, the yeasty smell.

dough with the 1 tablespoon cooled melted butter. Sprinkle with the cinnamon-sugar. Sprinkle with the raisins. Tightly roll the rectangle into a 9-inch-long cylinder and place it in the prepared pan, seam side down. Press the dough into the pan so that it touches the sides and reaches into the corners. Cover the pan with plastic wrap and let the dough rise in a warm, draft-free spot until doubled in size, 1 to 1½ hours.

6. Preheat the oven to 350 degrees.

7. Remove the plastic wrap from the loaf pan and place the pan in the oven. Bake the bread until it is golden brown and firm, 40 to 50 minutes. Remove the pan from the oven and turn the bread out onto a wire rack. Let it cool to room temperature before slicing and serving.

Cinnamon-Raisin Bread may be wrapped in plastic and then aluminum foil and frozen for up to 2 weeks.

Buying and Storing Yeast

Professional bakers use fresh yeast, which comes in little cakes and must be refrigerated. But active dry yeast, which is easier to store, has a longer shelf life, does the same job as fresh yeast, and is more convenient and easier to use. Active dry yeast should be stored in a cool, dry place. The pantry is fine. If you bake a lot of bread, you may want to buy active dry yeast in a jar instead of purchasing envelopes, which come in packs of three. That way you'll always have yeast on hand. One envelope of active dry yeast contains 2½ teaspoons of yeast, so if you've got a jar of yeast, simply measure that amount from the jar.

The only time I have ever had a problem with active dry yeast is when I inadvertently use a package that has passed its expiration date. Check the expiration date on the yeast before you buy it at the supermarket, and check it again (who knows how long ago you bought it?) before you use it for baking.

multigrain loaf

Makes one 9-inch loaf

My children prefer white bread, but I am a fiend for whole-grain loaves. This bread is simple to make and utterly satisfying. If you can't find rye flakes, whole wheat flour, or flax seeds at your supermarket, look for them at your natural foods store.

1½ cups warm water
1 envelope (2½ teaspoons) rapid-rise yeast
2¼ cups unbleached all-purpose flour
1 cup whole wheat flour
2 teaspoons salt
½ cup rye flakes
½ cup old-fashioned rolled oats (not instant)
¼ cup unsalted sunflower seeds
¼ cup flax seeds
2 tablespoons honey
2 tablespoons vegetable oil
Nonstick cooking spray

1. Measure the water into a glass measuring cup and sprinkle the yeast over the water. Let the mixture stand for 5 minutes to give the yeast a chance to dissolve.

2. Combine the flours, salt, rye flakes, oats, sunflower seeds, and flax seeds in a food processor and pulse 2 or 3 times to combine. With the motor running, pour the yeast mixture, honey, and vegetable oil in through the feed tube. Process until the dough forms a smooth ball. To knead, continue to process for 1 minute.

3. Coat the inside of a large mixing bowl with cooking spray. Shape the dough into a rough ball and place it in the bowl. Cover the bowl with plastic wrap and let the dough stand in a warm, draft-free spot until the dough has doubled in size, 1 to 1½ hours.

4. Coat the inside of a 9 x 5-inch loaf pan with cooking spray. Turn the dough onto a lightly floured work surface and gently press it into a rectangle measuring about 1 inch thick and 9 inches long. Tightly roll the rectangle into a 9-inch-long cylinder and place it in the prepared pan, seam side down. Press the dough into the pan so that it touches the sides and reaches into the corners. Cover the pan with plastic wrap and let the dough rise in a warm, draft-free spot until doubled in size, 1 to 1½ hours.

5. Preheat the oven to 350 degrees.

6. Remove the plastic wrap from the loaf pan and place the pan in the oven. Bake the bread until it is golden brown and firm, 40 to 50 minutes. Remove the pan from the oven and turn the bread out onto a wire rack. Let it cool to room temperature before slicing and serving.

Multigrain Loaf may be wrapped in plastic and then aluminum foil and frozen for up to 2 weeks.

A Good Excuse to Make Multigrain Loaf

I love to visit the natural foods store with my kids because there are so many great organic ingredients for baking. Next time you stop at your store, get inspired, go home, and bake a Multigrain Loaf.

crusty baguettes

Makes two 12-inch-long baguettes

One of the secrets to crusty French-style bread is a streamlined recipe; these loaves contain far fewer ingredients than any of the American-style breads I bake. Bread flour, which gives the bread a chewier texture, is a must. The other secrets are high oven temperature and some moisture in the oven during the initial stage of baking. So crank up the heat and don't forget to put some water in a baking pan at the bottom of the oven just before putting the loaves in to bake.

1⅓ cups warm water
1 envelope (2½ teaspoons) rapid-rise yeast
3½ cups bread flour, plus more if necessary
2 teaspoons salt
2 tablespoons olive oil
Nonstick cooking spray
2 cups water

1. Measure the warm water into a glass measuring cup and sprinkle the yeast over the water. Let the mixture stand for 5 minutes to give the yeast a chance to dissolve.

2. Combine the flour and salt in a food processor and pulse 2 or 3 times to combine. With the motor running, pour the yeast mixture and olive oil into the feed tube and process until the dough forms a smooth ball, scraping down the sides of the bowl with a rubber spatula once or twice if necessary. To knead, continue to process for 1 minute.

3. Coat the inside of a large mixing bowl with cooking spray. Shape the dough into a rough ball and place it in the bowl. Cover the bowl with plastic wrap and let the dough stand in a warm, draft-free spot until the dough has doubled in size, 1 to 1½ hours.

4. Lightly flour a baking sheet. Punch down the dough and divide it into 2 pieces. Turn the dough out onto a lightly floured work surface. Working with one piece at a time, pull and stretch each piece into a 12 x 4-inch rectangle. Fold the rectangle in thirds lengthwise and pinch the seam to seal. Flatten the tube and fold it in thirds again. Pinch to seal the seams. Place each shaped baguette on the baking sheet, seam side down, leaving at least 5 inches between the loaves. Cover the loaves with a clean, floured dishcloth wrap and let the dough rise in a warm, draft-free spot until doubled in size, 1 to 1½ hours.

5. Preheat the oven to 500 degrees. Arrange 2 oven racks, one in the middle and one at the bottom of the oven.

6. Bring the 2 cups water to boil and pour it into a small baking pan. Place the baking pan on the lower oven rack. Remove the dishcloth from the loaves and place the baking sheet on the middle rack. Bake the bread until it is golden brown, 18 to 20 minutes. Remove the bread from the oven and let it cool on a wire rack.

Crusty Baguettes may be wrapped in plastic and then aluminum foil and frozen for up to 2 weeks.

homemade hot dog and hamburger buns

Makes 12 hot dog or hamburger buns

My great-grandmother, who grew up close to Coney Island, loved a good hot dog as much as anyone else. So I hope she won't turn over in her grave because I've used her challah dough to make hot dog and hamburger buns. Every time I bake a batch of these shiny, golden buns I am very impressed with my skill as a baker, and almost forget how easy they are to make.

½ cup warm water
1 envelope (2½ teaspoons) rapid-rise yeast
2½ cups unbleached all-purpose flour
2 tablespoons sugar
1 teaspoon salt
5 large eggs, at room temperature
2 tablespoons vegetable oil
Nonstick cooking spray

 A Good Excuse to Make Homemade Hot Dog and Hamburger Buns

A homemade bun really transforms a plain old hot dog or hamburger. One summer weekend when you've invited another family over for a barbecue, make your own buns. Your guests will appreciate the effort. The rest of the meal won't take much work—buy some hot dogs and shape some hamburger patties, put out a plate of pickles, boil some corn, slice some tomatoes. (And may I suggest a do-ahead Coffee-Toffee Ice-Cream Pie, page 193, or Chocolate Chip Cookie Ice-Cream Sandwiches, page 86, for dessert?)

1. Measure the water into a glass measuring cup and sprinkle in the yeast. Let the mixture stand for 5 minutes to give the yeast a chance to dissolve.

2. Combine the flour, sugar, and salt in a food processor and pulse 2 or 3 times to combine. With the motor running, add 4 of the eggs, one at a time, through the feed tube. Pour in the vegetable oil. Process until the dough forms a smooth ball, scraping down the sides of the bowl with a rubber spatula once or twice if necessary. To knead, continue to process for 1 minute.

3. Coat the inside of a large mixing bowl with cooking spray. Shape the dough into a rough ball and place it in the bowl. Cover the bowl with plastic wrap and let the dough stand until it has doubled in size, 1 to 1½ hours.

4. Line a baking sheet with parchment paper. Punch down the dough and turn it out onto a lightly floured work surface. Divide it into 10 equal pieces. For hot dog buns: Press each dough piece into a 3 x 4-inch rectangle. Fold each rectangle in thirds lengthwise and pinch the seam to seal. Flatten the tube and fold it in

Braiding and Baking Challah

Of course, the dough from this recipe can also be used to make traditional braided challah:

Divide the punched-down dough into 3 equal pieces. Roll each piece between the palms of your hands to form three 12-inch lengths. Place the lengths side by side vertically on a lightly floured baking sheet. Begin braiding from the middle and work toward the bottom. When you reach the bottom, tightly pinch the dough lengths together and turn the pinched portion under. Turn the baking sheet around and braid from the middle to the other end, pinching and turning under the ends.

Place a clean, floured dishcloth over the loaf and let the dough rise in a warm, draft-free spot until doubled in size, about 1 hour. Lightly brush the loaf with a beaten egg and bake it in a preheated 400 degree oven until golden brown, 30 to 35 minutes. Let the bread cool completely before slicing.

thirds again. Pinch to seal. For hamburger buns: Form balls by gathering the rough edges of the dough piece together and pinching tightly to form a smooth, round top. Place each ball, pinched side down, on the parchment and flatten it slightly with the palm of your hand. Lay a clean, floured dishcloth over the dough pieces and let them rise in a warm, draft-free spot until almost doubled in size, about 1 hour.

5. Preheat the oven to 400 degrees.

6. Lightly beat the remaining egg. Remove the dishcloth from the dough and lightly brush each bun with some of the egg. Bake the buns until they are golden brown and well risen, 12 to 15 minutes. Remove them from the oven and let them cool on a wire rack. Slice each bun in half before using.

Homemade Hot Dog and Hamburger Buns may be wrapped in plastic and then aluminum foil and frozen for up to 2 weeks.

sticky buns

Makes 8 large
sticky buns

These sticky buns are a decadent treat, and not at all difficult to make. Why not try them sometime, and see how they compare to the mass-produced variety sold at your shopping mall's food court?

For the dough

- 1¼ cups whole milk
- 1 envelope (2½ teaspoons) rapid-rise yeast
- 3½ cups unbleached all-purpose flour
- 3 tablespoons granulated sugar
- 1 teaspoon salt
- ¼ cup (½ stick) unsalted butter, softened
- 1 large egg, at room temperature, lightly beaten
- Nonstick cooking spray

For the brown sugar filling and glaze

- ½ cup (1 stick) unsalted butter, cut into small pieces
- 1½ cups firmly packed dark brown sugar
- ¼ cup light corn syrup
- 1 cup finely chopped pecans

1. Make the dough: Heat the milk over low heat in a small saucepan until just warm to the touch. Pour it into a glass measuring cup and whisk in the yeast. Let the mixture stand for 5 minutes to give the yeast a chance to dissolve.

2. Combine the flour, granulated sugar, and salt in a food processor and pulse 2 or 3 times to combine. Add the butter and pulse several times until the mixture resembles coarse meal. With the motor running, pour the milk and yeast mixture and the egg into the feed tube and process until the dough forms a ball, scraping down the sides of the bowl with a rubber spatula once or twice if necessary. Do not overknead. The dough will be sticky.

3. Coat the inside of a large mixing bowl with cooking spray. Scrape the dough into the bowl. Cover the bowl with plastic wrap and let the dough stand in a warm, draft-free spot until the dough has doubled in size, 1 to 1½ hours.

4. Make the glaze: Combine the butter, brown sugar, and corn syrup in a small saucepan and heat over medium-low heat until the butter is melted and the sugar is dissolved.

5. Grease a 10-inch round cake pan. Pour 1 cup of the glaze across the bottom of the pan. Sprinkle in the pecans. Set aside the remaining glaze to cool.

6. Turn the dough onto a lightly floured work surface and roll it into a 12 x 18-inch rectangle. Spread the remaining glaze over the dough with a rubber spatula, leaving a 1-inch border all around. Tightly roll the rectangle along the long side, making a log. With a sharp chef's knife or serrated knife, cut an inch from either end of the log and discard that dough. Cut the log into eight 2-inch pieces. Place the pieces cut side down in the pan, 7 in a circle about 1 inch from the outer edge of the pan, one piece in the center. Cover the pan loosely with plastic wrap and let the dough rise in a warm, draft-free spot until the buns just begin to touch each other, 45 minutes to 1 hour.

7. Preheat the oven to 375 degrees. Bake the buns until they are golden, 25 to 30 minutes. Remove the pan from the oven and invert the buns onto a wire rack placed over a rimmed baking sheet to catch the dripping glaze. Let the buns cool for 10 minutes and then serve them warm.

Sticky Buns are best eaten on the day they are made.

sweet focaccia with grapes

Makes one 15-by-10-inch focaccia

This bread may seem a little bit out of the mainstream for a mom's baking book, but in Italy schoolchildren regularly consume grape-studded focaccia as an after-school snack, so why wouldn't your kids like it too? I like a little bit of chopped fresh rosemary in the dough; it gives the finished focaccia a wonderful aroma.

1⅓ cups warm water
1 envelope (2½ teaspoons) rapid-rise yeast
3½ cups unbleached all-purpose flour
1½ teaspoons salt
½ teaspoon finely chopped fresh rosemary (optional)
5 tablespoons unsalted butter, melted
Nonstick cooking spray
2 cups seedless red grapes
¼ cup sugar

1. Measure the warm water into a glass measuring cup and whisk in the yeast. Let the mixture stand for 5 minutes to give the yeast a chance to dissolve.

2. Combine the flour, salt, and rosemary, if you are using it, in a food processor and pulse 2 or 3 times to combine. With the motor running, pour the yeast mixture and 3 tablespoons of the melted butter into the feed tube and process until the dough forms a smooth ball. To knead, continue to process for 30 seconds.

3. Coat the inside of a large mixing bowl with cooking spray. Shape the dough into a rough ball and place it in the bowl. Cover the bowl with plastic wrap and let the dough stand in a warm, draft-free spot until the dough has doubled in size, 1 to 1½ hours.

4. Coat a 15½ x 10½-inch rimmed baking sheet with cooking spray. Punch down the dough and press it on the pan. Loosely cover the dough with plastic wrap and let it rise in a warm, draft-free spot until it is puffy and almost doubled in size, about 1 hour.

5. Preheat the oven to 425 degrees.

6. Press the grapes into the dough at 1-inch intervals. Drizzle the remaining 2 tablespoons melted butter over the dough, letting some collect in the grape indentations. Sprinkle the sugar over the loaf.

7. Bake the bread until it is golden brown, 25 to 30 minutes. Use a large spatula to remove the focaccia from the pan and slide it onto a wire rack to cool. Serve the bread warm or at room temperature.

Sweet Focaccia with Grapes is best served the day it is made.

A Good Excuse to Make Sweet Focaccia with Grapes

In Italy, people celebrate the grape harvest by baking this bread; I bake Sweet Focaccia to celebrate the fact that I can buy decent grapes almost any time of year.

buttermilk doughnuts

Makes about
20 doughnuts and
20 doughnut holes

Because these doughnuts are leavened with baking powder and baking soda rather than yeast, they are quicker to make than jelly doughnuts are. Just mix up the dough, cut out the doughnuts, and fry them. For the most tender doughnuts, be gentle with the dough. As with biscuits, overworking the dough will toughen it up. If you are going to coat the doughnuts in cinnamon sugar, do so as soon as they come out of the fryer. If you prefer powdered sugar, wait until the doughnuts have cooled so that the sugar doesn't melt and become gluey.

$3\frac{1}{2}$ cups unbleached all-purpose flour
$\frac{3}{4}$ cup granulated sugar
2 teaspoons baking powder
$\frac{1}{2}$ teaspoon baking soda
1 teaspoon salt
$\frac{1}{2}$ teaspoon ground cinnamon
$\frac{1}{4}$ teaspoon ground nutmeg
$\frac{3}{4}$ cup buttermilk, at room temperature
$\frac{1}{4}$ cup ($\frac{1}{2}$ stick) unsalted butter, melted and cooled
2 large eggs, at room temperature
1 teaspoon pure vanilla extract
Confectioners' sugar or Cinnamon Sugar (page 23) for coating

1. Whisk together the flour, granulated sugar, baking powder, baking soda, salt, cinnamon, and nutmeg in a medium mixing bowl.

2. Combine the buttermilk, cooled melted butter, eggs, and vanilla in a large mixing bowl. Add the flour mixture all at once and mix until all the ingredients are moistened.

3. Turn the dough out onto a lightly floured work surface. Pat it into a $\frac{1}{2}$-inch thickness. Cut the dough into rounds with a floured doughnut cutter, re-patting and cutting the scraps. Let the rounds and the holes stand, uncovered, on the counter, until slightly puffed, about 30 minutes.

4. Preheat the maximum amount of vegetable oil recommended by the manufacturer in an electric deep fryer to a temperature of about 370 degrees.

5. Place 2 or 3 doughnuts and a couple of doughnut holes into the fry basket and fry them until golden, 2 to 3 minutes. Transfer the cooked doughnuts to a paper towel–lined baking sheet to cool. Repeat with the remaining doughnuts and holes.

6. Place the confectioners' sugar or Cinnamon Sugar in a shallow bowl. If you are using Cinnamon Sugar, roll the doughnuts in the sugar when they are still warm. If you are using confectioners' sugar, allow the doughnuts to cool before coating them with sugar.

Buttermilk Doughnuts are best eaten on the day they are made.

jelly doughnuts

I only deep-fry in an electric fryer with a basket and cover, not only because I am terrified of stovetop grease fires, but also because these appliances regulate oil temperature wonderfully and don't splatter hot oil all over the place. They also somewhat contain any cooking odors, lessening the chance that the entire house will smell like McDonald's for days.

If you've put your fryer in the closet and can't remember the last time you used it, try making some homemade jelly doughnuts. Use a fresh bottle of oil. Resist eating the doughnuts straight out of the fryer—let them cool to a safe eating temperature—because the jelly in the center gets very, very hot.

½ **cup whole milk**
1 **envelope (2½ teaspoons) rapid-rise yeast**
2¼ **cups unbleached all-purpose flour**
⅓ **cup granulated sugar**
½ **teaspoon salt**
5 **tablespoons unsalted butter, softened**
2 **large eggs (separate one of the eggs and reserve the white), at room temperature**
1 **teaspoon pure vanilla extract**
Nonstick cooking spray
Vegetable oil for frying
¼ **cup best-quality raspberry, strawberry, or grape jelly**
½ **cup confectioners' sugar for coating**

1. Heat the milk over low heat in a small saucepan until just warm to the touch. Pour it into a glass measuring cup and whisk in the yeast. Let the mixture stand for 5 minutes to give the yeast a chance to dissolve.

2. Combine the flour, granulated sugar, salt, and butter in a food processor and pulse several times until the mixture resembles coarse meal. With the motor running, add the milk and yeast mixture, the whole egg, the separated egg yolk, and the vanilla. Process until the dough forms a smooth ball. To knead, continue to process for 30 seconds.

 Kids Can Help

Rolling the dough, spooning the jelly onto the dough rounds, brushing the dough rounds with egg white, and pinching the doughnut halves together are all good jobs for kids six years and older. Make sure they wash their hands well afterwards. Needless to say, keep all kids away from the deep fryer, and don't let them touch the doughnuts until you are sure they are cool enough to eat.

3. Coat the inside of a large mixing bowl with cooking spray. Shape the dough into a rough ball and place it in the bowl. Cover the bowl with plastic wrap and let the dough stand in a warm, draft-free spot until the dough has doubled in size, 2 to 2½ hours.

4. Punch down the dough and turn it out onto a lightly floured work surface. Pat it into a ¼-inch thickness. Cut the dough into rounds with a floured 2-inch biscuit cutter, re-patting and cutting the scraps. Let the rounds stand, uncovered, on the counter, until they are slightly puffed, about 30 minutes.

5. Preheat about 3 inches of vegetable oil in an electric deep fryer to a temperature of about 370 degrees.

6. Place ½ teaspoon of jelly on one of the rounds, brush the edges with the egg white, and place another round on top. Pinch the edges together to seal the doughnut. Repeat with the remaining rounds.

7. Place the doughnuts, 3 or 4 at a time, into the fry basket and fry until golden, about 1 minute per side. Transfer the cooked doughnuts to a paper towel–lined baking sheet and let them cool completely.

8. Place the confectioners' sugar in a shallow bowl and roll the cooled dough-nuts in the sugar to coat.

Jelly Doughnuts are best eaten on the day they are made.

thin and crispy pizza dough

Makes enough for two 14-inch pizzas

Since I discovered how easy it is to make pizza dough at home, homemade pizza has been a dinner staple in our house. Pizza dough is very forgiving. You can make it in the morning, punch it down, and refrigerate it until dinner time. If you want to make only one pizza, freeze the other portion of dough in an airtight container for another night. Just defrost the dough on the counter for a couple of hours. It will bake up just as beautifully as if it were made that day.

For the crispiest pizza, use bread flour, which is available in most supermarkets and by mail (see Mail-Order and Online Resources, page 273). Look for bags marked as specially made for bread machines; this flour is available in most supermarkets or by mail.

1¾ cups warm water
1 envelope (2½ teaspoons) rapid-rise
  yeast
4 cups bread flour
1½ teaspoons salt
2 tablespoons olive oil
Nonstick cooking spray

1. Measure the warm water into a glass measuring cup and whisk in the yeast. Let the mixture stand for 5 minutes to give the yeast a chance to dissolve.

2. Combine the bread flour and salt in a food processor and pulse 2 or 3 times to combine. With the motor running, pour the yeast mixture and olive oil into the feed tube and process until the dough forms a smooth ball. To knead, continue to process for 30 seconds.

3. Coat the inside of a large mixing bowl with cooking spray. Shape the dough into a rough ball and place it in the bowl. Cover the bowl with plastic wrap and let the dough stand in a warm, draft-free spot until the dough has doubled in size, 1 to 1½ hours.

4. Punch down the dough and cut it in half with a sharp chef's knife. Place each half in a separate bowl, cover each bowl with plastic, and let the dough rest for 20 minutes. Use the dough as directed in any pizza recipe. (After the dough is punched down and divided, it can be placed in an airtight container and frozen for up to 2 months. Defrost the dough on the counter for 5 to 6 hours before using.)

whole wheat pizza dough

**Makes enough for two
14-inch pizzas**

Whole wheat flour and bread flour together make a dough too tough. So if you want whole wheat pizza dough, combine whole wheat flour with all-purpose flour.

1¾ cups warm water
1 envelope (2½ teaspoons) rapid-rise
    yeast
2 cups unbleached all-purpose flour
2 cups whole wheat flour
1½ teaspoons salt
2 tablespoons olive oil
Nonstick cooking spray

1. Measure the warm water into a glass measuring cup and whisk in the yeast. Let the mixture stand for 5 minutes to give the yeast a chance to dissolve.

2. Combine the flours and salt in a food processor and pulse 2 or 3 times to combine. With the motor running, pour the yeast mixture and olive oil into the feed tube and process until the dough forms a smooth ball. To knead, continue to process for 30 seconds.

3. Coat the inside of a large mixing bowl with cooking spray. Shape the dough into a rough ball and place it in the bowl.

Cover the bowl with plastic wrap and let the dough stand in a warm, draft-free spot until the dough has doubled in size, 1 to 1½ hours.

4. Punch down the dough and cut it in half with a sharp chef's knife. Place each half in a separate bowl, cover each bowl with plastic, and let the dough rest for 20 minutes. Use the dough as directed in any pizza recipe. (After the dough is punched down and divided, it can be placed in airtight containers and frozen for up to 2 months. Defrost the dough on the counter for 5 to 6 hours before using.)

Kids Can Help

If you let your kids choose and arrange the toppings, they'll be even more excited than usual about having pizza for dinner.

pan pizza dough

Makes enough for two 10-inch round pan pizzas

A lot of kids prefer pan pizza to thin-crust pizza because the crust is softer and more doughy. All-purpose flour is actually better for this dough since it makes a more tender crust. If you have crust-haters in your house, try this variety and watch them eat it up. One nice thing about pan pizza is that it can accommodate a heavier load of toppings than thin-crust pizza can. In fact, this type of pizza is better with more stuff rather than less. So make pan pizza when you are in the mood for sausage, peppers, onions, eggplant, and extra cheese.

1²⁄₃ cups warm water
1 envelope (2¹⁄₂ teaspoons) rapid-rise yeast
4 cups unbleached all-purpose flour
2 teaspoons salt
¹⁄₄ cup olive oil
Nonstick cooking spray

1. Measure the warm water into a glass measuring cup and whisk in the yeast. Let the mixture stand for 5 minutes to give the yeast a chance to dissolve.

2. Combine the flour and salt in a food processor and pulse 2 or 3 times to combine. With the motor running, pour the yeast mixture and olive oil into the feed tube and process until the dough forms a smooth ball. To knead, continue to process for 30 seconds.

3. Coat the inside of a large mixing bowl with cooking spray. Shape the dough into a rough ball and place it in the bowl. Cover the bowl with plastic wrap and let the dough stand in a warm, draft-free spot until the dough has doubled in size, 1 to 1¹⁄₂ hours.

4. Punch down the dough and cut it in half with a sharp chef's knife. Place each half in a separate bowl, cover each bowl with plastic, and let the dough rest for 20 minutes. Use the dough as directed in any pizza recipe. (After the dough is punched down and divided, it can be placed in airtight containers and frozen for up to 2 months. Defrost it on the counter for 5 to 6 hours before using.)

Tomato Sauce for Pan Pizza

**Makes about 2 cups, enough to
top two 10-inch round pan pizzas**

I like this smooth, flavorful sauce for pan pizza. Make sure to simmer the tomatoes long enough so that all of the excess liquid cooks off. A watery sauce will make the crust soggy.

**2 tablespoons olive oil
2 tablespoons finely chopped onion
2 tablespoons peeled and finely chopped carrot
2 tablespoons finely chopped celery
2 medium garlic cloves, finely chopped
One 28-ounce can crushed tomatoes
Salt and freshly ground black pepper**

1. Heat the olive oil in a large saucepan over medium heat. Add the onion, carrot, and celery and cook until softened, stirring occasionally, 7 to 10 minutes. Stir in the garlic and cook an additional 2 minutes. Add the tomatoes and season with salt and pepper. Bring the sauce to a simmer and cook it until it is very thick, 20 to 25 minutes.
2. Season with salt and pepper again if necessary.

Pizza Equipment

The only piece of special equipment that's absolutely necessary for making homemade pizza is a heavy-duty food processor. But if you really get into pizza making, there are a couple of tools and ingredients that will make you feel like a pizza parlor pro. See Mail-Order and Online Resources (page 273) for purveyors of the following items:

* **Perforated pizza pans:** These thin, flexible round pans with holes punched in the bottoms allow the hot air from the oven to come in contact with the bottom of thin-crust pizza, making the dough extra crisp. Another nice thing about using one of these pans: Its round shape gives you a guide by which to shape your dough. If you are shaping your dough free-form on a rectangular baking sheet, you're on your own.

* **Baking stones and tiles:** Here's another item that will help crisp up your crust. Baking stones and tiles absorb and conduct heat very well. Pizza and Crusty Baguettes baked on stones develop extra-chewy crusts. One caveat: Pizza and bread bake more quickly on stones and tiles, so check the oven frequently and adjust cooking times accordingly.

* **Pizza peel:** The convenient thing about baking pizza on a baking sheet is that you can shape the dough right on the sheet and just pop the sheet in the oven. If you are going to use a baking stone, however, you'll need a pizza peel to get the shaped dough into and out of the oven. I recommend stainless-steel rather than wood peels. Wooden peels have a nasty habit of growing mold, and they are difficult to wash because they warp if immersed in hot soapy water.

* **Pizza wheel:** Pizza can be sliced with a sharp knife, of course, but a wheel works better and is more fun. Avoid the flimsy models with cheap plastic handles that are sold in the gadgets section of the supermarket. Instead look for an extra-large wheel with a soft rubber handle.

* **Wood-burning pizza oven:** Just kidding. When my husband and I were renovating our kitchen, we thought it would be neat to have one of these. Then we discovered that it would cost about $10,000 to build one. When you do the math, that's pretty expensive pizza. So I turn up the heat on my electric oven and enjoy my homemade pizza that much more, thinking of all the money I'm saving.

neapolitan pizza

**Makes two
14-inch pizzas**

Unless you live in New Haven or New York's Little Italy, you can probably make a better pizza at home than they do at your local takeout place. Your topping ingredients will be fresher, you can use real cheese (rather than the fake stuff that pizza places often buy), and your pie won't drip with grease. Here is a simple recipe for a thin-crust tomato pie. Serve it as is or top it with whatever your family usually orders.

Two 14½-ounce cans diced tomatoes
½ teaspoon salt
1 recipe Thin and Crispy Pizza Dough (page 260) or Whole Wheat Pizza Dough (page 261)
Add-ons of your choice (extra mozzarella cheese, pepperoni, pitted olives, roasted red peppers, sautéed mushrooms, sautéed onions, crumbled cooked Italian sausage, bacon or Canadian bacon, anchovies, pineapple chunks)
8 ounces part-skim mozzarella cheese, shredded
½ cup freshly grated Parmesan cheese

1. Preheat the oven to 500 degrees.

2. Place the tomatoes in a strainer over a bowl and let them stand, stirring once or twice, until most of the liquid has drained into the bowl, about 10 minutes. Discard the liquid, turn the tomatoes into the bowl, and stir in the salt.

3. Turn one portion of the pizza dough out onto a lightly floured baking sheet and press it into a 14-inch circle. Spread half of the diced tomatoes on top of the dough. Sprinkle half of any add-ons over the tomatoes. Sprinkle half of the mozzarella cheese over the add-ons. Bake the pizza until the edges of the crust are well browned and the cheese is golden and bubbling, 15 to 18 minutes. Sprinkle half of the Parmesan on top of the pizza and bake until it is melted, an additional minute or two. Remove the pizza from the oven and serve it immediately. Repeat with the remaining dough and topping ingredients.

broccoli and three-cheese pizza

Makes two 14-inch pizzas

This is a wonderful alternative to pizza with tomato sauce. The broccoli makes it a one-dish vegetarian meal. Using part-skim cheese cuts down on the fat but doesn't diminish the flavor. Go all the way health-wise and use Whole Wheat Pizza Dough. Make sure to chop the broccoli; large florets tend to poke out from the cheese and burn in the high heat of the oven.

1 medium head broccoli (about 1¼ pounds)
1 cup whole-milk or part-skim ricotta cheese
8 ounces whole-milk or part-skim mozzarella cheese, shredded
½ cup freshly grated Parmesan cheese
2 medium garlic cloves, finely chopped
½ teaspoon salt
Freshly ground black pepper
1 recipe Thin and Crispy Pizza Dough (page 260) or Whole Wheat Pizza Dough (page 261)

1. Preheat the oven to 500 degrees.

2. Bring several inches of water to a boil in a large saucepan. Trim the tough ends of the stems from the broccoli and discard. Cut the broccoli into small florets and cut the remaining stems into ½-inch pieces. Blanch the broccoli for 2 minutes, drain, and coarsely chop. Set it aside to cool slightly.

3. Combine the ricotta, mozzarella, Parmesan, garlic, salt, and black pepper to taste in a large mixing bowl. Stir the broccoli pieces into the cheese mixture.

4. Turn one portion of the pizza dough out onto a lightly floured baking sheet and press it into a 14-inch circle. Spread half of the broccoli and cheese mixture over the dough. Bake the pizza until the edges of the crust are well browned and the cheese is browned and bubbling, 15 to 20 minutes. Remove the pizza from the oven and serve immediately. Repeat with the remaining dough and topping ingredients.

 A Good Excuse to Make Broccoli and Three-Cheese Pizza

Even kids who hate broccoli can usually be coaxed into trying this pizza. Once they try it, they might even like it.

fresh tomato and parmesan pizza

Makes two
14-inch pizzas

Nothing can beat this pizza for simplicity. But when a pizza is this simple, the quality of the ingredients is paramount. I reserve this recipe for late summer and early fall, when local tomatoes are at their peak. I also use freshly grated imported Parmigiano-Reggiano.

4 medium-size ripe tomatoes
1 recipe Thin and Crispy Pizza Dough (page 260) or Whole Wheat Pizza Dough (page 261)
2 tablespoons olive oil
Salt and freshly ground black pepper
1/2 cup freshly grated Parmesan cheese
2 tablespoons finely chopped fresh basil leaves

1. Preheat the oven to 500 degrees.

2. Core the tomatoes and cut them into 1/4-inch-thick slices. Place the slices on paper towels to drain for 5 minutes.

3. Turn one portion of the pizza dough out onto a lightly floured baking sheet and press it into a 14-inch circle. Arrange half of the tomatoes on top of the dough, drizzle on 1 tablespoon of the olive oil, sprinkle with salt and pepper to taste, and

bake until the edges of the dough have begun to brown, 12 to 15 minutes. Sprinkle the grated cheese over the tomatoes and bake the pizza until the edges of the crust are well browned and the tomatoes are bubbling, an additional 3 to 5 minutes. Remove the pizza from the oven, sprinkle it with 1 tablespoon of the basil, and serve immediately. Repeat with the remaining dough and topping ingredients.

shrimp and goat cheese pizza

This might seem like a rather grown-up combination, but lots of kids love shrimp, and goat cheese is very mild, kind of like cream cheese but better. I think of shrimp as a quality convenience food; I buy bags of frozen peeled and cooked shrimp at the supermarket and keep it on hand for quick dinners. Shrimp is also a good source of low-fat protein.

Two 14½-ounce cans diced tomatoes
2 medium garlic cloves, finely chopped
½ teaspoon salt
1 recipe Thin and Crispy Pizza Dough (page 260) or Whole Wheat Pizza Dough (page 261)
10 ounces peeled and cooked small shrimp, cut into ½-inch pieces
7 ounces fresh goat cheese, crumbled
1 tablespoon finely chopped fresh oregano leaves
2 tablespoons extra-virgin olive oil

1. Preheat the oven to 500 degrees.

2. Place the tomatoes in a strainer over a bowl and let them stand, stirring once or twice, until most of the liquid has drained into the bowl, about 10 minutes. Discard the liquid, turn the tomatoes into the bowl, and stir in the garlic and salt.

3. Turn one portion of the pizza dough out onto a lightly floured baking sheet and press it into a 14-inch circle. Spread half of the diced tomatoes on top of the dough. Bake the pizza until the edges of the crust are well browned, 12 to 15 minutes. Scatter half of the shrimp, half of the goat cheese, and half of the oregano over the top of the pizza, drizzle with 1 tablespoon of the olive oil, and cook until the shrimp are heated through and the goat cheese is melted, another 2 to 3 minutes. Remove from the oven and serve immediately. Repeat with the remaining dough and topping ingredients.

white clam pizza

I include my version of this classic pizza because, for some unknown reason, my kids, who won't touch lobster, crabs, or scallops, actually like clams. Living near the ocean, I have never been able to bring myself to buy canned clams. Fresh clams are fantastic and definitely make this pizza special.

¼ cup olive oil

4 medium garlic cloves, finely chopped

24 fresh littleneck clams, shucked and coarsely chopped

1 teaspoon salt

¼ cup finely chopped fresh parsley leaves

1 recipe Thin and Crispy Pizza Dough (page 260) or Whole Wheat Pizza Dough (page 261)

½ cup freshly grated Parmesan cheese

1. Preheat the oven to 500 degrees.

2. Combine the olive oil, garlic, clams, salt, and parsley in a medium mixing bowl.

3. Turn one portion of the pizza dough out onto a lightly floured baking sheet and press it into a 14-inch circle. Distribute half of the clam mixture, including the juices, over the dough. Bake the pizza until the edges of the crust are golden, 12 to 15 minutes. Remove the pizza from the oven, sprinkle it with half of the grated cheese and serve immediately. Repeat with the remaining dough and topping ingredients.

pan pizza with turkey sausage and peppers

Makes two 10-inch round pan pizzas

I like to load up on extras when I'm making pan pizza. Turkey sausage, even when it's piled on, won't weigh the pie down with extra calories and fat.

2 tablespoons olive oil
2 yellow bell peppers, seeded and cut into ¼-inch dice
1½ pounds turkey sausage
Nonstick cooking spray
1 recipe Pan Pizza Dough (page 262)
1 recipe Tomato Sauce for Pan Pizza (page 263)
8 ounces Italian fontina cheese, grated

1. Preheat the oven to 400 degrees.

2. Heat the olive oil in a medium skillet over medium heat. Add the bell pepper and cook, stirring occasionally, until softened, about 10 minutes. Set aside.

3. Bring several inches of water to boil in a large saucepan. Prick the sausages all over with a fork and blanch them for 3 minutes. Drain them and let them cool slightly. Slice them into ⅓-inch-thick rounds.

4. Coat two 10-inch-round baking pans with cooking spray. Divide the dough into 2 pieces and press it into the pans and 2 inches up the sides. Prick the bottom of the dough all over with the tines of a fork and bake the dough until it begins to dry out, 5 to 7 minutes. Remove the pans from the oven. Spread half of the Tomato Sauce across the bottom of each pan. Distribute half of the sausage and half of the peppers over the sauce in each pan. Sprinkle the cheese on top. Return the pizzas to the oven and cook them until the cheese is browned and bubbling, about 25 minutes. Serve immediately.

pan pizza with eggplant

Even vegetable haters enjoy Parmesan-coated eggplant slices on top of pan pizza.

1 large eggplant (about 1 pound)
1/2 teaspoon salt
1 large egg, lightly beaten
3/4 cup freshly grated Parmesan cheese
1/2 cup olive oil
Nonstick cooking spray
1 recipe Pan Pizza Dough (page 262)
**1 recipe Tomato Sauce for Pan Pizza
  (page 263)**
8 ounces mozzarella cheese, grated
**2 tablespoons finely chopped fresh basil
  leaves**

1. Preheat the oven to 400 degrees.

2. Trim the ends from the eggplant and discard. Slice the eggplant into 1/4-inch-thick rounds. Sprinkle with the salt and place on a paper towel–lined platter. Let stand for 15 minutes. Blot the eggplant to absorb any moisture.

3. Place the beaten egg in a shallow bowl. Place the Parmesan cheese in another shallow bowl. Dip each piece of eggplant in the egg and then in the cheese to coat. Place the coated slices on a plate and set them aside.

4. Heat the olive oil in a medium skillet over medium-high heat. Dip one of the slices in the oil. When the oil sizzles, add the eggplant slices in batches and cook, turning once, until lightly browned on both sides, about 5 minutes. Transfer to a paper towel–lined plate to cool.

5. Coat the inside of two 10-inch round baking pans with cooking spray. Divide the dough into 2 pieces and press it into the pans and 2 inches up the sides. Prick the bottom of the dough all over with the tines of a fork and bake the dough until it just begins to set, about 7 minutes. Remove the pans from the oven. Spread some sauce across the bottom of each pan. Distribute the eggplant over the sauce. Sprinkle with the mozzarella cheese. Return the pizzas to the oven and cook until the cheese is browned and bubbling, 20 to 25 minutes. Sprinkle with basil and serve immediately.

mail-order and online resources

Almost every ingredient and piece of equipment used in these recipes is available at a supermarket or local housewares shop. Once in a while, however, I'll use a mail-order source to stock up on supplies that may be difficult to find. Here are the sources I turn to when I can't find baking ingredients or equipment locally, or when I just want to find something new and fun for my kitchen without running all over town.

The Baker's Catalogue
58 Billings Farm Road
White River Junction, VT 05001
1-800-827-6836
www.kingarthurflour.com

If you can't find the ingredients you need at your local supermarket or natural foods store, this is the place to go. This is where I get specialty flours, seeds, meringue powder, sprinkles, and sanding sugar. I also buy parchment paper in bulk, pastry bags and tips, and pizza equipment (stones, peels, pizza pans, and wheels) from King Arthur. As a bonus, the catalogue and Web site run wonderful, simple recipes for a variety of baked goods.

Crate & Barrel
P.O. Box 3210
Naperville, IL 60566-7210
1-800-323-5461
www.crateandbarrel.com

Crate & Barrel carries a wide range of well-designed, reasonably priced kitchen equipment and serving pieces. Order from their "Best Buys" catalogue for low prices on measuring cups and spoons, canisters, cookie sheets, aprons and oven mitts, baking racks, mixing bowls, springform pans, and cake decorating sets.

Sur La Table
5701 Sixth Avenue South, Suite 486
Seattle, WA 98108
1-800-243-0852
www.surlatable.com

This high-end, French-inspired catalogue has beautiful bakeware and serving pieces. Although I can't afford the copper-plated KitchenAid mixer offered through Sur la Table, I have splurged on a wall-mounted maple rolling pin and a set of ceramic mini-loaf pans from Provence. And there are always some affordable surprises here: an ergonomically designed apple wedger by OXO, or a set of heart and teddy bear pancake rings, each for less than $10.

Williams-Sonoma
P.O. Box 7456
San Francisco, CA 94120-7456
1-877-812-6235
www.williams-sonoma.com

This outfit carries pricey but pretty decorating supplies—icing pens, glitter, confetti, and dragées. Very often the company runs specials on top-of-the-line appliances such as Cuisinart food processors and KitchenAid mixers. VillaWare waffle makers, offered exclusively through Williams-Sonoma, are a great investment for the baking mom.

www.cooking.com

This easy-to-navigate Web site has a well-stocked bakeware shop with competitive prices.

www.amazon.com

Amazon has a good selection of baking equipment, as well as a lot of helpful articles on general baking and some simple, classic recipes. After you shop, you can check out their cookbook recommendations.

www.cookiecutterfactory.com

Need to make cookies that look like guitars, cowboy boots, or the state of Montana? Here's the place to go. Over six hundred cookie cutter shapes are available through this site, all priced at a dollar or so.

measurement equivalents

Please note that all conversions are approximate.

Liquid Conversions

U.S.	Metric
1 tsp	5 ml
1 tbs	15 ml
2 tbs	30 ml
3 tbs	45 ml
1/4 cup	60 ml
1/3 cup	75 ml
1/3 cup + 1 tbs	90 ml
1/3 cup + 2 tbs	100 ml
1/2 cup	120 ml
2/3 cup	150 ml
3/4 cup	180 ml
3/4 cup + 2 tbs	200 ml
1 cup	240 ml
1 cup + 2 tbs	275 ml
1 1/4 cups	300 ml
1 1/3 cups	325 ml
1 1/2 cups	350 ml
1 2/3 cups	375 ml
1 3/4 cups	400 ml
1 3/4 cups + 2 tbs	450 ml
2 cups (1 pint)	475 ml
2 1/2 cups	600 ml
3 cups	720 ml
4 cups (1 quart)	945 ml (1,000 ml is 1 liter)

Weight Conversions

U.S./U.K.	Metric
1/2 oz	14 g
1 oz	28 g
1 1/2 oz	43 g
2 oz	57 g
2 1/2 oz	71 g
3 oz	85 g
3 1/2 oz	100 g
4 oz	113 g
5 oz	142 g
6 oz	170 g
7 oz	200 g
8 oz	227 g
9 oz	255 g
10 oz	284 g
11 oz	312 g
12 oz	340 g
13 oz	368 g
14 oz	400 g
15 oz	425 g
1 lb	454 g

Oven Temperature Conversions

°F	Gas Mark	°C
250	1/2	120
275	1	140
300	2	150
325	3	165
350	4	180
375	5	190
400	6	200
425	7	220
450	8	230
475	9	240
500	10	260
550	Broil	290

index